Theologizing Friendship

Theologizing Friendship

How Amicitia in the Thought of Aelred and Aquinas Inscribes the Scholastic Turn

NATHAN LEFLER

With a Foreword by Austin G. Murphy, OSB

☙PICKWICK *Publications* • Eugene, Oregon

THEOLOGIZING FRIENDSHIP
How Amicitia in the Thought of Aelred and Aquinas Inscribes the Scholastic Turn

Copyright © 2014 Nathan Lefler. All rights reserved. Except for brief quotations in critical publications or reviews, no part of this book may be reproduced in any manner without prior written permission from the publisher. Write: Permissions, Wipf and Stock Publishers, 199 W. 8th Ave., Suite 3, Eugene, OR 97401.

Pickwick Publications
An Imprint of Wipf and Stock Publishers
199 W. 8th Ave., Suite 3
Eugene, OR 97401

www.wipfandstock.com

ISBN 13: 978-1-62564-104-5

Cataloging-in-Publication data:

Lefler, Nathan.

    Theologizing friendship : how amicitia in Aelred and Aquinas inscribes the scholastic turn / Nathan Lefler ; with a foreword by Austin G. Murphy, OSB.

    xvi + 178 pp. ; 23 cm—Includes bibliographical references.

    ISBN 13: 978-1-62564-104-5

    1. Aelred, of Rievaulx, Saint, 1110–1167. 2. Thomas, Aquinas, Saint, 1225?–1274. 3. Friendship—Religious aspects—Christianity—Early works to 1800. 4. Spiritual life—Catholic church—Early works to 1800. I. Murphy, Austin G. II. Title.

BX2349 L234 2014

Manufactured in the USA

From Connor, Elizabeth, OCSO, trans. *The Mirror of Charity* by Aelred of Rievaulx. © 1990 by Cistercian Publications, Inc. Excerpts used by permission of Cistercian Publications, Inc.

From Laker, Mary Eugenia, SSND, trans. *Spiritual Friendship* by Aelred of Rievaulx. © 1977 by Cistercian Publications, Inc. Excerpts used by permission of Cistercian Publications, Inc.

From Southern, R. W. *Medieval Humanism and Other Studies.* © 1984 by Basil Blackwell. Excerpts from Chapter 4, "Medieval Humanism," used by permission of Blackwell Publishing, Inc.

To three friends,
Aelred, Thomas, and Annie,
Who have helped me in their various ways
out of a dark wood.

Ecce quam bonum et quam iucundum, habitare fratres in unum.

Ps. 132:1

Contents

Foreword ix

Preface xiii

Acknowledgments xv

Abbreviations xvi

Introduction 1

1 Differences between the More Experiential Approach of Monastic Theology and the More Conceptual Approach of Scholastic Theology 9

2 The Theological Account of Friendship in Aelered of Rievaulx 43

3 The Theological Account of Friendship in Thomas Aquinas 89

4 Aelred and Thomas Compared: Analysis, Conclusions, Final Speculations 133

Selected Bibliography 171

Foreword

There is a certain irony to the modern university. On the one hand, a university has the advantage of bringing scholars together into a community. One scholar need only walk across campus, or simply down the hall, to converse with another. The exchange of ideas is immediate, lively, personal. Many of us have experienced this as students or teachers. Meeting in the lounge, in hallways, over lunch, or for coffee, we speak, often as friends, sharing our thoughts and growing in insight as a consequence. But on the other hand, the fruit of university scholarship is so often impersonal. Hard scientific knowledge, *Wissenschaft*, is privileged, and subjective detachment encouraged in the interest of objectivity and a supposed neutrality. The fruit of intellectual inquiry is often impersonal, as a result, and also insipid. Ironically, the lively exchange of ideas among a community of scholars leads to the production of texts that are detached and impersonal.

The privileging of objective, scientific knowledge is certainly a cause. According to Newman, this privileging has its roots in the modern desire to be emancipated "from the capricious *ipse dixit* of authority,"[1] while at the same time wanting to have an authoritative, objective means for ascertaining the truth. Newman narrates the pursuit of this objective means for finding the truth in a style that tellingly echoes the biblical story of the Tower of Babylon:

> As the index on the dial notes down the sun's course in the heavens, as a key, revolving through the intricate wards of the lock, opens for us a treasure-house, so let us, if we can, provide ourselves with some ready expedient to serve as a true record of the system of objective truth, and an available rule for interpreting its phenomena; or at least let us go as far as we can in providing it.

---

1. John Henry Newman, *An Essay in Aid of a Grammar of Assent* (Notre Dame: University of Notre Dame Press, 2003), 211.

> One such experimental key is the science of geometry, which, in a certain department of nature, substitutes a collection of true principles, fruitful and interminable in consequences, for the guesses, *pro re natâ*, of our intellect, and saves it both the labour and the risk of guessing. Another far more subtle and effective instrument is algebraical science, which acts as a spell in unlocking for us, without merit or effort of our own individually, the *arcana* of the concrete physical universe. A more ambitious, because a more comprehensive contrivance still, for interpreting the concrete world is the method of logical inference. What we desiderate is something which may supersede the need of personal gifts by a far-reaching and infallible rule. Now, without external symbols to mark out and to steady its course, the intellect runs wild; but with the aid of symbols, as in algebra, it advances with precision and effect. Let then our symbols be words: let all thought be arrested and embodied in words.[2]

Notice the ambitious desire to "supersede the need of personal gifts by a far-reaching and infallible rule." In Newman's celebrated comparison of reasoning to rock climbing, he speaks of it as trying to reason "by rule" and he says that, in the last analysis, this is not how we reach the truth.[3] Rather than the detached, impersonal application of rules, the pursuit of truth, especially sublime truths, requires personal engagement and certain personal qualities.

Ultimately Newman finds Aristotle's *phronesis* useful for describing the matter. Aristotle correctly noted that the exercise of right moral judgment cannot be reduced to rules. No system of moral precepts automatically (and impersonally) produces correct moral decisions. The person must discern the right path in ways more fluid and subtle than can be articulated in prescribed rules. Moreover, to do this well one needs a personal attribute called *phronesis* (that is, the virtue of prudence). Newman argues that, likewise, correct reasoning about the truth is more fluid and subtle than can be delineated in the premises and conclusion of a syllogism. The rules of logical inference cannot completely map out for us the way to the truth, but we must rely on personal gifts and qualities—intellectual, moral, or otherwise—to get there.

---

2. Ibid.

3. John Henry Newman, *Sermon* 13.7 in *Fifteen Sermons Preached before the University of Oxford* (Notre Dame: University of Notre Dame Press, 2003), 257.

But Newman's critique of reasoning by *a priori* rules is not unsympathetic of their value. The rules of logical inference, like moral precepts, are useful. This makes the ironic tension of the modern university hard to resolve. There is indeed an indispensable personal and also communal dimension to the pursuit of truth, but the value of objective, methodological thinking cannot be altogether dismissed.

Nathan Lefler's study touches upon this tension. It explores a most personal subject, friendship, and it considers how two personally gifted thinkers in the Catholic tradition, St. Aelred and St. Thomas Aquinas, sought to understand friendship. Friendship is not peripheral to either thinker's system of thought. Aelred finds it to be a perfection, through grace, of inter-human relations and Aquinas defines the highest of all the virtues, charity, as friendship with God. Therefore both speakers, albeit in different respects, place friendship at the heart of the moral project. Human life, and in a sense all of reality, is ordered toward friendship. This is surely a very personalist view of things. Lefler examines how such a view manifests itself in each thinker's writings and also how the thinker's understanding of friendship relates to community, the Trinity, the eschaton, and the reading of the Bible.

Aelred and Aquinas consider friendship in different respects, with Aelred focusing on inter-human relationships and Thomas on the human-divine relationship, but in addition to this, their approaches and styles differ. Do differing approaches and styles matter? Lefler argues yes. He proposes that "a certain recognizable correspondence between the mode in which a subject is presented and the nature of that subject itself has great merit, especially in terms of its capacity for being fruitfully received by a hearer or reader." This is "one of the great strengths of Aelred's account," whereas Aquinas' scholastic approach is not exactly aglow with the warmth that corresponds to friendship. At the same time, Lefler entertains the possibility that "the charm of Aelred's account, for all its power to seduce us, may risk intermittently obscuring our Lordly Friend from our vision, in his less comely guise as a Suffering Servant" (p. 165). Lefler further entertains, by way of Leclercq, that monastic theology, typified by Aelred, and scholastic theology, typified by Aquinas, may complement each other.

Lefler is appreciative of both thinkers, but in the end his sympathies are with the monastic style of St. Aelred. One senses that this is especially in resistance to the dominance that the scholastic style gained at the end of the Middle Ages. But such a resistance to scholastic dominance in theology

Foreword

may be a favor shown to scholastic theology. To this writer at least, the scholastic mode of inquiry is like that of a commentary which presupposes familiarity with the texts, ideas, and realities upon which it comments. If, then, these texts, ideas, and realities are forgotten, the scholastic style loses its purpose and lends itself to caricature. It was never meant to monopolize the way in which Christian truths were presented. Other texts and media were meant to present these truths and to be the means, even the primary means, for gaining access to them. Accordingly, I have found that the brilliance of St. Thomas' writings shines forth most brightly when they are kept in conversation with other thinkers, especially the Fathers and biblical authors.

While I would not read Aquinas' scholastic approach in substantial continuity with modernity's detached, impersonal mode of pursuing the truth, still Lefler forces us to consider the impersonal style of Aquinas. What are we to make of it? Does it hinder his aims? Is it at odds with the personal, enlivening faith it aims to present? Or if his style is indeed valuable, how is this to be understood? In turn, if we look to the writings of Aelred, we might ask: How is their more charming style not to be mistaken for sentimental theologizing? Or granted that Aelred's thinking does not lack rigor, can that rigor be explicated academically without using a more scholastic or dry and impersonal style? Reading Lefler's study is an invitation to exercise the mind on such questions, in addition to questions concerning friendship itself. But the two sets of questions may be related, especially if friendship is at the heart of the intellectual endeavor. In that case, the greatness of a university may lie not simply in how strictly it adheres to scientific and critical methods, but in the quality of relationships between its scholars, not to mention between the scholars and God.

Austin G. Murphy, OSB

Preface

The following work constitutes a lightly edited version of my dissertation, originally defended in 2008. As the project is anchored in a comparison of the writings of two men whose floruits were many centuries ago, I have not deemed it necessary to update the essentially speculative argument derived from my original analysis: though there has been a good deal of work done on each author over the past several years and some work drawing Aelred and Aquinas into the same ambit under one rubric or another, no one that I know of has placed their thinking on friendship head to head in an extended discussion, much less as an entrée into the comparative evaluation of monastic and scholastic theology. There is a further, positive reason for leaving my original argument essentially as-is, namely, that, as the reader shall see in my introduction, I deliberately draw attention to the genre of the dissertation, noting some of the implications of that form for academic discourse and proposing to engage that form in my own case in what may be deemed somewhat problematic ways, at any rate according to the canons of modern scientific discourse. Whether the outcome is beneficial or deleterious to the common good is for the reader to decide.

The dissertation investigates the theological accounts of friendship offered by Aelred of Rievaulx and Thomas Aquinas, compares these accounts, and applies this localized comparison as an index of the relationship between monastic and scholastic theology in general.

Through close reading of the key texts in which the subject of friendship is treated, Aelred's *Speculum caritatis* and *De spiritali amicitia* and Thomas's *Summa Theologiae*, the two authors are found to epitomize their different theological milieux, the monastic and the scholastic respectively. This judgment pertains as much to the content of the two accounts as it does to the form. Thus, not only each author's theological approach, but his distinctive understanding of friendship itself, proves to be profoundly

Preface

congruent with his spiritual-theological matrix, whether twelfth-century monasticism on the one hand, or thirteenth-century scholasticism on the other.

In fact, a loose, tripartite analogy may be seen to obtain among friendship, reading and theology in the monastic milieu, while a parallel analogy is to be found, *mutatis mutandis*, in the scholastic realm. Taking due care to demonstrate this relationship according to the rigors of comparative textual analysis, the earnest effort is made at the same time not to minimize the heterogeneity of the texts and theological perspectives in question. Granting Jean Leclercq's wise dictum that the Church has but "one theology," we recognize as well the risk of misconstruing that theological unity as monolithic.

In short, monastic theology, like monastic friendship according to the exemplary account of Aelred of Rievaulx, is ideally a balanced activity of reason and will, profoundly Christ-centered, existentially grounded in both sensible and spiritual experience, and quintessentially expressed in the perfect union of will and ideas between the persons involved. Scholastic theology, on the other hand, seeks to elucidate as clearly as possible both nature and supernature and the relation between them, in the bright light of natural reason, yet simultaneously elevated by the brighter light of supernatural grace. In doing so, the enterprise strongly resembles Thomas's notion of friendship as the ideal relation between God and man.

Acknowledgments

I would like to thank several people for their especial support in bringing to completion the original form of this book, namely, my dissertation. First, I must acknowledge the faithful work of my director, Father James Wiseman, O.S.B., whose unwavering consistency and extraordinary efficiency made the project far less onerous than it might have been. I would also like to thank my readers: Father Regis Armstrong, O.F.M.Cap., for his willingness to read my dissertation, but also and particularly for one of the finest seminars in medieval theology I have had the privilege of attending, and Father Raymond Studzinski, for stepping into the proverbial breach. I should add that Father Studzinski's recent book, *Reading to Live: The Evolving Practice of* Lectio Divina, has provided welcome confirmation of part of the background argument for my opening chapter. To these older debts of gratitude I must now append those accrued through the process of editing and preparing my manuscript for publication as a book. Above all in this latter category, I must thank Father Austin Murphy, OSB, Abbot of St. Procopius Abbey and old friend, for his willingness to read my dissertation and write a foreword, in the midst of overseeing a large Benedictine community and its numerous adjoining apostolates. Next, I am deeply grateful to Mary Ann Smith, whose sharp eye and editorial prowess when thrown suddenly into the breach enabled her quickly and unerringly to accomplish what would have taken me months of fretting and probably years off my life. I am also grateful to Patricia Mecadon for her professional typesetting skills. I would like to acknowledge as well the spiritual and emotional support of my parents, Charles and Susan Lefler, who have never doubted my abilities or my heart, no matter how frequent and great have been my own mistrust of both. Finally, I would like to acknowledge my wife, Annie, for whom this work in many ways has been principally executed, and without whom it would never have taken the shape it has.

Abbreviations

DDN	*In Librum Beati Dionysii De divinis nominibus*
De am.	*De amicitia*
Eth.	*Sententia Libri Ethicorum*
Iesu puero	*De Iesu puero duodenni*
Ioannis	*Super evangelium S. Ioannis lectura*
NE	*Nichomachean Ethics*
O. past.	*Oratio pastoralis*
RB	*The Rule of St. Benedict*
SA	*De spiritali amicitia*
SC	*Speculum caritatis*
SCG	*Summa contra Gentiles*
Sent.	*Scriptum Super libros Sententiarum*
ST	*Summa Theologiae*

Introduction

*A**mare et amari*: these lapidary words of St. Augustine's haunted the high Middle Ages and its theologians, both in the monasteries and in the Schools.¹ The phrase not only captured Augustine's romantic pre-Christian notion of friendship, thereby bearing importantly on humanistic questions of an anthropological or psychological cast; since "God is love," according to St. John, "to love and to be loved" must in some way pertain to the heart of theology as well.² But if *amor* describes in the most general terms an action or disposition that could be further specified as one of either *amicitia* or *caritas*, what, in turn, is the relationship between these latter two notions? In one way or another, both monks and schoolmen came to be exercised by these questions, and the revival of the Roman rhetorical tradition in the twelfth century, including crucially Cicero's *De Amicitia*, along with the translation of Aristotle's *Nicomachean Ethics* in the following century, only added fuel to the flame. Among those who became keenly interested in the issue were the Cistercian abbot, Aelred of Rievaulx, and the Dominican friar, Thomas Aquinas.

Not surprisingly, the theological treatments of friendship produced by these two authors—the twelfth-century monk on the one hand, the thirteenth-century scholastic theologian on the other—differ in many significant ways. It is precisely the central thesis of the following dissertation that the differences between these two accounts of friendship exhibit a certain congruence with fundamental differences between monastic and scholastic theology *tout court*. However, this thesis may be further subdivided, inasmuch as we will argue that the correspondence asserted is not merely

---

1. Augustine, *Confessions*, II, 2. For allusions by our own two authors, see Aelred of Rievaulx, *SC* I.25.71, *SA* Prologus.1, and Thomas Aquinas, *Sent.* distinction 27, question 2, article 1.

2. Deus caritas est. 1 Jn. 4:8 (Vulgate).

formal, limited, for example, to ways in which each of our two authors' accounts of friendship respectively instantiates monastic or scholastic theological method *per se*. Rather, we contend that the discovered correspondence touches also the particular subject matter in question, namely, *friendship* under its Christian theological aspect. What is true, therefore, about the monastic notion of friendship can be seen to characterize the monastic theological project as well, and the same reasoning applies, *mutatis mutandis*, to the scholastic notion and enterprise. In order, then, to facilitate the reader's progress through the dissertation, we will now briefly outline the procedure whereby we arrive at these conclusions.

In chapter 1, we undertake a preliminary survey of the distinguishing features of monastic and scholastic theology in the period spanned by the lives of our two authors. The aim of this preparatory chapter is twofold: first, to provide ourselves with a general sense of the very different cultural and theological milieux within which Aelred and Thomas lived and wrote;[3] second, to delineate a number of more particular criteria, drawn from our assessment of these milieux, by which we may gauge the theological projects of Aelred and Thomas in the ensuing chapters.[4] It is here that we find reasons for our expectations of significantly different approaches on the parts of our two authors. The chapter also contains a brief survey of the typical sources employed by the two milieux in their theological endeavors, noting both the commonalities and some significant differences.[5] On all of these points, our principal guidance comes from the lifework of Dom Jean Leclercq, whose defense of monastic theology provides one of the seminal impulses behind our own inquiry. In the final major section of the chapter the choice of Aelred and Thomas, as both typical and at the same time outstanding representatives of their respective milieux, is defended.[6] A brief

---

3. The monastic and scholastic milieux are, however, carved out of the much larger common culture of high medieval educated Western Europe, in consequence of which it is possible to overdraw the differences between these two sub-cultural units. On this point, see the sections entitled: "Common Culture" and "Cautionary Paragraph " from chapter 1 and "Conclusions, Challenges, Possible Avenues for Further Exploration" from chapter 4.

4. See especially the conclusion of the section entitled: "Differences between Monastic and Scholastic Theology" in chapter 1, below.

5. See the section on "Sources" in chapter 1, below.

6. See sections "Aelred: How Typical; How Understanding" and "Thomas: How Typical; How Understanding" in chapter 1, below.

argument is also made for the choice of friendship as the theological *topos* for investigation.[7]

Chapters 2 and 3 comprise the bulk of our investigation of primary sources, namely, the writings of Aelred of Rievaulx and Thomas Aquinas. We begin each of these chapters with a summary of contemporary scholarship,[8] followed by a sketch of the author's own major sources.[9] Having surveyed each author's corpus as a whole, we train our attention on those works in which are to be found their most trenchant and comprehensive theological treatments of friendship: Aelred's *Speculum caritatis* (hereafter referred to as *SC*) and *De spiritali amicitia* (hereafter referred to as *SA*), on the one hand, and the *Secunda Pars* of the *Summa Theologiae* (hereafter referred to as *ST*) of Thomas on the other.

The principal task of chapter 2 is to provide a close analysis of the two major works by Aelred that bear significantly on the subject of friendship.[10] In addition to elucidating the content of each work in detail, the chapter gives careful consideration to the relationship between them, with respect not only to their theological content, but also to the formal and historical relations between the texts themselves. In the course of the textual analysis of these works, the distinctive features of Aelred's theological account of friendship are delineated. A brief treatment of Aelred's approach to Scriptural exegesis is appended to the main discussion, in consequence of our conviction of the impact of one's mode of *reading*—especially the Bible—on the way one does theology.[11] In conclusion of the investigation of our first major author, we argue that Aelred presents a splendid spiritual vision of holy friendship and its eschatological telos, in the idiom of medieval monastic theology.[12] Neither argumentative nor systematic, Aelred's account bespeaks his own innocence and purity of heart. Thus, his theology of friendship proves to be an integral and harmonious expression of his monastic life, a life defined by prayer, both in solitude and in choir, and by the virtually unceasing practice of *lectio divina*.

---

7. See the section "Why Their Accounts of Friendship" in chapter 1, below.

8. See the sections in chapter 2 and 3 on "Contemporary Scholarship," below.

9. See section "Aelred's Sources" in chapter 2 and "Thomas's Sources" in chapter 3, below.

10. See the section entitled "Aelred's 'Synthesis' and Original Position" in chapter 2, below.

11. See the section "Aelred's Friendly Exegesis" in chapter 2, below.

12. See the section "Conclusion: Aelred's Monastic Theology of Friendship" in chapter 2, below.

Theologizing Friendship

In chapter 3 an analysis of Thomas Aquinas's theological account of friendship is carried out, in deliberate parallel with the analysis of Aelred's account in chapter 2.[13] Thomas's most mature and thorough treatment of friendship is discovered to transpire wholly within the bounds of what is technically a single work, the *Summa theologiae*.[14] Nevertheless, we find that this treatment is readily parsed out between two subsections of that work, namely, the *Prima Secundae*, where Thomas first deals with love and friendship in the natural realm, and the *Secunda Secundae*, in which he brings his previous explanation of friendship to bear on the subject of supernatural charity.[15] Thus, we find an immediate parallel with Aelred, in terms of both the structure and the constitutive elements of the two authors' accounts: on the one hand, each of the accounts spans two major textual loci; on the other hand, each of these loci, in turn, is preoccupied with one of the two key theological terms, *amicitia* or *caritas*. As with Aelred, we proceed through a close analysis of Thomas's texts to enumerate the signal features of his theological account of friendship,[16] again ending with a brief look at his exegetical practice.[17] In conclusion of our inquiry into his work, we contend that Thomas's finely wrought definition of charity as man's friendship for God embodies *in nuce* one of scholasticism's most remarkable achievements: the harmonization of Christian revelation with Aristotelian philosophy.[18] In anticipation of chapter 4, we also observe that Thomas's theological account of friendship exhibits the major characteristics of scholastic theology in general, described in chapter 1.

The fourth and final chapter of the dissertation draws together the key findings from the three preceding chapters. More specifically, here our assessments of the two theological accounts of friendship are directly juxtaposed and compared point by point, with respect both to their material characteristics, and also to their form. That is to say, first, the distinctive features of the content of each of the two accounts, to which we have drawn attention in the two preceding chapters, are set side by side

---

13. See the section "Thomas's Synthesis and Original Position" in chapter 3, below.

14. See the section "Rousselot's 'Problem of Love' and Vansteenberghe's 'Amitié'" in chapter 3, below.

15. See the section "Thomas's Sources" in chapter 3.

16. See the section "Thomas's Synthesis and Original Position" in chapter 3, below.

17. See the section "Thomas's Exegesis: *Lectio utilis?*" in chapter 3, below.

18. See the section ""Conclusion: Thomas's Scholastic Theology of Friendship" in chapter 3, below.

Introduction

and each characteristic is evaluated relative to the parallel characteristic of the alternative account.[19] The outcome of this comparative analysis is then supplemented by a formal comparison between the accounts, again based on the findings of chapters 2 and 3, only this time with further reference to the formal comparative framework established in chapter 1.[20] Finally, the results of this stereoscopic analysis are distilled into a single formulation, articulated in terms of an analogy of friendship.[21] This pithy conclusion is in turn elaborated in terms of an Aelredian and monastic expression on one side and a Thomistic and scholastic version on the other.[22] In both cases it is asserted that the analogy spans three elements treated in the dissertation: the author's notion of friendship itself, his way of reading, and ultimately the way he does theology. So, too, *mutatis mutandis*, with the two authors' respective milieux. In light of this general conclusion, several challenges are proposed to each of our two authors' accounts, either from the perspective of the alternative account, or independently.[23] The dissertation ends with four brief speculative suggestions for further inquiry.[24]

Two further points are in order, which will prove in the final analysis to be complementary aspects of the same underlying reality. One point concerns the dissertation's principal subject matter, the other the intellectual approach entertained by the author of the dissertation towards the dissertation itself. First, there is a mild degree of intellectual embarrassment, never adverted to explicitly in the dissertation, resulting from a profound asymmetry between the two notions of friendship treated by Aelred of Rievaulx and Thomas Aquinas, respectively. This is not to say that the two perspectives share no common ground, much less that they cannot be placed in counterpoint and conversation with each other. Nevertheless, such a project presents a dilemma likely to appear initially rather daunting, particularly—and precisely—when such a project is undertaken according to the constraints of the peculiarly modern genre called the doctoral dissertation. The dilemma is, in the words of the old but durable cliché,

---

19. See the section "Content of the Two Accounts Compared" in chapter 4, below.
20. See the section "Form of the Two Accounts Compared" in chapter 4, below.
21. See the section "The Analogy of Friendship" in chapter 4, below.
22. See the sections "Aelred and Monastic Friendship" and "Thomas and Scholastic Friendship" in chapter 4, below.
23. See the section "Challenges: Evaluations of the Two Analogies and Beyond" in chapter 4, below.
24. See the section "Speculative Suggestion for Further Inquiry" in chapter 4, below.

how to compare an apple with an orange. Furthermore, the fathers of the Enlightenment generated a ratiocinative apparatus that has often tempted its users, when faced with such a comparison, to begin by trying to turn the orange into an apple, or vice versa, in order to carry out the much easier comparison between two specimens of the same fruit. Originally erected in service of the so-called hard sciences, this apparatus gradually made its way into humanistic intellectual endeavors as well,[25] influencing in the process all genres of academic writing—preeminent among them, the dissertation. And with the seductive tool came the besetting temptation noted. The effort by the current dissertation's author to employ the tool judiciously while resisting the temptation brings us to the second point.

So far as was deemed compatible with the conventional scholarly requirements of the genre, we have attempted *not* to succumb to the occasional academic weakness for prestidigitation, touching either fruit or friendship. Consequently, the reader will find rather drastic disparities between the lengths of sections treating the same or parallel themes in our respective authors. Yet to have forced these sections into the same-sized outfits, as it were, would have falsified both positions, and thereby also necessarily undermined our comparison between them, ultimately rendering our conclusions and the whole enterprise intellectually suspect. Similarly, while the reader will find in the following pages a great deal of careful, logical argumentation, shored up by regular appeal to both primary and secondary sources, he will not find the presumption that the conclusions arrived at are to be received as indisputable, scientifically watertight propositions: quite the contrary. Moreover, we insist that this state of things, however unsatisfactory it may be to some, is no decoy for desultoriness on our part: rather, we believe we wander closer to the truth (often in spite of ourselves) when we allow it a certain amount of room to play. Consider, for example, such relatively recent oddities as Goedel's Incompleteness Theorem, chaos theory, or fuzzy mathematics: all essentially post-modern responses—now each more or less well-respected—to modern rationalism and its totalizing agenda. We engage our topic, then, deliberately in somewhat the mode of a juggler, or particle physicist, keeping elements of the discussion alive and in the air, knowing full-well that they are liable to change in bumping into one another. This is not sloppy science in a modern register: it is more like the highly rational yet non-restrictive activity of

---

25. Cf. Hans-Georg Gadamer's classical treatment of this complex process in *Truth and Method*, especially 171–379.

dancing, and dancing in a post-modern key. Indeed, if it is conceded that the dissertation is a thoroughly modern genre, we predict that the genre will eventually implode, if it cannot expand to allow the self-confrontation invited by the post-modern challenge to a rationalism ultimately imperiling the very search for truth it claims to champion.

In brief, the following dissertation seeks, as its title indicates, to shed further light on the relationship between monastic and scholastic theology, both historically and *in se*, through the high-filter lens of friendship, construed as a theological *topos* or category, focused narrowly on two personal subjects, Aelred and Thomas, both of whom had important things to say about the topic. As suggested above, we are also concerned to guard against the superficial and false homogenizing of the two accounts that would result if we reduced our analysis to questions of method. This would be, in our opinion, to cede the field of debate to one side, namely, that of scholasticism, before the discussion had even been joined. In this connection too, we may construe our own project as one that, loosely, employs both more monastic approaches—the existential and historical—and more scholastic approaches—the speculative and systematic—in order to elucidate the differences between Aelred and Thomas on friendship. More than this, we have sought to draw attention to some elements of a genuine monastic theology that have indeed been muted, if not even altogether lost, in the wake of the ascendancy of scholasticism and its continuous dominance of the Church's professional theological enterprise until the present. Without, then, we trust, giving short shrift to the genuine benefits of the basic formalities of the academic dissertation, we have aimed at the same time for a modest transcendence of those long established boundaries. It is for the reader to judge whether, and to what extent, we have succeeded in our endeavor.

1

Differences between the More Experiential Approach of Monastic Theology and the More Conceptual Approach of Scholastic Theology

CONTEMPORARY SCHOLARSHIP

In service of our comparison between the particular theological accounts of friendship given by St. Aelred of Rievaulx and St. Thomas Aquinas, a preliminary description of the relationship between monastic and scholastic theological approaches *per se* will provide the most helpful point of departure. In this preparatory chapter, our preeminent guide will be the great twentieth-century Benedictine scholar, Jean Leclercq. The conclusions of Leclercq's extensive and profound researches will be supplemented principally by the work of R. W. Southern, Beryl Smalley, David Knowles and Ivan Illich.

Common Culture

Between the birth of Aelred of Rievaulx in 1110 and the death of Thomas Aquinas in 1274, a substantial homogeneity of culture obtained throughout Western Europe. David Knowles comments that "For three hundred years, from 1050 to 1350, and above all in the century between 1070 and 1170, the whole of educated Western Europe formed a single undifferentiated cultural unit."[1] Jean Leclercq, who tends to insist on the non-monolithic character of medieval life and culture, nevertheless confirms Knowles's assertion in a somewhat peculiar way when he argues that, "jusqu'alors [xiie siècle], toute la culture médiévale porte l'empreinte monastique, et qu'en ce sens et dans cette mesure elle est une culture monastique."[2] To the extent, then, that medieval culture, at least up until the twelfth century, can be said to be monastic, it necessarily maintains a certain uniformity of character. Moreover, as Knowles's chronologically broader claim suggests, such a deeply ingrained uniformity of Christian worldview and practice was by no means easily shed, even through Aquinas's lifetime and well beyond. In *The Love of Learning and the Desire for God*, Leclercq is furthermore earnestly concerned to stress the fundamental unicity of the Church's theology, however divergent or even disparate may appear its sundry expressions from one era, or nation, or school, to another:

> Fundamentally, as there is but one Church, one faith, one Scripture, one tradition, and one authority, there is but one theology. Theology cannot be the specialty of any one milieu, where it would be, as it were, imprisoned. Like every great personality, every culture, and even more, necessarily, every reflection on the Catholic faith, every theology is, by its essence, universal and overflows the confines of specialization. It is only within the great cultural entities which have succeeded one another in the life of the Church that different currents can be observed; but they cannot be separated.[3]

In this dissertation, we will be very much concerned with a number of significant *differences* between monastic and scholastic theology. Precisely for this reason, we must heed attentively Leclercq's salutary reminder concerning theology, along with the generally acknowledged evidence of broad cultural homogeneity spanning the lifetimes of Aelred and Thomas and the years in between.

---

1. Knowles, *The Evolution of Medieval Thought*, 80.
2. Leclercq, *Aux Sources de la Spiritualité Occidentale*, 283.
3. Leclercq, *The Love of Learning*, 193.

Differences between Monastic and Scholastic Theology

Midway through his project of delineating a true "monastic theology," Leclercq affirms "real continuity between the patristic age and the medieval monastic centuries, and between patristic culture and medieval culture." He continues:

> And it is this continuity which gives medieval monastic culture its specific character: it is a patristic culture, the prolongation of patristic culture in another age and in another civilization. From this point of view, it seems possible to distinguish, from the eighth to the twelfth centuries in the West, something like two Middle Ages. The monastic Middle Ages, while profoundly Western and profoundly Latin, seems closer to the East than to the other, the scholastic Middle Ages which flourished at the same time and on the same soil. Our intention here is by no means to deny that scholasticism represents a legitimate evolution and a real progress in Christian thought, but rather to point out this coexistence of two Middle Ages. To be sure, the culture developed in the monastic Middle Ages differs from that developed in scholastic circles. The monastic Middle Ages is essentially patristic because it is thoroughly penetrated by ancient sources and, under their influence, centered on the great realities which are at the very heart of Christianity and give it its life. It is not dispersed in the occasionally secondary problems discussed in the schools. Above all, it is based on biblical interpretation similar to the Fathers' and, like theirs, founded on reminiscence, the spontaneous recall of texts taken from Scripture itself with all the consequences which follow from this procedure, notably the use of allegory.[4]

Bearing in mind Leclercq's provocative notion of "two Middle Ages," let us proceed to consider more carefully some of the significant ways in which monastic and scholastic theology diverge, in keeping with the differences between their respective milieux.[5]

If we begin at the most generic level, already we discover a striking contrast between the metaphors employed by monks and schoolmen to

---

4. Ibid., 106–7.

5. In *The Monastic Order in England*, David Knowles observes that "from 1150 onwards an ever-increasing number of monks, and those the intellectual *elite*, owed their training to the schools, not to the cloister" (502). Notwithstanding the usefulness of Leclercq's schema, we are continually, and rightly, reminded of the semi-permeability of the boundary between the medieval monastery and the non-monastic clerical world of the day.

describe their respective theological activities. Thus, R. W. Southern says of the monks that "they liked to think of themselves as bees gathering nectar far and wide, and storing it in the secret cells of the mind."[6] Leclercq recalls St. Bernard's description of himself and his fellow-monks as "lowly gleaners," in comparison with those great reapers, Sts. Augustine, Jerome, and Gregory, not to mention the other Fathers.[7] And Ivan Illich highlights the medieval characterizations of monks, by themselves and others, as "mumblers and munchers," ruminating, or chewing, on the divine words of Scripture.[8] The scholastics, on the other hand, when compared with the great thinkers of antiquity in the memorable description of Bernard of Chartres, were like "dwarfs perched on the shoulders of giants," able to see a little farther, however much lesser their stature, than those by whose accomplishments they hoisted themselves up.[9] Even more significantly, it was the schoolmen for whom the most compelling image of Heaven came to be the Beatific Vision. We find, then, that whereas the theological enterprise of the monks is depicted by various metaphors of eating, the work of the schools is chiefly conceived under the metaphorical rubric of sight, or vision. The evident privileging of different senses here—the highly concrete sense of taste, and by extension, touch and smell, on the one hand; the most spiritual of the senses, sight, on the other—is not arbitrary. Rather, it proves to be congruent with the contrast between the fundamentally more experiential, tactile, aesthetic mode of being and thinking embraced by the monks, and the more strictly conceptual, abstract mode of thought cultivated in the scholastic milieu.

Ways of Reading

These metaphorical differences are expressive in imaginative terms of a whole range of more empirically verifiable differences embodied in the practices of reading, writing and theological inquiry typically employed by monks and schoolmen respectively. The most foundational of all such activities, the one without which would-be practitioners of the others cannot venture the first step, is reading. Though an authentically secular meaning

---

6. Southern, *The Making of the Middle Ages*, 190.
7. Leclercq, *The Love of Learning*, 202.
8. Illich, *In the Vineyard*, 54–57; citation at 54.
9. Leclercq, *The Love of Learning*, 202; cf. Southern, *The Making of the Middle Ages*, 203.

Differences between the More Experiential Approach of Monastic Theology

of the word is inevitably promoted by the pursuit of the strictly non-ecclesial disciplines of medicine and secular law, *lectio*, for the medieval churchman, whether monk, friar, or secular cleric, means above all else the reading of Scripture. Leclercq explains the profound divergence between monastic and scholastic *lectio* in the following illuminating passage:

> Since Scripture is a book, one must know how to read it, and learn how to read it just as one learns how to read any other book. . . . However, this application of grammar to Scripture has been practiced in monasticism in a way which is entirely its own because it is linked with the fundamental observances of monastic life. The basic method is different from that of non-monastic circles where Scripture is read—namely, the schools. Originally, *lectio divina* and *sacra pagina* are equivalent expressions. For St. Jerome as for St. Benedict, the *lectio divina* is the text itself which is being read, a selected passage or a 'lesson' taken from Scripture. During the Middle Ages, this expression was to be reserved more and more for the act of reading, 'the reading of Holy Scripture.' In the school it refers most often to the page itself, the text which is under study, taken objectively. Scripture is studied for its own sake. In the cloister, however, it is rather the reader and the benefit that he derives from Holy Scripture which are given consideration. In both instances an activity is meant which is 'holy', *sacra, divina*; but in the two milieux, the accent is put on two different aspects of the same activity. The orientation differs, and, consequently, so does the procedure. The scholastic *lectio* takes the direction of the *quaestio* and the *disputatio*. The reader puts questions to the text and then questions himself on the subject matter: *quaeri solet*. The monastic *lectio* is oriented toward the *meditatio* and the *oratio*. The objective of the first is science and knowledge; of the second, wisdom and appreciation. In the monastery, the *lectio divina*, which begins with grammar, terminates in compunction, in desire of heaven.[10]

The monastic emphasis on compunction, with its correlative spiritual desire,[11] ultimately has important eschatological implications, which will be taken up below. It also tends inevitably to entail a certain privileging of the will. The particular point at stake here is that the relative weights

---

10. Ibid., 72.

11. The most important literary roots of the monastic notion of *compunctio* are in the writings of St. Gregory the Great and receive a new infusion from St. Bernard. See ibid., 25–34, 67–68, passim.

13

accorded intellect and will have implications even for the ways in which readers engage texts.

Ivan Illich, in his treatment of Hugh of St. Victor's great work, the *Didascalicon*, articulates the distinction between monastic and scholastic reading in equally stark terms, though he arrives at his conclusions via an entirely different mode of inquiry from that of Leclercq. Illich advances the thesis that "By emphasizing *exemplum* as the task of the teacher, and *aedificatio* as its result in the town community at large, Hugh recognizes that the new Canons Regular, and not just he as a person, stand on a watershed between monastic and scholastic reading."[12] He goes on to argue that this exemplary and edifying role does not persist in the schools: rather, the Canons occupy what proves shortly to have been an anomalous position, atop the watershed, as it were, where reading has not yet lost

> its analogy to the bell which is heard and remembered by all the townsfolk, though it principally regulates the hours of canonical prayer for the cloister. Scholastic reading then becomes a professional task for scholars—and scholars who, by their definition as clerical professionals, are not an edifying example for the man in the street. They define themselves as people who do something special that excludes the layman.[13]

Illich's haunting image of remembered tintinnabulation points to another characteristic difference between monastic and scholastic modes of reading, one which leads to a watershed in exegetical technique between the two milieux. This is the way memory functions in the two environments. Reminiscences, according to Leclercq, "are not quotations, elements of phrases borrowed from another. They are the words of the person using them; they belong to him."[14] So highly developed, in fact, was the monks' aptitude for graphic recollection of texts that

> The monastic Middle Ages made little use of the written concordance; the spontaneous play of associations, similarities, and comparisons are sufficient for exegesis. In scholasticism, on the contrary, much use is made of these *Distinctiones*, where, in alphabetical order, each word is placed opposite references to all the

---

12. Illich, *In the Vineyard*, 79. For a recent, lucid distillation of the work of Illich, Leclecq and others on the transition from monastic to scholastic reading, see Studzinski, *Reading to Live*, 12–17 and 140–76, especially 141–46, 149, 161–66, 172–76.

13. Ibid., 81.

14. Leclercq, *The Love of Learning*, 75.

Differences between the More Experiential Approach of Monastic Theology

texts in which it is used; these written concordances can be used to replace, but only in a bookish and artificial manner, the spontaneous phenomenon of reminiscence.[15]

With reminiscence, in contrast with the *Distinctiones*, "one becomes a sort of living concordance."[16]

Ways and Kinds of Writing

STYLE

In their writing, too, the monks and the schoolmen differ significantly, both in style and in preferred genres, as well as in the uses they make of those genres they have in common. Leclercq identifies three distinct humanisms, those of monasticism and scholasticism, and a third "neo-classic" humanism represented by such "worldly clerics" as Peter of Blois and John of Salisbury, who belong neither to the university nor to the cloister. Comparing the writing styles that emerge from these three humanisms, Leclercq observes that

> Monastic style keeps equally distant from the clear but graceless style of the scholastic *quaestiones* and the neo-classic style of these humanists. . . . In this sense, one can rightly speak, with regard to the most representative types of monastic culture . . . of a 'monastic style.' The literary heritage of all of antiquity, secular and patristic, can be found in it, yet less under the form of imitation or reminiscences of ancient authors than in a certain resonance which discloses a familiarity, acquired by long association, with their literary practices. . . . This was both a way of thinking and a way of expressing oneself. Thus the *lectio divina* complemented harmoniously the grammar that was learned in school.[17]

Leaving aside the neo-classic category, the monastic and scholastic styles tend to express their respective cultural biases, the one more literary, the other more speculative. Where the monks embrace grammar, music and rhetoric, the schoolmen prefer dialectics, to the detriment of the rest of the

---

15. Ibid., 77.

16. Ibid. The distinction between the living and the written concordance corresponds as well with Illich's fascinating theory of the place of "alphabetic technologies" in the transition in medieval Europe from an essentially monastic to an essentially scholastic way of reading. Cf. especially the sixth chapter of Illich, *In the Vineyard*, 93–114.

17. Leclercq, *The Love of Learning*, 143.

seven liberal arts; they forfeit "artistry of expression," in favor of "clarity of thought" at all costs. For the monks' genuine concern for beauty of expression, the schoolmen substitute "words originating in a sort of unaesthetic jargon, provided only that they be specific." Consequently, "the language of orators and poets gives place to that of metaphysicians and logicians."[18] Simply put, "the modes of expression and the processes of thought [of monastic theology] are linked with a style and with literary genres which conform to the classical and patristic tradition."[19] With the masters of the urban schools, on the other hand,

> the accent is no longer placed on grammar, the *littera*, but on logic. Just as they are no longer satisfied with the *auctoritas* of Holy Scripture and the Fathers and invoke that of the philosophers, so clarity is what is sought in everything. Hence the fundamental difference between scholastic style and monastic style. The monks speak in images and comparisons borrowed from the Bible and possessing both a richness and an obscurity in keeping with the mystery to be expressed.[20]

Leclercq proceeds with a revealing contrast between St. Bernard's understanding of "biblical language," as the essential mode appropriate for theological activity, and the burgeoning new scholastic terminology:

> St. Bernard sees in the biblical tongue a certain modesty which respects God's mysteries; he admires the tact and discretion God used in speaking to men. Hence, he says: *Geramus morem Scripturae*. The scholastics are concerned with achieving clarity; consequently they readily make use of abstract terms, and they never hesitate to forge new words. . . . For [Bernard], this terminology is never more than a vocabulary for emergency use and it does not supplant the biblical vocabulary. The one he customarily uses remains, like the Bible's, essentially poetic; his language is consistently more literary than that of the School. . . . In answering doctrinal questions put to him by Hugh of St. Victor . . . he transposes into the biblical mode what his correspondent had said to him in the school language.[21]

---

18. Hubert, "Aspects du latin philosophique," 227–31, cited by Leclercq, *The Love of Learning*, 142 n. 130. The previous brief citations are from the same passage in Leclercq.
19. Leclercq, *The Love of Learning*, 199.
20. Ibid., 200.
21. Ibid., 200–201.

Differences between the More Experiential Approach of Monastic Theology

In general, then, the monastic style tends to be biblical, literary, aesthetically self-aware, even poetic, whereas the scholastic style is dialectical, logical, technical and abstract.

Apropos of Leclercq's observation of the fundamental dichotomy between rhetoric in the monasteries and logic in the schools, R. W. Southern describes the basic distinction between rhetoric and logic and the gradual shift in emphasis from the one to the other in the period spanning the late tenth to the early thirteenth century. He begins his historical account of this transition with a discussion of the revolutionary teaching career of Gerbert of Rheims, later to become Pope Silvester II. Southern writes:

> it is a striking thing that though this impulse to the study of logic was probably Gerbert's most important contribution to medieval learning, he did not allow it that pride of place among the arts which it later attained. Gerbert aimed at restoring the classical past, and nowhere was he more faithful to this aim than in the preeminence which he gave to the art of rhetoric. He had no room for the forward-reaching spirit of enquiry which animated the study of logic in the twelfth century. His energies were concentrated on the task of conservation, and on the worthy presentation of long-acquired, and sometimes long-lost, truths. Hence he was drawn to the art of rhetoric by a double chain: first because it was the chief literary science of the ancient world; secondly because it was congenial to his own spirit of conservatism. Rhetoric is static; logic dynamic. The one aims at making old truths palatable, the other at searching out new, even unpalatable truths—like the *invidiosi veri*, syllogized, in Dante's phrase, by Siger of Brabant [*Paradiso*, x, 138]. Rhetoric is persuasive, logic compulsive. The former smooths away divisions, the latter brings them into the open. The one is a healing art, an art of government; the other is surgical, and challenges the foundations of conduct and belief. To persuade, to preserve, to heal the divisions between past and present—these were Gerbert's aims, and in this work rhetoric and statesmanship went hand in hand, with logic as their servant. . . . Hence for Gerbert rhetoric, not logic, was the queen of the arts.[22]

Though Southern's point in this particular context is not to distinguish monasticism from scholasticism—Gerbert was not even a monk, but one of the itinerant masters that became such a common phenomenon in the tenth and eleventh centuries—nevertheless, the fundamental distinction between rhetoric and logic provides an important lens for appreciating

22. Southern, *The Making of the Middle Ages*, 176.

the gap, ever-widening from Gerbert's day onward, between monastic and scholastic formation and sensibilities. Indeed, the above characterizations of Gerbert's outlook could virtually be applied wholesale to the monastic point of view, possibly excepting the specifically political orientation noted in the penultimate sentence of the passage cited.

Genre

In addition to stylistic differences in their approaches to writing in general, the two milieux vary in their preferences for particular forms, or genres, of writing, as well as in the ways they use genres they have in common. Thus, "the monks prefer the genres which might be called concrete,"[23] including especially history and hagiography. Whereas the interest of the schoolmen

> goes chiefly to the *quaestio*, the *disputatio*, or the *lectio* taken as a basis for formulating *quaestiones*, the monks prefer writings dealing with actual happenings and experiences rather than with ideas, and which, instead of being a teacher's instruction for a universal and anonymous public, are addressed to a specific audience, to a public chosen by and known to the author.[24]

Furthermore, the monastic genres, like the cloisters themselves, remain essentially stable over centuries, while the basic scholastic genres multiply rapidly, keeping pace with their ever-changing *Sitze im Leben*: from schools in small towns, to the cathedrals of cities, to the classrooms of academic consortia that then become universities. Soon, "the *quaestio* will give birth to the *quaestio disputata*, the *quaestiuncula*, the *articulus*, and the *quodlibet*; to the *lectio* will be added a *reportatio*, and each of these genres, as well as the sermon itself, will obey a more and more precise plan and a more and more complicated technique."[25] Over against these distinctively scholastic genres, we must now look briefly at the genres of *history*, *sermon*, and *florilegium* and their respective relations to the monastic and scholastic milieux.

Leclercq says that "The monks loved history very much. More than any other writers, they concentrated on it, and sometimes they were almost the only ones to do so."[26] In contrast, "not one of the masters of the schools

---

23. Leclercq, *The Love of Learning*, 153.
24. Ibid., 153.
25. Ibid., 155.
26. Ibid.

of Chartres, Poitiers, Tours, Rheims, Laon, or Paris, in spite of the renown of their teaching, had any concern for historical work." In England also, the historians are almost always monks."[27] Accordingly, Aelred of Rievaulx himself produced an impressive corpus of historical and hagiographical works, following in the footsteps of his great English monastic forebear, Bede the Venerable. In tentative explanation of the monastic interest in history, Leclercq ventures only to point out the genre's antiquity and its inherent conservatism, both characteristics perennially appealing to the traditionalist tendencies of the monastic enterprise *per se*. Commenting further on the monks' use of the genre, he observes that

> The manner of presentation is determined by the end in view; to incite to the practice of virtue and promote praise of God, the events once recorded must, to a certain extent, be interpreted. Above all they must be situated in a vast context; the individual story is always inserted in the history of salvation. Events are directed by God who desires the salvation of the elect. The monks devote to the interests of this conviction a comprehension of the Church which was developed in them by the reading of the Fathers and the observance of the liturgy. They feel they are members of a universal communion. The saints, whose cult they celebrate, are, for them, intimate friends and living examples. In similar fashion, thinking about the angels comes naturally to them. Liturgical themes permeate their entire conception of what takes place in time.[28]

Here, Leclercq verges on an insight that he only makes explicit much later in *The Love of Learning*, namely, the link between history and eschatology and the corresponding monastic concern with both. In his climactic chapter on "Monastic Theology" he argues that

> the importance the monks attribute to history also explains the great weight they give to considerations of eschatology: for the work of salvation, begun in the Old Testament and realized in the New, is brought to completion only in the next world. Christian knowledge here below is only the first step toward the knowledge that belongs to the life of beatitude. Theology, here below, demands that we be detached from it, that we remain oriented

---

27. Ibid. For Leclercq's citation (J. de Ghellinck) see 185 n. 10.

28. Ibid., 158. As we shall see, the theme of the universality of friendship, with men and angels, in the glorified communion of saints, is one of the hallmarks of Aelred's theological enterprise.

toward something else beyond it, toward a fulfillment of which it is merely the beginning. This is yet another of the differences which distinguish the monks' intellectual attitude from that of the scholastics. As has been correctly observed, eschatology occupies practically no place in the teaching of Abailard.[29]

On the other hand, Leclercq offers no corresponding explanation for the *lack* of interest in history—or, for that matter, the relative lack of interest in eschatology—on the part of the schoolmen. In the first instance, the best explanation is probably to be found precisely by inverting the argument Leclercq offers for the monks' striking propensity for the genre. In their relentless search for clarity and scientific knowledge, the schools accord no special authority to *any* literary form, however ancient. The same motives militate against traditionalism and conservatism, whenever authority is perceived as a tool, willful or not, of obfuscation. There are also important philosophical issues to be considered here, namely, the matters of time, contingency and particularity. In their increasingly programmatic concern to reduce the bewildering complexity of the universe to a series of demonstrable propositions, the schoolmen inevitably attempted to abstract from time and the particularity and contingency of individual historical persons and events, whenever possible. In the case of eschatology, we must be even more cautious in our speculations. Nevertheless, it is quite reasonable, given the homogenizing tendencies of scholastic method with respect to the multiplicity of disciplines, to expect a certain indisposition in the realm of theology analogous to the one just described in the anthropological order, given the intrinsic relationship between history and eschatology. The reasons for such a disinclination to eschatological inquiry, like the disinclination itself, are analogous to the prior indisposition to the genre of history, whether or not these reasons were ever sufficiently examined.

Unlike the genre of history, the genre of the sermon was necessarily employed by all clerics who had pastoral responsibilities, whether in the cloister, the cathedral, or the academic hall. The differences, however, between style, method, and even content of the preaching done in the monasteries and that done elsewhere, were great, and only increased as the Middle Ages progressed. The monastic sermon is fundamentally patristic in tone and style, and pastoral in intention. It takes place within the context of a "rite" which was both "solemn" and "intimate," sometimes in the cloister, sometimes, after the day's work was over, "at the very spot where the

29. Ibid., 220.

Differences between the More Experiential Approach of Monastic Theology

work was being done, for example under a tree or some other spot where all could sit around the superior."[30] In stark contrast, the preaching of the schools

> came to be governed as much by dialectics as by rhetoric. Sermons were composed which were rigidly logical, but which bear a much closer resemblance to *quaestiones disputatae* than they do to homilies, and the laws which govern them are codified in the vast literature of the *artes praedicandi*. In scholasticism, the technique of the sermon becomes more and more subtle and complicated: one manual on the art of preaching teaches, for example, eighteen ways to 'lengthen a sermon.' The end result is a very clear, very logical oration which may be doctrinal and occasionally not devoid of stylistic or theological merit; but from this category, there is not in existence today one work of genius still worth reading.[31]

Here Leclercq records the telling comment of M. D. Chenu, that "The scholastics are professors.... Their sermons, like St. Thomas's, will themselves be scholastic. And the Church will consider the greatest of them as 'doctors,' no longer as its 'Fathers.'"[32] That the schoolmen took seriously their roles as teachers does not necessarily entail that they denigrated their pastoral responsibilities to their students and religious communities. Nonetheless, it is fair to affirm Leclercq's assertion that "to say the least, it was not in their sermons that they gave the best they had to offer."[33] In brief, then, the two ways of preaching correspond to their respective milieux: where the monastic sermon tends to be pastoral and biblical, the scholastic sermon is professorial and dialectical.

Another important genre employed in both the monasteries and the urban schools, though like the sermon, in remarkably different ways, was the *florilegium*. According to Leclercq, the fundamental distinction between the two uses amounts to that between a spiritual and an intellectual tool. Thus:

> The grammar schools had collections of examples taken from the authors. These collections of excerpts, either from the classics or, more frequently, from the Fathers and the councils, were used by the urban schools in particular as a veritable arsenal of

---

30. Ibid., 167.
31. Ibid., 173.
32. Chenu, *Introduction à l'étude*, cited in Leclercq, *The Love of Learning*, 173.
33. Leclercq, *The Love of Learning*, 173.

> *auctoritates*. They were seeking important, concise, and interesting extracts for doctrinal studies, something of value for the *quaestio* and the *disputatio*. . . . Always conveniently ready for use . . . , these collections facilitated research; they eliminated the necessity of handling numbers of manuscripts. Consequently, they were primarily working tools for the intellectuals.[34]

Pressing the point a step further, Southern contends that scholastic method *per se* was in fact

> a development of the *florilegium*. In its simplest form, it was an attempt to solve by infinitely patient criticism and subtlety of distinction the problems posed by the juxtaposition of related but often divergent passages in the works of the great Christian writers. It was, one might say, the attempt of the intellect to discover and articulate the whole range of truth discoverable in, or hinted at in, the seminal works of Christianity.[35]

In the monasteries, on the other hand, the notion and its application are entirely different. There, the *florilegium* was the organic fruit of spiritual reading:

> The monk would copy out texts he had enjoyed so as to savor them at leisure and use them anew as subjects for private meditation. The monastic *florilegium* not only originated in the monk's spiritual reading but always remained closely associated with it. For this reason the texts selected were different from those required in the schools. . . .[36]

The monastic is almost certainly the older of the two forms of *florilegia*. Moreover, it did not cease to exist, nor was its spiritual function forgotten, with the ingenious recasting of the genre by the schools. Rather, it persisted alongside the scholastic version, at least into the thirteenth century.[37]

Though admittedly not so much itself a genre as an interpretive activity or tool, nevertheless exegesis is a specialized mode of writing, often embedded within wider contexts, though sometimes characterizing the whole of a particular work (most especially the commentary, but sometimes sermons

---

34. Ibid., 182.
35. Southern, *The Making of the Middle Ages*, 191.
36. Leclercq, *The Love of Learning*, 182.
37. Cf. ibid., where Leclercq cites a work of Helinand of Froidmont as an example from the early thirteenth century.

Differences between the More Experiential Approach of Monastic Theology

as well). Differing significantly in style and application from the monastic to the scholastic milieu, it demands brief attention here.

In her great work, *The Study of the Bible in the Middle Ages*, Beryl Smalley writes:

> Gradually in the twelfth and thirteenth centuries exegesis as a separate subject emerges. It had its own technical aids to study, and its auxiliary sciences of textual criticism and biblical languages. Even though the personnel of its teachers was still undifferentiated, a scholar distinguished between his work as a theologian and his work as an exegete.[38]

By contrast, "in the early part of our period [the whole of which is the eighth to the fourteenth century] sacred doctrine resembled secular government in being undifferentiated and unspecialized."[39] Though Smalley does not at this point advert to Leclercq's fundamental distinction, it is clear that specialization in biblical studies, for better or for worse, is strongly associated with the rise of the schools. Moreover, says Smalley, "we are invited"—by the early medieval commentators, as by the Fathers themselves—"to look not at the text, but through it."[40] This somewhat obscure description Smalley intends as an aphorism for allegorical interpretation, the predominant ancient mode of "spiritual exposition" and the form of interpretation overwhelmingly favored in the monastic milieu. To "literal exposition," on the other hand, belongs "what we should now call exegesis, which is based on the study of the text and of biblical history, in its widest sense."[41] In her juxtaposition of the monastic and cathedral schools, Smalley observes:

> The innumerable problems arising from the reception of Aristotelian logic and the study of canon and civil law, the new possibilities of reasoning, the urgent need for speculation and discussion, all these produced an atmosphere of haste and excitement which was unfavourable to biblical scholarship. The masters of the cathedral schools had neither the time nor the training to specialize in a very technical branch of Bible study.[42]

---

38. Smalley, *The Study of the Bible in the Middle Ages*, xv.
39. Ibid.
40. Ibid., 2.
41. Ibid.
42. Ibid., 54.

Theologizing Friendship

All in all, Smalley's appraisal of both monastic and scholastic exegesis is fairly negative.[43] Leclercq's estimation of monastic exegesis, on the other hand, is predictably far more positive. In addition to taking the letter of the Bible with the utmost seriousness, the monks read Scripture as

> not primarily a source of knowledge, of scientific information; it is a means for salvation, its gift is the 'science of salvation': *salutaris scientia*. This is true of Scripture in its entirety. Each word it contains is thought of as a word addressed by God to each reader for his salvation. Everything then has a personal, immediate value for present life and for the obtaining of eternal life.[44]

Furthermore, the monastic theme of *desire* finds its biblical correlates first in the prophetic character of the Old Testament, in "desire for the Promised Land or desire for the Messiah," then in the anticipation of eschatological fulfillment, as these desires get "interpreted spontaneously by the medieval monks as desire for Heaven and for Jesus contemplated in His glory." As already noted, there is no comparable eschatological emphasis in the exegesis of the schools. Concerning scholastic exegesis generally, we cannot finally bypass Smalley's authoritative censure:

> the main tendency of the cathedral schools is clear; it leads away from old-fashioned Bible studies. St. Gregory had identified theology with exegesis. The eleventh- and early twelfth-century masters were inclined to identify exegesis with theology. Their work appears to be brilliant but one-sided, if we remember the promise of the eighth and ninth centuries. We find the theological questioning but not the biblical scholarship.[45]

---

43. In fact, it is Smalley's thesis that only the Victorines, particularly in the person of Hugh, conceived of a comprehensive program of biblical scholarship *informed* by *lectio divina*, a program that might have realized a kind of *via media* between monasticism and scholasticism—precisely congruent with their hybridized form of religious life. We have already noted a similar conviction on the part of Ivan Illich. For all its grandeur, the program was ultimately destined for failure, as Smalley recounts in her trenchant chapter, "The Victorines" (58–85; see especially, 80).

44. Leclercq, *The Love of Learning*, 79–80.

45. Smalley, *The Study of the Bible in the Middle Ages*, 54.

Differences between the More Experiential Approach of Monastic Theology

DIALECTICS

We need now to take up more intentionally a subject already alluded to several times above, that of dialectics. Relevant to style and to genre but transcending both categories, it is a topic about which the monks and the schoolmen were much exercised and deeply divided.[46] Leclercq deals with the problem of dialectics—the need for it and its inherent vulnerability to abuse—in a series of sections[47] that highlight monasticism's attentiveness to mystery and simplicity, and its inclination to draw learning and love so close together as almost to make an equation between them. The great monastic heroes here are St. Bernard and, behind him, St. Gregory the Great, whose dictum Leclercq reproduces as: "Love itself is knowledge: the more one loves, the more one knows."[48] Leclercq points out that dialectics was taught in the monastery schools, as the complement to grammar,[49] but that when the monastic teachers or their students disputed a point, "it was almost always on the subject of the liberal arts." In contrast, "in the town schools the same procedure was applied to sacred doctrine."[50] Granted the legitimacy in principle of the basic development of the back-and-forth activity of *quaeritur* and *respondendum est*,[51] there was general recognition

---

46. Prior even to other ideological concerns, David Knowles suggests that the response to dialectics was determined by a fundamental divide between the monasteries' otherworldly concerns and the generally more utilitarian perspective of the schools. Thus: "By the second half of the eleventh century [dialectic] was becoming increasingly the province of the cathedral schools, and canon law was finding a natural home in the entourage of the bishops, and with the gradual emergence of dialectic and law, canon and civil, as the higher education of Europe and the corresponding development of the career of the professional master, the gulf grew ever wider between the meditative, literary culture of the Norman monasteries and the speculative and practical learning of the schools, which were dependent in a peculiar degree upon the personality of the master and the free play of debate among the students" (Knowles, *The Monastic Order in England*, 98). What is true for Normandy may be accepted as essentially valid for Europe as a whole. Note that "schools" here means cathedral schools, not the universities, which do not take clear shape for another century.

47. Leclercq, *The Love of Learning*, 202–9.

48. Ibid., 208. The precise Gregorian source for the whole reference appears somewhat elusive, though the first half, at least, can be found in *In Evangelia*, 27.4. See 32, along with the corresponding nn. 51 and 52, as well as 208 n. 99.

49. Ibid., 202.

50. Ibid., 203.

51. Cf. David Knowles's comment that "the term 'scholastic' cannot rightly be applied to the content, as opposed to the method, of medieval philosophy; it is essentially a term of method. If by a scholastic method we understand a method of discovering and

Theologizing Friendship

already by the early twelfth century of the possibility of abuse. Theology was at risk of becoming "one technique among the others," and the academic *disputatio* "began to assume a value of its own."[52]

In reaction to this mode of theological inquiry, the monks, with St. Bernard very much in the vanguard, came more and more to conceive of the monastery as

> a 'school of charity,' a school for the service of God. They maintained a certain reserve toward any intellectual research carried on outside of this setting and without the guarantees it offers of sincerity and humility. They feared it would be wanting in respect for divine truth to attempt to penetrate it as if by forcible entry after breaking the seal of mystery.[53]

Leclercq notes here also an important and long-standing prejudice in the monasteries, concerning the Greeks:

> [Plato], more than others, was considered a religious man. The few writings of his they possessed and those which showed his influence were represented in monastic libraries. More than one monastic author felt a sort of secret sympathy for what Plato, in their belief, said about God and the good. Aristotle, on the other hand, who was known only through his works on logic,[54] passed for being the master *par excellence* of the very dialectics whose abuses they feared.[55]

Indeed, the monks quoted St. Paul against the scholastic abuse of dialectics: *Scientia inflat* (1 Cor 8:1). The problem is that knowledge not deliberately linked with the pursuit of holiness tends to a puffing up, a self-inflation

> both psychological and moral. In the domain of psychology, it is that complexity which is the characteristic of a mind attracted to multiple and varied objects. It incurs the risk of giving rise to a sort of agitation hardly compatible with 'contemplative repose' or pure prayer. It also risks distracting the spirit from the undivided search for God and diverting its attention to numerous and superfluous

---

illustrating philosophical truth by means of a dialectic based on Aristotelian logic, then 'scholastic' is a useful and significant term" (Knowles, *The Evolution of Medieval Thought*, 87).

52. Leclercq, *The Love of Learning*, 203.
53. Ibid., 204.
54. Prior, that is, to the thirteenth century.
55. Leclercq, *The Love of Learning*, 204.

problems. Questions, objections, argumentations rapidly lead into an inextricable forest: *nemus aristotelicum*; like a deer, one laboriously makes one's way through it.[56]

In the moral domain, the same unnecessary complexity "jeopardizes humility," the titular virtue of the famous seventh chapter of St. Benedict's *Rule*, and not coincidentally the signal quality of the Benedictine ideal. The alternative to both the moral and the more strictly spiritual dilemmas, for which Bernard and his fellow monks constantly strive, is holy simplicity.

In general, the monk-scholars, adhering to the mystical doctrine of their own beloved St. Gregory the Great, cited above, counsel a knowledge bound up inextricably with Christian charity. Gregory's equation between love and knowledge contrasts strikingly even with such a sympathetic figure as Hugh of St. Victor, who, in spite of his appreciation for the monastic tradition and ethos,[57] already grants a clear division between the intellectual habits, or virtues, and those belonging to the will. Thus, for Hugh there is a strict distinction between science on the one hand and moral action on the other.[58] Such a division is inevitably at odds with Gregory's statement, and not less with the Bernardine programme built upon it, however much one should insist that the difference is one of emphasis, rather than of absolute opposition.

Positive Correlatives to Dialectics

The monks' generally critical relationship to dialectics, then, constitutes in important part a negative, because reactive, element of the monastic approach to theological activity. Yet alongside and even within the conscious

---

56. Ibid., 205.

57. Ivan Illich points out that Hugh is in fact still writing for an essentially monastic audience: see Illich, *In the Vineyard*, 54, 66–67, and 74–92, especially 84.

58. Accordingly, Hugh says of his book, "in the first part, it instructs the reader of the arts, in the second, the reader of the Sacred Scripture" (*Didascalicon*, preface): hence, two different readers. Again: "The integrity of human nature, however, is attained in two things—in knowledge and in virtue and in these lies our sole likeness to the supernal and divine substance" (ibid., chapter 5). However ancient may be the distinctions between intellect and will, and between knowledge and virtue, the latter has become conspicuous by the early twelfth century, particularly in the schools—so much so that the two habits would appear to be quite separable (See, e.g., Aquinas, *ST*, I–II, q. 12, a. 1, to cite only one of many significant contexts.). If the grounds for this separation are already present in Aristotle, the chasm has undoubtedly deepened by the High Middle Ages.

tension felt by monastic thinkers between their own use of dialectics and its employment by the schools, there developed numerous positive bases for furthering the Church's theological enterprise as well. We have already noted the powerful Gregorian-Bernardine intuition that knowledge and love, intellect and will, ought to be kept closely allied and aligned by every practicing, praying Christian. In addition to this influential perspective, Leclercq remarks that monastic traditionalism, whatever impetus it undoubtedly receives from the instinctive reaction to scholastic novelty, at times unquestionably facilitates theological advance. Leclercq's favorite example is that of St. Anselm's disciple, Eadmer, whom a number of scholars now credit with anticipating Scotus in providing a theological articulation of the dogma of the Immaculate Conception—albeit one much less expressly worked-out than that of Scotus.[59]

Finally, the monastic stress on personal experience, in the forms of both contemplation and charity, diffuses itself throughout monastic theological work and shapes it in ways that elude scholasticism's generally detached, scientific approach to research and argumentation. According to Leclercq, "altogether the great difference between the theology of the schools and that of the monasteries resides in the importance which the latter accord the experience of union with God."[60] This experience is one of "lived faith;"[61] it is both profoundly *communal*[62] and *biblical*,[63] and ultimately, in consequence of these characteristics also *spiritual, pastoral,* and *sapiential*.[64] In these ways it stands over against a scholastic ethos always running the risk, albeit in the laudable name of science, of incautiously embracing an arid intellectualism.

Conclusion

Drawing together the many strands of the preceding discussion, we may appeal to one more pithy formulation by Jean Leclercq:

---

59. Leclercq, *The Love of Learning*, 209–11, 218–20.
60. Ibid., 212.
61. Ibid.
62. Ibid., 213.
63. Ibid.
64. Ibid.

Differences between the More Experiential Approach of Monastic Theology

> The difference between scholastic theology and monastic theology corresponds to the differences between the two states of life: the state of Christian life in the world and the state of Christian life in the religious life. The latter was what was, in fact, until the end of the twelfth century, unanimously called the "contemplative life."[65]

Leclercq further notes the universal awareness at the time "of a profound difference between scholastic and monastic milieux, and, consequently, between the kinds of religious knowledge to be acquired in each. Monastic knowledge is determined by the end of monastic life: the search for God."[66] He concludes:

> Thus in the opinion of medieval men, monks or not, a contrast exists between the two milieux where Christian thought flourishes. In the cloister, theology is studied in relation to monastic experience, a life of faith led in the monastery where religious thought and spiritual life, the pursuit of truth and the quest for perfection, must go hand in hand and permeate each other. This orientation, proper to the cloistered life, was to affect the methodology used in Christian reflection and the subject matter of this reflection."[67]

We ought particularly to note here Leclercq's typically conscientious affirmation of the flourishing of Christian thought in the *scholastic* context, notwithstanding his pardonable tendency, in keeping with his subject-matter and his thesis, not to mention his own vocation, to favor the monastic approach to theological activity.[68]

Our findings may be usefully recapitulated in terms of the following criteria: First, we have discovered that monastic theology tends to have a biblical 'flavor,' whereas scholastic theology, while still permeated with Scripture and oriented towards its explication, has deliberately departed

---

65. Ibid., 196.
66. Ibid., 197.
67. Ibid., 199.
68. It was, after all, precisely the egregious imbalance of scholarly attention, in conspicuous favor of scholastic theology, that propelled Leclercq into his life's work in the first place. Should the suspicion lurk that a similar bias informs the current author's perspective, it is sufficient to observe that, in that author's opinion, Leclercq's corrective enterprise, salutary and inspiring though it was, by no means accomplished a full righting of the vessel. There is, moreover, the gravest need in the academy for intellectual—and psychological—honesty with respect to one's own presuppositions, notwithstanding the perennial need for such an "objectivity" as may adequately, one hopes, correct for one's overweening prejudices.

from what can be characterized as the "biblical style"[69] of monastic writing. Second, monastic theology tends to be poetic; more broadly, we might say that the monks are acutely attentive to aesthetic considerations.[70] Scholastic theology, on the other hand, self-consciously eschews all literary artistry in favor of clarity, characteristically producing not theologically informed "poems," but disquisitions on theological *topoi*.[71] Third, monastic theology is erotic: in a tradition indelibly stamped by the personality and writing of St. Gregory the Great, it is not only concerned with, but fundamentally shaped by, desire—essentially, the desire for God, fueled by *compunctio*.[72] In contrast, the whole scholastic enterprise is predicated upon the ideal of a scientific neutrality which must check the motion of the inquirer's will at all costs: the goal is the static, indisputable (because demonstrable) proposition, not a moving target.[73] Fourth, we have noted the typically "personal" character of monastic theology, where that term is to be taken in both the psychological and in the grammatical sense. Thus, the deep

---

69. I.e., "style biblique": Leclercq, *Aux Sources de la Spiritualité Occidentale*, 276. Cf. also Leclercq, *The Love of Learning*, 62, as well as the whole of chapter 5 ("Sacred Learning"), 71–88.

70. "And, just as in music and in poetry, art consists in making 'variations' on simple yet rich themes, so the true worth of monastic language lies in its evocative powers. This could not be otherwise, since it is a biblical language, concrete, full of imagery, and consequently poetic in essence. But, although not abstract, these modes of expression must not be taken any the less seriously" (Leclercq, *The Love of Learning*, 54–55). Cf. also, e.g., 55, 59, 75, 134, 173, etc.

71. See ibid., 142, 175, 200, etc. We ought also to note here that monastic theology is profoundly *liturgical*, while scholastic theology is not. Of the monastic liturgy, Leclercq writes that "the liturgy . . . is the medium through which the Bible and the patristic tradition are received, and it is the liturgy that gives unity to all the manifestations of monastic culture" (Leclercq, *The Love of Learning*, 71). Leclercq's complete silence regarding liturgy in the scholastic milieu, in a chapter entitled "The Poem of the Liturgy" (ibid., 236–54), is fairly deafening. Further inquiry into this elusive, yet enormously important distinction is beyond the scope of this dissertation. It warrants a study all to itself.

72. See ibid., 29–32, 67–68. Note that Leclercq does not use the term "erotic," in this context, though there is no reason to avoid it in its strict denotation. Indeed, the monastic debt to Augustine, and through him, to Plato, argues strongly in favor of explicit scholarly consideration of the "erotics" of the Christian theological enterprise.

73. One need only thumb through the *ST* of St. Thomas to demolish the curious notion that the methodological hypothesis of scientific neutrality is invented by the thinkers of the seventeenth-century Enlightenment. This is not at all to deny that Thomas clearly acknowledges his own Christian presuppositions: on the contrary. Yet the *methodological* stance assumed at every stage of inquiry is one of a strict logical relationship between the various propositions adduced in constructing an argument.

personal investment of the monastic author in his subject, as well as his earnest concern for the spiritual well-being of his readers, both evident in so many stylistic nuances, are made transparent through the frequent use of the first and second grammatical persons. The master of the school, on the other hand, meticulously distances himself from his text, both emotionally and linguistically speaking. Here the third person is the predominant grammatical form employed. Finally, to what has been already explicitly adduced we may add that monastic theology is characteristically "sweet," where we understand that English word as translating at least two different Latin words: *suavis* and *dulcis*. Both of these terms, though especially the latter, can connote the most ordinary, concrete sense of sweetness to the physical palate, as well as a metaphorical spiritual sense deriving from the physical. The first term, however, has a further resonance, highly amenable to the monastic theological sensibility: this arises from its obvious etymological connection to *suasion*, or *per*suasion.[74] In a connection that can be traced back to Augustine, the *sweetness* of God's Word, especially his Incarnate Word, Jesus, has the ultimate power to persuade, and so to win man's wayward heart to himself.[75] By christological extension, the words (both spoken and written) produced by a member of Christ's Body ought always, sweetly, to urge the sinner to conversion. The schoolmen, in striking contrast, seek not to sway men's hearts with rhetoric, but through the application of logic to change men's minds.[76] The preceding criteria are intended less as an exhaustive list than as a kind of level, analogous to the carpenter's tool, whereby, in the ensuing chapters of this dissertation, we

74. Cf. the Latin verb forms *suadeo* and *persuadeo*, as well as the related noun forms *suasio* and *persuasio*.

75. For a thorough treatment of the argument from the Augustinian side, see Cavadini, "The Sweetness of the Word," 164–81.

76. Leclercq offers a comparable, though not identical, set of criteria for "monastic culture" in *Aux Sources de la Spiritualité Occidentale*: "Tout d'abord, il y a des constantes culturelles monastiques. Lesquelles? Quels sont ces caractère déterminants et intrinsèques au monachisme? Il suffira ici de les énumérer. Il faut citer d'abord la liturgie, qui exerça une influence capitale sur le style de vie des moines de partout, par conséquent sur leurs préoccupations et sur leur style littéraire. Il faut nommer ensuite le culte de la Bible: la *lectio divina* est pratiquée dans les monastères plus qu'ailleurs et y fait apparaître un certain 'style biblique.' De plus un certain sens traditionnel fait que les moines se tournent spontanément vers le passé du monachisme, y compris celui de l'Orient, vers le passé de l'Eglise et les écrits des Pères: d'où un certain 'style patristique.' Enfin une certaine tendance ascétique et spirituelle, plus accentuée que dans les milieux de laïcs ou de clercs séculiers, se manifeste, par exemple, en une production poétique plus exclusivement religieuse, moins 'mondaine'" (276–77).

may gauge within a single horizon, so to speak, the respective theological projects of St. Aelred of Rievaulx and St. Thomas Aquinas.

Sources

To the above framing observations, we must now add some brief notes on the use of sources by monks and schoolmen between 1110 and 1274. What follows is intended only to provide a general picture; certain precisions will need to be made in subsequent chapters, in reference to the sources used specifically by Aelred and Thomas.

Biblical

The Bible was far and away the most important source for monastic theology and remained the guiding force for scholastic theology as well, at least through the high Middle Ages, in spite of the increasing importance of Aristotle. In general, both monks and schoolmen show a thorough familiarity with the biblical text, from beginning to end, though each milieu reveals certain clear preferences for particular books or types of biblical material. Thus, the Song of Songs is perennially and by far the favorite book of the monks,[77] whereas the schoolmen of the thirteenth century prefer other sapiential literature, especially Proverbs and Ecclesiastes.[78] Considering the canon in its entirety, Smalley records the following order of preferences among commentators in the schools during the eleventh and early twelfth centuries:

> the two favourite books for commentators were the Psalter and the Pauline Epistles, their creative energy being centred in the latter; St. Paul provided the richest nourishment to the theologian and logician. Next came the Hexaemeron, because it provided an opportunity to discuss the questions of Creation and angelology. Original work on the Law, the historical books of the Old

---

77. See Leclercq, *The Love of Learning*, 84–86, passim. "The monks," Leclercq writes at the close of his extended treatment of the monastic devotion to the Song, "have associated themselves with the canticle of love. An anonymous commentator on the *Rule of St. Benedict* sees the Canticle of Canticles as the complement of the monks' rule: it is, he says, the rule of love" (86).

78. See Smalley, "Some Thirteenth-Century Commentaries," 267–69.

Testaments, the Prophets, the Gospels, and the Acts seems to be lacking.[79]

By contrast, the monks make much of both the historical and the prophetic materials, in part, at least, for reasons already discussed. As for two of the greatest Cistercians, Bernard and Aelred, they incorporate Scripture effortlessly into everything they write, skillfully interweaving passages from every book in both Testaments.[80]

Patristic

After the Bible, the next most-read texts in the Middle Ages are the collective works of the Church Fathers. As should be expected, availability, and hence knowledge, of the works of the Latin Fathers exceeds that of the Greek works. Nevertheless, Leclercq notes that

> In the twelfth century, Latin monks took the initiative of having Greek texts translated whenever it was possible. But a considerable part of the patristic legacy inherited from the Greeks had already been translated: it was preserved and handed on, as was all that remained of ancient culture, especially in Italy and in England.[81]

In the peculiarly significant case of Origen, Leclercq makes the following interesting observation:

> If we read the introductions to the different volumes of the critical edition of the Latin Origen, we note that almost all the manuscripts are of monastic origin and that most date from the ninth and the twelfth centuries. Other indications point to the conclusion that in every period or place where there was a monastic renewal, there was a revival of Origen. It is true of the Carolingian reform; it is even more . . . readily apparent in the monastic revival of the twelfth century.[82]

79. Smalley, *The Study of the Bible in the Middle Ages*, 54.

80. Of St. Bernard's use of Scripture, Leclercq writes: "Many of his pages are simply mosaics of scriptural expressions, skillfully chosen, compared and arranged; one casting light on the other." Moreover, "He had a precise, vast and profound knowledge of the sacred text. He had so woven it into the very fabric of his personal psychology that he made use of it, perhaps at times unawares, even when he did not quote it explicitly" (*Bernard of Clairvaux and the Cistercian Spirit*, 21). For a more detailed inventory of Aelred's use of the Bible, see chapter 2, below.

81. Leclercq, *The Love of Learning*, 91.

82. Ibid., 94.

Theologizing Friendship

In contrast with this strong evidence of Origen's influence on the monasteries, "Origen is less frequently represented in the libraries of the cathedral churches."[83] In general, however, it is reasonable to assume that such manuscripts as were at the disposal of the monasteries were at least accessible to the masters of the schools as well, and in time, the more important works inevitably became part of the universal intellectual patrimony.

As for the Western Fathers, the Latin patristic corpus diffused among the medieval monasteries is virtually complete.[84] The Fathers whose works are most frequently copied, and the widest range of whose works are represented, are Sts. Ambrose, Jerome and Augustine. In the case of the Latins, the thorough familiarity of the schoolmen would not have varied substantially from that of the monks. Leclercq observes, however, that the *uses* made of patristic sources, and consequently the parts of works given most attention, differed significantly between the two milieux.[85]

Finally, in addition to complete works by particular authors, by about 1130, medieval churchmen had also at their disposal the massive biblical *Glossa Ordinaria*, a six-volume digest of patristic commentary on the Scriptures, organized into an elaborate series of interlinear and marginal glosses, superimposed on the biblical text itself. Of this "tremendous work" Beryl Smalley notes that "the range of authors quoted in the *Gloss* is wide. The better known of the Latin Fathers down to Bede, Origen and Hesychius in translation, Raban, Strabo, Paschasius, John the Scot, Haimo, Lanfranc, Berengar have all been laid under contribution."[86]

Pagan

The humanist renaissance that swept across Europe in the twelfth century entailed a renewed interest in the classics of antiquity, especially in the monasteries. Within this variegated body of literature, the Roman rhetorical tradition undoubtedly had pride of place. Thus, alongside their reading in the Church Fathers, the monks became well acquainted with Virgil, Horace, Terence, Statius, Lucan, and above all others, Cicero. However paradoxical

---

83. Ibid.

84. "Almost all its texts had been preserved and handed down" (ibid., 97).

85. So, for example, "Whereas the scholastics valued a whole arsenal of metaphysical proofs in the *Confessions*, monasticism's teachers retained only the testimony of the mystic" (ibid., 98).

86. Smalley, *The Study of the Bible in the Middle Ages*, 44.

in its superficial aspect, there was at bottom nothing revolutionary about the cloister's integration of these pagan works into their own living literary tradition: Cicero's moral, aesthetic and rhetorical concerns the monks easily recognized as profoundly congruent, if not always perfectly identical, with their own. It was rather in the schools that pagan literature provoked a real and lasting revolution, as Latin translations of the entirety of Aristotle's work became available in the West, the better part of it for the first time. How truly seismic the change was can be glimpsed in R. W. Southern's juxtaposing of the pattern of citation in Peter Lombard's *Sentences*, written in the mid-twelfth century, with that of Aquinas's *ST*, a century later. The former work contains "thousands of quotations from the Church Fathers, . . . only three from secular philosophy, and all these were borrowed from St. Ambrose or St. Augustine." In contrast, "the *Summa Theologica* of Thomas Aquinas contains about 3500 quotations from Aristotle, of which 1500 come from the *Nichomachean Ethics* and 800 from the *Meteorology* or *Metaphysics*, works wholly unknown a century earlier."[87] Moreover,

> by 1250 virtually the whole corpus of Greek science was accessible to the western world, and scholars groaned under its weight as they strove to master it all. The days had gone when two large volumes could hold all that was essential for the study of the liberal arts. There was no time for artistic presentation and literary eloquence. This was a grave loss, but the achievement was there all the same. The main ideas of the earlier masters—the dignity of man, the intelligibility of the universe, the nobility of nature—not only remained intact, but were fundamental concepts in the intellectual structures of the thirteenth century.[88]

Yet the Bible refused to go away, or even to be ignored. In Southern's words, "medieval thought became a dialogue between Aristotle and the Bible."[89] Elaborating on this lapidary formulation, he continues: "here lay the main tension which transformed the thought of Europe in the two centuries after 1150. Paradoxical though it may seem, it was the Bible that did most for humanism in its medieval form simply because it provided the

---

87. Southern, *Medieval Humanism*, 46. (The quotation comes from the title essay in the volume.)

88. Ibid., 48. With the reference to "two large volumes," Southern alludes to "the two volumes of texts put together by Thierry of Chartres, formerly in the library of Chartres cathedral."

89. Ibid., 47.

most difficult problems."[90] Recalling the monastic prejudice against Aristotle, we may note that Southern's comments here pertain first and foremost to the schools, though the "transformation of thought" taking place there could not help but spill over eventually into the cloister. In further explanation of his insight, Southern maintains that "Men learn after all by being puzzled and excited, not by being told." Thus:

> Aristotle standing alone had no power to excite thought: at best, like alcohol, he first stimulated and then stupefied. What he said was so complete, so incontrovertible, so far beyond the range of conflicting authorities, that he hammered reason into submission. Curiously enough, therefore, the paradoxes of the Bible did more for rational argument by stimulating discussion than all the reasons of Aristotle which were swallowed whole.[91]

In the end, then, Southern's observations regarding the scholastic engagement with Aristotle have brought us back to the fundamental significance of Scripture for the medieval scholar, a significance of which the medieval monasteries never lost sight.

Aelred of Rievaulx and Thomas Aquinas

In this preparatory chapter, there remains only the task of saying something briefly about the choice of Aelred and Thomas as representatives of their respective milieux, in a comparison between theological accounts of friendship. Why them? Why *their* accounts of friendship? Finally, why their accounts of *friendship*? Of the many theological *topoi* taken up by monks and schoolmen alike, why focus on a subject seemingly far removed from such central dogmatic issues as the Trinity, Christology, or ecclesiology?

Why Them? (Why Their Accounts of Friendship?)

Aelred: How Typical; How Outstanding

Aelred of Rievaulx is ideally suited to represent the monastic theological enterprise, as an outstanding example, but one nonetheless typical, of monastic life and thought throughout the ages. Thus, Amédée Hallier speaks

---

90. Ibid.
91. Ibid., 47–48.

Differences between the More Experiential Approach of Monastic Theology

in general terms of the "penetrating originality of Aelred's theology."[92] In a more specific delineation of Aelred's theological contribution, Charles Dumont observes that it was Aelred who took Bernard's synthesis of "the spiritual doctrine of the school of charity" and gave its principles "a new attractiveness by a pedagogical and even systematic application, particularly in the practice of meditation on the Gospels."[93] Commenting on Aelred's longest and most significant work, *SC*, Aelred Squire asserts that Aelred arrived through his reflections "at a valuable, original insight. At least there appears to be no other patristic or medieval writer who explores these matters quite in Aelred's way."[94] Furthermore, referring to the same work, Dumont contends that "Aelred's scriptural argumentation is remarkable enough to be considered unique, both in its scope and in its precision."[95]

On the other hand, Dumont also reminds us that Aelred "had never attended the schools and so received his formation in both theology and monastic life at the same time within the monastic tradition."[96] Aelred differed, then, from Lanfranc and St. Bruno, both of whom turned aside from established academic careers in favor of monachism. Rather, Aelred's entire spiritual and intellectual formation was thoroughly monastic. Consequently, while many of his writings are of exceptional quality, they are in kind precisely the sorts of works to be found ubiquitously in the medieval monastic milieu: histories, hagiographies, prayers, a *De Anima*, a *Speculum*, liturgical sermons. So, too, his skill as a biblical exegete should not divert us from recognizing the sources for his basic principles of interpretation.[97] These are, first, the patristic tradition, and second, the virtually ceaseless practice of *lectio divina*: both integral elements of the common patrimony of European monasticism. In short, Aelred of Rievaulx is a true monk, and while the quality of his thought in its own right justifies scholarly attention, that thought always possesses a genuinely *monastic* character. So, too,

---

92. Hallier, *The Monastic Theology of Aelred of Rievaulx*, 39.
93. Dumont, introduction to *The Mirror of Charity*, 13.
94. Squire, *Aelred of Rievaulx*, 39.
95. Dumont, introduction to Aelred of Rievaulx, *The Mirror of Charity*, 33.
96. Ibid., 12.
97. E.g., the interpretation of Old Testament figures as types of Christ, as well as allegorical reading beyond the immediately christological purview: closely related principles, both belonging to the common practice of "spiritual reading" of the biblical text. The most thorough treatment of medieval exegetical practice remains Henri de Lubac's seminal work, *Exégèse médiévale*.

Thomas: How Typical; How Outstanding

To some extent attempts to justify the choice of Thomas Aquinas as our representative scholastic theologian risk degenerating into embarrassing commonplaces: widely accepted as the most complete synthesis of Christian theology ever executed, his work must in the same fora be recognized *a fortiori* as the high-water mark of medieval scholastic theology. In terms more specific and relevant to our own purposes, R. W. Southern writes:

> The work of Thomas Aquinas is full of illustrations of the supremacy of reason and nature.... He reversed the ancient opinion that the body is the ruined habitation of the soul, and held with Aristotle that it is the basis of the soul's being. Everywhere he points to the natural perfection of man, his natural rights, and the power of his natural reason. The dignity of human nature is not simply a poetic vision; it has become a central truth of philosophy.
>
> Thomas Aquinas died in 1274, and it is probably true that man has never appeared so important a being in so well-ordered and intelligible a universe as in his works. Man was important because he was the link between the created universe and the divine intelligence. He alone in the world of nature could understand nature. He alone in nature could understand the nature of God. He alone could use and perfect nature in accordance with the will of God, and thus achieve his full nobility.[99]

To this eloquent tribute to Aquinas's towering achievement, we may add the authoritative voices of two great Dominican scholars: James Weisheipl, who speaks of the "transcendent significance" of Thomas's thought,[100] and

---

98. In this connection, James McEvoy makes the following observation: "Among the early Cistercians *consensio*, or agreement, was, at least in the very best cases, capable of being almost ideally complete, since the same content filled their minds, through the continuous practice of *lectio divina*, and their hearts, through the Blessed Eucharist, and even their affections, through the kiss of peace, which was exchanged between the Pater Noster and the communion at every Mass. The very core of Aelred's teaching on spiritual friendship intuits, in the experienced unity of wills and feelings, only a difference of degree from that friendship with God which consists in perfect conformity with His will" ("The Theory of Friendship," 21).

99. Southern, *Medieval Humanism*, 50.

100. Weisheipl, *Friar Thomas D'Aquino*, x.

Differences between the More Experiential Approach of Monastic Theology

Jean-Pierre Torrell, who refers to Thomas from the vantage point of the late twentieth century simply as "the Master."[101]

That Thomas's thought, superlative as it is in every respect, is also thoroughly characteristic of the scholastic milieu, is formally self-evident: in his massive corpus, the genre and fundamental structure of every one of his major works find more or less exact parallels in the works of innumerable other schoolmen. Moreover, the various subjects that most absorbed him were those that occupied universities all across the Europe of his day—above all Scripture, dogmatic and moral theology, and the philosophical and scientific work of Aristotle. It may fairly be asked what impact his early years in the abbey of Monte Cassino, from about the age of six until he was fifteen, would have had on his intellectual and spiritual development.[102] Here it is sufficient to note with Torrell that at this time "the abbey was in a period of decadence,"[103] and as such, "would not have much attracted a young man taken with the absolute."[104] No doubt Thomas did receive his first training in reading and writing at the hands of the Cassinese monks[105] and even conceived during this period what would become a lifelong "esteem for the Benedictine ideal."[106] Nevertheless, his spiritual and intellectual formation took place substantially at the hands of the Dominicans, whose studium in Naples he had joined upon leaving the abbey. Five years later, at the age of twenty, Thomas took the habit of the Order of Preachers. From these facts we may rest assured that St. Thomas's singular theological insights into the subject of friendship have been profoundly shaped by the scholastic milieu and will be articulated in the finest expressions possible in that mode.

Cautionary Paragraph: Distinction between the Two Milieux Semi-Permeable

These reminders of St. Thomas's youthful experience of monastic life suggest a salutary caution to anyone seeking to understand better the complex

---

101. Torrell, *Saint Thomas Aquinas*, xix.

102. We shall return once more to this question in our consideration of Thomas's sources in chapter 3.

103. Torrell, *Saint Thoma Aquinas*, 4.

104. Ibid., 14.

105. Ibid., 5.

106. Ibid., 14.

relationship between the monastic and the scholastic milieux, and consequently between their respective theological approaches. As Jean Leclercq warns repeatedly in *The Love of Learning*, the commerce between monastery and school, if erratic and occasionally contentious, was not slight. Thus, we know, for example, that by the ninth century, abbots were sending a few of their monks to the town schools to be educated,[107] while schoolmen sometimes left the world permanently to become monks.[108] And lest we suppose that Aelred, at least, at the far reaches of civilized Europe, must have lived in splendid monachistic isolation, C. H. Talbot observes that

> for the greater part of his twenty years in office at Rievaulx he was a constant visitor to France and must have been aware of the controversies in which Saint Bernard was involved. The possibility that he may have met on these occasions John of Salisbury, Robert Pullus and Robert of Melun cannot be ruled out.[109]

In short, though the differences between the monastic and scholastic milieux in our period are real and significant, we must be alert not to envision too radical a cultural or ideological partition between the two. The distance between medieval monastery and school is by no means negligible, but it is probably far smaller than the distance between either of these institutions and its twenty-first century counterpart.

Why Their Accounts of Friendship?

Regarding our final important question—Why these two theologians' accounts of *friendship*?—a few comments are in order. R. W. Southern's acute analysis of the respective roles of the monasteries and schools in the twelfth-century renaissance provides a useful point of departure. Southern believes the period from 1100 to 1320 "to have been one of the greatest ages of humanism in the history of Europe."[110] The change that marks the

---

107. Leclercq, *The Love of Learning*, 195.

108. Ibid., 196–97.

109. Talbot, introduction to *Dialogue on the Soul*, 26. Talbot notes too that Aelred's "closest friendships were with men of the highest intellectual standing" (26), many of whom were abbots and other monks, but who also included Gilbert Foliot, bishop of London, and undoubtedly other secular clerics.

110. Southern, *Medieval Humanism*, 31.

beginning of this period "took the form of a greater concentration on man and on human experience as a means of knowing God."[111] But

> if self-knowledge is the first step in the rehabilitation of man, *friendship*—which is the sharing of this knowledge with someone else—is an important auxiliary. This was understood by the humanists of the Renaissance; but the discovery was made in the monasteries of the late 11th century.[112]

Moreover, "the experience of friendship lay along the road to God. . . . So here again we start with nature and end with God."[113] In fact, "of all the forms of friendship rediscovered in the twelfth century, there was none more eagerly sought than the friendship between God and man."[114] Such influential monastic thinkers as St. Anselm, St. Bernard and St. Aelred helped to realize this theological and spiritual epiphany. Popularly, too, for a multitude of reasons difficult to isolate one from the other, Christian piety and thought began to shift in focus from averting and appeasing God's anger, to relating to God as a friend. Southern notes the plethora of prayers and poems from this time onward dominated by the theme of "the humanity of God."[115] He makes as well the astute and original point that the "sentimentality" of much of this poetry is itself an expression and form of "humanism in religion"—a form "that has survived all the religious divisions of Europe. . . . Popular piety has never lost this sentimental familiarity."[116] Indeed, "The greatest triumph of medieval humanism was to make God seem human. The Ruler of the Universe, who had seemed so terrifying and remote, took on the appearance of a familiar friend."[117]

If the monasteries rediscovered friendship and gradually cultivated the revolutionary notion of a friendly God, then the complementary scholastic feat was, according to Southern,

111. Ibid., 33.

112. Ibid., 34; my emphasis. In a beautiful passage that effectively distills the whole history of medieval friendship into a few well-chosen lines, Leclercq confirms Southern's claim, arguing that "it was the monks who contributed most to the rediscovery of a type of friendship which had almost disappeared from literature after the invasions: pure, disinterested friendship which solicits no favors" (Leclercq, *The Love of Learning*, 181).

113. Southern, *Medieval Humanism*, 35.

114. Ibid.

115. Ibid.

116. Ibid., 36. Southern's observation evokes the work of the twentieth-century poet-theologian Charles Péguy.

117. Ibid., 37.

> to make the universe itself friendly, familiar, and intelligible. This is an essential part of the heritage of western Europe which we owe to the scholars of the twelfth and thirteenth centuries. The experience of earlier centuries had suggested that so far as man could see, the universe was a scene of chaos and mystery, and that renunciation, submission to the supernatural, and a grateful acceptance of miraculous aid were the best that men could aim at. But in the late eleventh century, secular schools began to multiply which were dedicated to the task of extending the area of intelligibility and order in the world in a systematic way....
>
> The importance of these schools for the intellectual development of Europe is very great. They provided permanent centres of learning which faced the world instead of facing away from it.[118]

Friendliness, then, was everywhere, it seems, in the period spanning the birth of St. Aelred and the death of St. Thomas, on both the theological and the cosmological scenes, and in a way that it had probably never been before. It was therefore inevitable that friendship should become a conscious part of theological discussion in both monastic and scholastic settings. We should reasonably expect to find many of the underlying differences discussed in this chapter reflected in the two theologians' accounts of friendship, and we will not be disappointed. A more elusive, and surprising discovery is that the different ways Aelred and Thomas engage the topic of friendship have significant implications for the approaches to theology *per se* engaged by their respective institutions.

---

118. Ibid.

2

The Theological Account of Friendship in Aelred of Rievaulx

Contemporary Scholarship

The twentieth century has witnessed an extraordinary growth in scholarly interest in the life and thought of the early Cistercians, an interest inspired by the prodigious work of Etienne Gilson and fueled by the more narrowly focused efforts of Dom Jean Leclercq, OSB. The consequent outpouring of publications has been effectively channeled in significant part into two series, the Cistercian Fathers Series, dedicated to translations of original works of the early Cistercians, and the Cistercian Studies Series, consisting of both monographs and collections of articles by modern authors. The latter series engages a wide range of topics and perspectives, though the center of gravity is clearly the ongoing evaluation of the theological legacy of the twelfth- and thirteenth-century Cistercians. In addition, a stream of papers and books both scholarly and popular and associated with neither of these series flowed forth steadily over the latter half of the century. In all this wealth of material, Saint Aelred of Rievaulx looms large, to say the least. Critical editions of almost the entire Aelredian corpus are now available in the *Corpus Christianorum Continuatio Mediaevalis (CCCM)*. The critical edition of the *Sermones Inediti*, a collection of twenty-six liturgical sermons not included in *CCCM*, was published in 1952, with an excellent introduction and annotation by C. H. Talbot, as the first volume of the *Series Scriptorum S. Ordinis Cisterciensis* (Rome). Most of Aelred's major works are now available in English, many also in French and German. Finally, there are a great number of articles and a few major studies of his thought. From these secondary sources, we may limit our attention to a small handful of authors for whom Aelred is either the main or at least a major object of theological interest.

Amédée Hallier

In *The Monastic Theology of Aelred of Rievaulx: An Experiential Theology*,[1] published in 1969, the Cistercian Amédée Hallier devotes the first of three major sections, "Man and God," to a synthesis of Aelred's "experiential" theology. The section is subdivided into two chapters, the first, "Man the Image of God," a careful account of Aelred's anthropology, the second, "God is Friendship," an exposition of the culmination of that anthropology in the theology of friendship. Drawing heavily on Saint Augustine, Aelred elaborates the patristic anthropology of image and likeness, wherein man is made in both the image and the likeness of his Creator, but at the fall loses God's likeness, while maintaining his image. Wandering in "the land of unlikeness,"[2] man can only return to God if his divine likeness is somehow restored. This restoration is initiated through the Incarnation, when "the Uncreated Image restored the created image by meriting for it the grace to be recreated in the divine likeness."[3] However, man's restoration is only fully accomplished "progressively by Christ and by the Holy Spirit,"[4] and ordinarily with a great deal of hard spiritual labor on the part of the converted soul. This labor is greatly facilitated by the serviceableness (*utilitas*) of one Christian to another in spiritual friendship. In fact, Aelred argues, God deliberately made men with this need for each other:

> But since the rational soul could confer nothing upon God, *many were created of the same nature, so that in this respect also the*

---

1. Hallier, *The Monastic Theology of Aelred of Rievaulx*, first published under the title *Un Éducateur Monastique, Aelred de Rievaulx*.
2. *Regio dissimilitudinis*, a common trope among the early Cistercian writers. Cf. Squire, *Aelred of Rievaulx*, 68.
3. Hallier, *The Monastic Theology of Aelred of Rievaulx*, 24.
4. Ibid.

The Theological Account of Friendship in Aelred of Rievaulx

likeness of the divine goodness, which flows out upon many, might appear through the mutual good offices of one to another.[5]

This created mutual need of human beings for each other will prove to be a central and distinctive feature of Aelred's theology of friendship. Then again, Hallier also recalls Aelred's endorsement in his dialogue on friendship, after only brief hesitation, of the proposition that "God is friendship."[6] The tension between the understanding of an intrinsic relationship between spiritual friendship and human need on the one hand, and the proposition that God, who is a sufficient good to himself,[7] is friendship, will be taken up in our own discussion of Aelred's theology. Hallier also correctly observes the significance of Aelred's theology of the three sabbaths[8] and hints at a convergence between these two key aspects of Aelred's thought.[9]

The final point to be taken from Hallier is that "the basic originality of [Aelred's] doctrine consists primarily in the fact that it was rethought and experienced by a man who was intensely alive and it became his own personal property."[10] It is for good reason that Hallier's actual synthesis of Aelred's theology takes up less than a third of his entire text. Through his carefully crafted biographical introduction, coupled with parts two and three of the body of his text, Hallier justifies the English subtitle of his work, "An Experiential Theology": Aelred's theology, including his theology of friendship, is worked out not so much through detached systematic reflection as it is through his own struggle for holiness in his monastic vocation, most particularly in his tireless activities as abbot and spiritual father of the burgeoning community at Rievaulx. Besides spiritual friendship with his fellow monks, the principal tools at Aelred's disposal are Scripture and the peculiarly monastic tradition of reading it termed *lectio divina*—"not

---

5. Sed quia anima rationalis deo nil conferre potuit, creati sunt eiusdem nature plures, ut in hac etiam parte similitudo divine bonitatis, que refunderet in multos, mutuis beneficiis apareret. *Serm. In.*, 108 (my translation and emphasis). Hallier gives the sermon in which this passage occurs, the first of several sermons for the Feast of Pentecost, particular attention and weight as bringing together many of the highpoints of Aelred's theology in a single well-focused context. See Hallier, *The Monastic Theology of Aelred of Rievaulx*, 37–38, 54–55.

6. Deus amicitia est. See *SA* I.69–70.

7. Sufficiens bonum sibi. *Serm. In.*, 108.

8. See the section entitled, "Aelred's Doctrine of the Three Sabbaths" in chapter 2 below, for our own discussion of this central element in Aelred's theological reflection.

9. See Hallier, *The Monastic Theology of Aelred of Rievaulx*, 35–36.

10. Ibid., 52–53.

simply an intellectual exercise, but a communing with the living God who reveals himself to us through his Word."[11]

Aelred Squire

In the same year that the English translation of Hallier's work was issued, the English Dominican Aelred Squire published his *Aelred of Rievaulx: A Study*.[12] Like Hallier, Squire approaches his subject existentially, situating his theological consideration of each of Aelred's major works within a more or less chronological narration of Aelred's life. Squire, too, concedes Aelred's cautious approval of the formulation "God is friendship,"[13] though he is more concerned to illuminate the movement in Aelred's life and thought from worldly to spiritual friendship, and thence to the eschatological friendship experienced in the communion of saints in heaven.[14] Concerning Aelred's theology of sabbath, Squire goes into more detail than Hallier, observing that "there appears to be no other patristic or medieval writer who explores these matters quite in Aelred's way."[15] Squire spends several pages showing how Aelred has taken an idea found in Augustine and proceeded to integrate and then go beyond it, forging a link between Old and New Testaments and thus clarifying the christological implications of the Hebrew idea.[16] Interestingly, the Dominican who has taken Aelred as his name in religion also sees evidence here of the twelfth-century monk anticipating an essentially scholastic insight: "there is in man, as in every creature, a natural force which impels him, even unconsciously, to seek the bliss which is appropriate to him . . . an objective apprehension of [his] central situation in a confident, panoramic view of creation such as the masters of the schools were already beginning to work out."[17] What is less evident

---

11. Ibid., 94.
12. Squire, *Aelred of Rievaulx*.
13. Squire, *Aelred of Rievaulx*, 105–6.
14. See ibid., chapter 5: "God is Friendship," 98–111.
15. Ibid., 39. Hallier, however, notes in passing "a school of thought whose chief exponent seems to be St. Maximus the Confessor," crediting Hans Urs von Balthasar with this discovery. See Hallier, *The Monastic Theology of Aelred of Rievaulx*, 49–50; cf. also n. 148.
16. Squire, *Aelred of Rievaulx*, 39–43, 45. The key Augustinian passage in question is found in the fourth book of *De Genesi ad litteram* (cf. Squire, 39).
17. Ibid., 43.

in Squire's exposition than in Hallier's is the implicit connection in Aelred's work between sabbath rest and friendship.

Charles Dumont

Another of Aelred's Cistercian children, Charles Dumont, has written for more than three decades on Aelred and unquestionably brings to his subject one of the most original perspectives to be found among contemporary authors writing on twelfth-century theology. Like Hallier and Squire, Dumont approaches Saint Aelred existentially, intent on listening to the man, not merely analyzing his ideas. Whereas both Hallier and Squire confine themselves quite strictly to their medieval sources, however, Dumont brings Aelred unapologetically into conversation with the philosophy and theology of the modern period, especially the twentieth century. Thus, over the course of several articles and one major introduction, he cites Gabriel Marcel, Hans Urs von Balthasar and Henri de Lubac, as well as Henri Bergson, Max Weber, Martin Heidegger, and William Sadler—not to speak of Shakespeare, Hegel, Kierkegaard, and Newman! To suppose, however, on the grounds of such an eclectic list, that Dumont must surely be an unserious dilettante would constitute a grave error in judgment: he also cites effortlessly and extensively from the entire Latin corpus of Aelred's works. On the contrary, Dumont plainly intends not only to argue for the continued relevance of St. Aelred's thought today, but to insist on inviting the twelfth century Cistercian into direct, personal conversation with theologians of our own time. Thus, with a nod to Kierkegaard, Dumont states that "Aelred spoke by being. And it is thus that we should read, listen to, and understand the words he has left us."[18] Such an assertion itself amounts to a kind of diachronic act of friendship, a gesture by a Christian scholar urging his fellow Christian scholars to join him in reaching out to a great mind and heart of an earlier age. As for Aelred's own doctrine of friendship, Dumont recalls Aelred's protest in *SC*, presumably directed toward a critic, which he neatly expounds as follows:

> "If you want to criticize this doctrine of mine, remember that Christ had a friend, Saint John."[19] He thus shows that Christ

18. Dumont, "Personalism in Community according to Aelred of Rievaulx," 254.
19. Not a direct quote of *SC*, rather, Dumont's elegant distillation of several sentences from the penultimate chapter of book III: ". . . we especially take enjoyment in those who are linked to us more intimately and more closely than others by the pleasant

sacramentalized friendship, for every word or gesture performed by Christ has been sacramentalized, and friendship is included among these."[20]

Worthy of note, too, is Dumont's observation in his introduction to *The Mirror of Charity* that "Aelred's scriptural argumentation is remarkable enough to be considered unique, both in its scope and in its precision."[21]

Katherine TePas

The 1992 doctoral dissertation by Katherine Yohe, née TePas, "Aelred of Rievaulx: The Correlation between Human Friendship and Union with God," provides the most thoroughgoing account to date of Aelred's theological treatment of friendship. Several points bear brief mention here. In her third chapter ("Spiritual Perfection in Aelred"), in a subsection entitled "Union with God: In Heavenly Glory," TePas states: "Each soul's life in union with God is described by Aelred more as a great communal celebration of a wedding than as a bridal couple's private embrace."[22] This notice complements Hallier's concerning Aelred's doctrine of the divinely created need in man for the help and friendship of others: both observations point toward the deeply communitarian character of Aelred's thought, a quality which has profound implications for his theology of friendship. Turning to the Trinity, however, where we might naturally expect to find this notion developed analogically with respect to the divine Persons, TePas asserts that "in his extant writings, Aelred never called the three persons in the

---

bond of spiritual friendship. Lest someone think that this very holy sort of charity should seem reproachable, our Jesus himself, lowering (Himself) to our condition in every way, suffering all things for us and being compassionate towards us, transformed it by manifesting his love. To one person, not to all, did he grant a resting-place on his most sacred breast in token of his special love. . . .": [frui possumus] his maxime, qui nobis spiritalis amicitiae gratissimo foedere caeteris familiarius arctiusque iunguntur. Cuius caritatis sacratissimum genus, ne cui improbandum videretur, ipse Iesus noster per omnia nobis condescendens, per omnia nobis patiens et compatiens, in suae dilectionis exhibitione transformans, uni, non omnibus, suavissimi pectoris sui reclinatiorium in signum praecipue dilectionis indulsit. . . . SC III.39.110 (Citations from *Speculum caritatis* will be given, according to the order in *CCCM* I, as follows: book number, chapter number, section or paragraph number.).

20. Dumont, "Aelred of Rievaulx's *Spiritual Friendship*," 195–96.
21. Dumont, introduction to Aelred of Rievaulx, *The Mirror of Charity*, 33.
22. TePas, "Aelred of Rievaulx," 258.

The Theological Account of Friendship in Aelred of Rievaulx

Trinity friends with each other."[23] Though an argument from silence can hardly be conclusive, TePas insists that Aelred "did not dwell very much on [friendship] in terms of the inner workings of the Trinity," admitting in a footnote that she is disagreeing here with both Hallier and Gaetano Raciti.[24] This question will demand closer consideration in our own exposition.

We have already characterized as existential both Aelred's own approach to theology and the theological treatments of his thought by Hallier, Squire and Dumont. In light of such a perspective, a comment by Squire, cited with approval by TePas, might seem to strike an ambivalent note. In an article published two years before his major monograph, Squire contended that Aelred "is much less autobiographical than is often supposed."[25] Whether or not careful reading of Aelred's texts ultimately bears out this claim, I would contend that "less autobiographical" by no means entails "less personal": that is to say, an author may for valid reasons choose to dramatize or color certain elements of his message and may nevertheless address his audience as sincerely and earnestly—with as authentic a "voice"—as if he had employed no literary artifice at all. An appreciation of this personal, or even "personalist," character of his writing is indispensable not only for understanding Aelred's whole theological outlook, but for comparing it with that of St. Thomas and of scholasticism in general. A final point from TePas's dissertation also pertains directly to the comparison between Aelred's and Thomas's accounts of friendship. TePas argues that "Aelred has described two very different types of love and affection."[26] The first is a classical model of friendship, "motivated by the perception that the other is good for oneself," whereas the second type of love is "based on overflowing generosity" and is "completely gratuitous"—first and foremost, the love of God, and of Christ, for the sinful world.[27] Though TePas says that Aelred "does not sufficiently distinguish" between the two,[28] she offers a detailed evaluation of the ways the two loves diverge in one aspect while simultaneously merging in another in Aelred's vision.

---

23. Ibid., 122.
24. Ibid.
25. Ibid., 277 n. 6.
26. Ibid., 422.
27. Ibid., 423.
28. Ibid., 422.

Theologizing Friendship

Brian Patrick McGuire

Finally, Brian Patrick McGuire's *Friendship and Community: The Monastic Experience, 350–1250*[29] is an outstanding and virtually exhaustive historical treatment of the topic, with a late chapter devoted wholly to Aelred's doctrine. In a programmatic statement in his introduction, McGuire states that "the aelredian point of view that sees no conflict between individual friendship and christian universal love does not gain universal acceptance."[30] Here, McGuire takes issue with James McEvoy for going too far in disputing the opinion that Christianity actually vitiated friendship, finally so exalting it that he sees "no conflict between the good of friendship and the highest good."[31] At the root of this dispute is McGuire's observation of a deep tension from the beginning of the Christian tradition onward between two basic biblical notions of friendship: (1) the "uncompromising" universalizing position championed by Paul and given articulation also by Jesus in John 15:12–17 (This is an ideal of friendship that effectively rules preferential friendship—*amicitia*—out of bounds in service of one's all-consuming love for Christ and His Body the Church.); (2) The particular and frankly preferential friendship iconically captured most of all by the relationship between Jesus and his "beloved disciple," especially as epitomized in their physical intimacy at the Last Supper, but also by Jesus' relationship with Lazarus (Jn. 11, etc.).[32] We note here only that this is not precisely the same tension discovered by TePas in Aelred's thought, already mentioned. Both seeming paradoxes will be considered in the conclusion of our own treatment.

We should note, too, that in *Friendship and Community* McGuire is completely matter-of-fact in his rejection of various fallacious modern historicizing and hermeneutical conceits, among the most important being the tendency to read every text in a Freudian light. But of equal weight is McGuire's correction of the tendency to over-politicize every text (especially correspondence), or, only slightly more subtly, to assume that if a clear political motive may be discerned, there cannot at the same time be other (non-sinister!) motives for writing. Such a fundamentally friendly approach to one's subject helps the contemporary scholar to attune himself

---

29. McGuire, *Friendship and Community*.
30. Ibid., xlix.
31. Ibid., xlviii.
32. Ibid., xxv–ix.

to the authentic voice of Aelred, Thomas, or any other writer from the distant past.[33] Though McGuire is more of a historian and less of a theologian than Hallier, Squire or Dumont, his mode of engaging his topic savors of a comparable existential impulse.

Other Scholarship

Brief mention should also be made of the work of Louis Bouyer, John Sommerfeldt, James McEvoy, Adele Fiske, and Marsha Dutton. The prolific theologian Louis Bouyer, by no means a specialist on Aelred, included in his mid-twentieth century volume on Cistercian spirituality[34] a chapter judged "one of the most complete and penetrating expositions of Aelred's thought available at the time."[35] This assessment is rendered by John Sommerfeldt, founder of Kalamazoo's renowned annual International Congress on Medieval Studies. Sommerfeldt himself has published two books on Aelred in the past three years,[36] each including brief sections on Aelred's doctrine of friendship. The intellectual historian James McEvoy, among numerous articles on friendship in the ancient, medieval and modern periods, published in 1981 an erudite close reading and translation of the Prologue to Aelred's *SA*.[37] Here, McEvoy adds his voice to those of other medieval

---

33. Within a few years of the publication of *Friendship and Community*, McGuire published *Brother and Lover*, in which he seems unfortunately to have succumbed to the very political pressure he so consistently and eloquently challenged in his earlier work. The question of Aelred's homosexuality—or not—has no significant bearing on the current project and will not be discussed further. For the interested reader there are the works of Boswell, *Christianity, Social Tolerance, and Homosexuality*—and of McGuire himself, as well as the refutations—to this author's mind compelling—of Dutton, "The Invented Sexual History of Aelred of Rievaulx"; TePas, "Aelred of Rievaulx," 408–13; and John Sommerfeldt. For a pithy summary of the debate, see Sommerfeldt, *Aelred of Rievaulx: Pursuing Perfect Happiness*, 8–9.

34. Bouyer, *The Cistercian Heritage*.

35. Sommerfeldt, *Aelred of Rievaulx: Pursuing Perfect Happiness*, 5.

36. Sommerfeldt, *Aelred of Rievaulx: On Love and Order in the World* and *Aelred of Rievaulx: Pursuing Perfect Happiness* (cf. n. 176, above).

37. McEvoy, "Notes on the Prologue," 396–411. Note the *u* in the variant spelling of *spiritual(i)*: Latin orthography in the mid-twelfth century remains somewhat unstable, particularly in the case of certain diphthongs and other vowel combinations (witness also the final—*ae/-e* variants in the feminine first declension, e.g.). The contemporary author is often forced to choose one or another option, rather arbitrarily, and thereafter to strive for consistency. I have opted against the *u* in this case, except in citations of other modern authors who have chosen otherwise.

studies experts who recognize the originality of Aelred's thought in his last great complete work, in spite of the conspicuous presences of Cicero and St. Augustine. In the early 1960s, Adele Fiske published a thoughtful treatment of Aelredian friendship, in two installments in *Citeaux*.[38] Lastly, Marsha Dutton has published numerous articles on Aelred, though none of them focuses on his theology of friendship.[39] Notwithstanding the importance of the contributions by these and other scholars to the general study of Aelred's life and thought, their treatments of friendship are comparatively cursory and do not require further remark here concerning Aelred's doctrine of friendship, much less regarding the question of the relationship between monastic and scholastic theological approaches.

Aelred's Sources

The question of Aelred's sources must be taken up briefly, principally for the purpose of remarking how typical he was of the mainstream of twelfth-century monasticism in his recourse to the written works at his disposal. Aelred did not aspire to be a great scholar or innovator: neither his disposition nor his circumstances urged him along the path of an Anselm of Canterbury, or of a Hugh of St. Victor. His early education had taken place locally, near his family home at Hexham, at the hands of a priest from the priory there, possibly with the help of his uncle Aldred, "reputed to be well-versed in holy scripture."[40] While still in his early youth, he was adopted by King David of Scotland into the royal household. Squire speculates that his education would have continued at court, probably at the hands of monastic tutors.[41] Somewhat ironically, perhaps, Aelred's favor with both the king and his sons was so great that they kept him home, and so he "lost the opportunity of being trained, as were many of his contemporaries, in the schools beyond the seas,"[42] at Paris, Laon, Chartres or Bologna. Moreover,

---

38. See Fiske, "Aelred's of Rievaulx."

39. See, e.g., Dutton-Stuckey, "The Conversion and Vocation of Aelred of Rievaulx," 31–49; Dutton-Stuckey, "The Cistercian Source," 151–78; etc.

40. Squire, *Aelred of Rievaulx*, 12. TePas contends that Aelred was also probably taught at Durham, by Laurence of Durham; see TePas, "Aelred of Rievaulx," 88–89.

41. Ibid., 13.

42. Talbot, introduction to *Aelred of Rievaulx*, 25. Aelred was born in 1110, and by the mid-twenties there were even the rudiments of a school system at Oxford, though it would be more than a century before England's great universities would come to rival

the community Aelred joined was a new foundation and initially very poor. Soon made novice-master, Aelred would have had little time in his early years as a monk to peruse even the few volumes in Rievaulx's modest library. Consequently, we should not expect to find anything exceptional in Aelred's reading, as the following cursory survey confirms. What Aelred read, he read thoroughly, and often with penetrating insight. By the standards of the twelfth-century monastic renaissance in which he lived, however, his reading was not especially remarkable in either breadth or depth.

Scripture

By far the most important of Aelred's sources, both quantitatively and qualitatively speaking, is the Bible. In this, he exemplifies a virtually monolithic tendency, not only encompassing the whole sweep of the monastic tradition up to and well beyond his own period, but even including most scholastic work before the early thirteenth century, the dawning of the age of Aristotle. Thus, in *SC*, his longest major work, he cites twenty-seven out of forty-six Old Testament books and every New Testament book except for the Second and Third Letters of John. The density of biblical quotation is no less in a much shorter spiritual work such as the *Oratio pastoralis*, in whose scant few hundred lines Aelred manages at least sixty scriptural references to twenty-five different books. Turning to Aelred's historical works, scriptural references are hardly less prominent, with upwards of four hundred citations spread across the pages of three major works, *Genealogia regum Anglorum*, *Vita sancti Edwardi*, and *De bello standardi*. In all of these cases, the references to the Psalms preponderate overwhelmingly, as we are prepared to expect of a monk continuously engaged in the *opus Dei*, as prescribed in St. Benedict's *Rule* and observed according to the strict Cistercian interpretation.[43] Among the Gospels, Matthew has pride of place; again, this is no surprise, given the availability of copies of the first Gospel, which far exceeded that of the other three Gospels, even in St. Thomas's day. The important question of *how* Aelred employed Scripture in his own writing will be considered in our main treatment of his thought.

---

those of Europe. David's court was unusually enlightened for the time, as Squire points out, and perhaps the king felt no urgency to export and risk losing local talent.

43. See ch. 18 of *RB*, which prescribes that the entire Psalter must be chanted each week.

Theologizing Friendship

Augustine and the Fathers

After Scripture, Aelred's next most important source is St. Augustine. He cites the other great Western Fathers, Sts. Ambrose, Jerome and Gregory the Great with some frequency,[44] and other fathers occasionally. Now and again appear citations from Isidore's *Etymologiae*, one of the most influential works in the common patrimony of medieval Europe. Aelred Squire even sees evidence for the influence of Origen, though he terms this influence "elusive."[45] We should not be surprised in Aelred's case to find John Cassian, for two reasons: first, because St. Benedict explicitly recommends his works in the *Rule*, and second, because one of Cassian's *Conferences* is devoted to the subject of friendship, one of Aelred's favorite topics.[46] Also to be expected is a relative preference for the great Englishman Bede, among the many fathers Aelred draws on less regularly. When all is said, however, Aelred's preference for Augustine is conspicuous. In this the twelfth-century English abbot is hardly atypical of his time or station, though his particular use of Augustine is very much his own, as will become more apparent in our analysis of Aelred's theology of friendship. Within the vast Augustinian corpus, Aelred draws most heavily on the *Confessions* and on Augustine's literal commentary on Genesis (*De Genesi ad litteram*).[47] Finally, Aelred

---

44. These references are generally scattered throughout the Aelredian corpus, though Aelred has frequent recourse to Ambrose's *Duties of the Clergy* in the third book of *SA*.

45. Squire, *Aelred of Rievaulx*, 32; cf. also 68. Louis Bouyer is far less reserved in asserting Aelred's familiarity with Origen. See Bouyer, *The Cistercian Heritage*, especially 132; also 135, 142.

46. *RB*, ch. 73. Cassian's sixteenth Conference concerns friendship.

47. For an extended treatment of the patristic and medieval sources Aelred had at his disposal, see TePas, "Aelred of Rievaulx," 73–107. Even such a careful historian as TePas, however, does not spend time piling up isolated references by Aelred to specific sources. Such a toilsome undertaking would arguably do little to enhance our understanding of the original theological contribution of one whose selection of source material hardly differentiates him from a whole host of eleventh- and twelfth-century monastic authors. Consider in this connection the comment cited above by David Knowles: "For three hundred years, from 1050 to 1350, and above all in the century between 1070 and 1170, the whole of educated Western Europe formed a single undifferentiated cultural unit" (*The Evolution of Medieval Thought*, 80). Cf. also Leclercq, *The Love of Learning*, chapter 6, on the ubiquitous and homogenizing influence of the patristic legacy on twelfth-century monasticism. Leclercq says quite simply that "medieval monastic culture . . . *is* a patristic culture, the prolongation of patristic culture in another age and in another civilization" (106, my emphasis).

also cites, though comparatively rarely, his contemporaries, especially his fellow Cistercians, Bernard of Clairvaux and William of St. Thierry.

Cicero

Among the range of non-Christian sources newly rediscovered during the humanist renaissance of the late eleventh and twelfth centuries, Cicero is far and away the most important for Aelred. Indeed, Aelred was predominantly interested in a single text of the great Roman rhetorician, *De am.*, which he cites at least sixty-five times in *SA*, his own radical Christian reworking of the classic text. In the same work, Aelred also cites Pseudo-Seneca and Terence, once each. Squire notes in book 3, chapter 39 of *SC* a faint echo of the language of Plato's *Symposium*, but does not argue for any textual dependency: on the contrary, he proposes that Aelred probably culled the phrase *solus cum solo* from one of Jerome's letters.[48] In more general terms, we may observe that the comparatively high quality of Aelred's Latin, often remarked,[49] undoubtedly owes much to the revival in his day of widespread interest in the Roman rhetorical tradition.

Aelred's "Synthesis" and Original Position

Speculum caritatis and De spiritali amicitia

Aelred's two most important theological works both deal with love. The earlier of these, *SC*, treats love under its supernatural aspect, that is, love as *caritas*. The later work, *SA*, completed near the end of Aelred's life, considers the special love relationship termed *amicitia*—friendship—again, especially as a Christian phenomenon. To arrive at a true understanding of Aelred's theological notion of friendship necessarily involves working out its relationship to charity. This relationship, in turn, finds a structural

---

48. "Epistle 52"; see Squire, *Aelred of Rievaulx*, 50; cf. also, 160 nn. 57 and 58.

49. See, e.g., Alexander Penrose Forbes, who notes that Aelred's "style, for the eleventh century [sic], is exceedingly good" (*Lives of S. Ninian and S. Kentigern*, x) and Louis Bouyer, who observes that "Aelred wrote a Latin which was in general correct, limpid, abounding in well-chiseled formulae, but without brilliance" (*The Cistercian Heritage*, 125–26). Bouyer notes evidence of Sallust and of the Roman poets, in addition to Cicero; see ibid., 126.

parallel in the relationship between the works devoted to the two notions in question. A consideration of this textual relationship will provide a useful approach to resolving the underlying theological question of the relationship between these two kinds of love.

The whole of SC, comprising an impressive 161 pages in CCCM, seems to have been composed in the space of not more than two years, between Aelred's return to England from a trip via Clairvaux to Rome, in 1142[50] and his appointment as first abbot of Revesby in 1143. During this brief period Aelred served as novice-master at Rievaulx, while reading over and assimilating notes he had made over the years since his entry in 1134 into the new Cistercian foundation of Rievaulx.

The history of composition of SA is somewhat more complicated. Sometime in the late 1140s, Ivo, a young monk of the new foundation at Wardon, put the request to his visiting abbot, Aelred, that he might

> teach me something about spiritual friendship, namely, its nature and value, its source and end, whether it can be cultivated among all, and, if not among all, then by whom; how it can be preserved unbroken, and without any disturbance of misunderstanding be brought to a holy end.[51]

The request and consequent composition of the first book of the treatise came no more than five years after the redaction of SC, though both Bouyer and Douglass Roby propose that Aelred may have begun work several years earlier, even as early as 1142.[52] In any case, the ideas developed in SC are still at the forefront of Aelred's mind as he engages in dialogue with Ivo

---

50. Whatever brief encounter may have occurred between St. Bernard and Aelred during this visit was enough to inspire Bernard to urge, as a matter of monastic obedience to himself, Father Immediate of the monks of Rievaulx, a daughter house of Clairvaux, the writing by Aelred of "a little something for me" (*mihi pauca quaedam scriberes*) concerning charity. Cf Dumont, introduction to *The Mirror of Charity*, 65.

51. Aliquid de spiritali amicitia doceas; videlicet quid sit, quid pariat utilitatis; quod eius principium, quis finis; utrum inter omnes esse possit; et si non inter omnes, inter quos; quomodo etiam possit indirupta servari, et sine aliqua dissensionis molestia sancto fine concludi. SA I.5 (Citations for *De spiritali amicitia* will be given according to the order in CCCM I. Note that, unlike SC, SA lacks chapter divisions. Thus the order is simply book number, followed by section or paragraph number. English translations of SA, unless otherwise noted, are those of Mary Eugenia Laker, from *Spiritual Friendship*.

52. Bouyer, *The Cistercian Heritage*, 155. Roby, in his introduction to the 1974 English translation of SA, appears inconsistent, initially giving explicit endorsement to the later date (10), but a few pages later proposing "the early 1140's" as the text's *terminus a quo* (22). See Aelred of Rievaulx, *Spiritual Friendship*.

in the opening pages of *SA*: he recalls the argument from the completed text, counting on Ivo's familiarity as necessary background for the current discussion.[53] Between the end of book one and the opening of book two, however, roughly twenty years have elapsed. In the interim, Ivo has died, as we learn early in the dialogue between Aelred and another monk, Walter. Nevertheless, Aelred carefully weaves the dramatic elements of his narrative in such a way as to strengthen the ties between the earlier and the later parts of his work. He recalls Ivo fondly and in terms which anticipate his climactic conclusion to the third book. Furthermore, it is the recent discovery of the "notes" to the earlier dialogue with Ivo which has inspired Walter to press his abbot to share further insights on spiritual friendship. Through these sundry literary devices, Aelred forges links not only between the first book and the last two books of *SA*, but also between the work as a whole and his earlier treatise on charity. In addition, there are a number of noticeable textual echoes of the earlier work in the later, mostly, if not all, occurring in the third book of *SA*.[54]

Friendship and Charity

More important than any of these formal connections, however, is the relationship in content between the two works. Louis Bouyer states bluntly that "the conclusion of the *Mirror of Charity* is the point of departure of the three dialogues *On Spiritual Friendship*,"[55] and goes so far as to say that "the chief interest of [the latter] work . . . lies in what it adds to the *Mirror of Charity*."[56] In point of fact, though the better part of *Speculum* does not deal specifically with friendship, spiritual or otherwise, both the climactic final chapter of the first book (ch. 34) and the concluding movement of the entire work, comprised by the last three chapters of book III (chs. 38–40), dwell on spiritual friendship at length and to the virtual exclusion of any other subject matter. Thus Aelred offers *prima facie* evidence of the significance in his mind of spiritual friendship as a particular expression of charity.

---

53. Cuius affectus et motus in Speculo nostro, quod satis cognitum habes, quam lucide potuimus ac diligenter expressimus. *SA* I.19.

54. Compare, e.g., *SA* III.2–3 with *SC* III.20.48; *SA* III.92–95 with *SC* III.29.69–71; and the pithy description of "well-ordered friendship" at the end of *SA* III.118 with *SC* III.18.41.

55. Bouyer, *Cistercian Heritage*, 155.

56. Ibid., 157.

Granted, then, that the literary and dramatic[57] structures of Aelred's two greatest theological works imply a strong fundamental relationship of some sort between these two theological *topoi*, we must inquire more particularly into the precise manner in which charity and friendship are related in these works, and ultimately in Aelred's wider theological perspective.

The relationship between spiritual friendship and Christian love or charity is a special, indeed the most exalted, case of the relationship between friendship and love, taken in their most general terms. In the beginning of the third book of *SA*, Aelred summarizes this relationship as follows:

> The fountain and source of friendship is love. There can be love without friendship, but friendship without love is impossible. Love proceeds either from nature, or from duty, from reason alone, or from affection alone, and sometimes from both simultaneously—from nature, as a mother loves her child; from duty, when through giving and receiving, some men are joined by special affection; from reason alone, as we love our enemies, not as the result of a spontaneous inclination of the heart but from the necessity of precept;[58] from affection alone, when anyone, because of bodily qualities only, such as beauty, strength, eloquence, inclines the affection of others to himself. From reason and affection simultaneously, when he, whom reason urges should be loved because of the excellence of his virtue, steals into the soul of another by the mildness of his character and the charm of a praiseworthy life. In this way reason unites with affection so that the love is pure because of reason and sweet because of affection.[59]

---

57. The importance of the dramatic character of Aelred's writing and thought will be elucidated shortly.

58. Note that while Aelred uses the generic word *amor* throughout this passage, in this particular example he clearly has supernatural *caritas* in mind, since it is only according to the Christian precept "Love your enemies and pray for those who persecute you" (Mt. 5:44) that one considers such a love the dictate of reason. In general, Aelred is neither systematic nor consistent in his use of *amor*, *dilectio*, and *caritas*, his employment of the three terms reflecting so much semantic overlap as to suggest that they are virtually interchangeable in his mind. In chapter 4, we will have occasion to comment further on this point.

59. Fons et origo amicitiae amor est, nam amor sine amicitia esse potest, amicitia sine amore numquam. Amor autem aut ex natura, aut ex officio, aut ex ratione sola, aut ex solo affectu, aut ex utroque simul procedit. Ex natura, sicut mater diligit filium. Ex officio, quando ex ratione dati et accepti, quodam speciali affectu coniungimur. Ex sola ratione, sicut inimicos, non ex spontanea mentis inclinatione, sed ex praecepti necessitate diligimus. Ex solo affectu, quando aliquis ob ea sola, quae corporis sunt, verbi gratia pulchritudinem, fortitudinem, facundiam, sibi quorumdam inclinat affectum. Ex ratione

A very similar passage occurs midway through the third book of *SC*:

> Love arises from attachment when the spirit gives its consent to this attachment, and from reason when the will joins itself to reason. A third love can also be brought about from these two when the three—reason, attachment, and will—are fused into one. The first is pleasant, but dangerous; the second is harsh, but fruitful; the third, having the advantages of the other two, is perfect. The sense of the sweetness we experienced draws us to the first; the evidence of reason impels us toward the second; and in the third, reason itself savors [the sweetness]. This last differs from the first because, although in the first we sometimes love what we ought to love, we love it more for the sake of the sweetness of attachment. In this last we love it not because it is pleasant, but because it deserves love and it is consequently sweet.[60]

Though each passage is carefully situated within its own argument, concerning friendship and love respectively, we see that Aelred remains profoundly consistent across the twenty years spanned by these texts: the most perfect love between persons—still prescinding for the most part[61] from the matter of whether the love in question is supernaturally infused—is one dually motivated, by both reason and affective attachment. It is this "pure" and "sweet" love that is most "advantageous to friendship," as Aelred establishes with Walter at the end of the above-cited passage in *SA*. Pursuing this line of reasoning to its logical terminus, spiritual friendship can only be that rare species of relationship, motivated by reason and affection, between members of the Body of Christ, and inspired by the Holy Spirit acting in the heart of each.

---

simul et affectu, quando is quem ob virtutis meritum ratio suadet amandum, morum suavitate, et vitae lautioris dulcedine, in alterius influit animum; et sic ratio iungitur affectui, ut amor ex ratione castus sit, dulcis ex affectu. *SA* III.2–3.

60. Est ergo amor ex affectu, cum affectui animus consenserit; ex ratione, cum se voluntas rationi coniunxerit; potest et tertius amor ex his duobus confici; cum scilicet haec tria, ratio, affectus et voluntas in unum coierint. Primus dulcis, sed periculosus; secundus durus, sed fructuosus; tertius utriusque praerogativa perfectus. Ad primum sensus expertae dulcedinis illicit, ad secundum ratio manifesta compellit, in tertio ipsa ratio sapit. Differt autem hic ultimus a primo, quia, licet illo et quod amandum est, aliquando ametur; magis tamen propter ipsius affectus dulcedinem amatur; hoc autem amatur, non quia dulce est, sed quia amore dignum; ideo dulce est. *SC* III.20.48. English translations of *SC*, unless otherwise noted, are those of Elizabeth Connor, from *The Mirror of Charity*.

61. Cf. n. 201.

Spiritual Friendship is Christological

If there can be no friendship of any sort without love, it is equally clear that friendship by no means necessarily presupposes the supernatural form of love known as charity. In fact, the essential difference between the most virtuous natural friendship and that friendship properly termed "spiritual" corresponds precisely to the difference between the sources of the love shared between the friends. This distinction is at the heart of Aelred's choice of Cicero's famous *De am.* as both model and foil for his own reflections on the same subject, considered in the light of Christian revelation. As a young man at the Scottish court, Aelred had been much captivated by Cicero's descriptions of the intimate, affectionate friendships possible between virtuous men. From the moment of his conversion and subsequent entry into the monastery, however,

> Sacred Scripture became more attractive and the little learning which I had acquired in the world grew insipid in comparison. The ideas I had gathered from Cicero's treatise on friendship kept recurring to my mind, and I was astonished that they no longer had for me their wonted savor.[62]

Whereas before, Aelred had desired nothing more than mutual affection—*amari et amare*[63]—now "nothing which had not been sweetened by the honey of the most sweet name of Jesus, nothing which had not been seasoned with the salt of Sacred Scripture, drew my affection so entirely to itself."[64] Thus, Aelred anticipates the succinct statement, put in the mouth of Ivo a few pages later, of the distinction between classical, Ciceronian friendship and the spiritual friendship to which Aelred and his interlocutors (and presumably his readers) aspire: "For it is evident that Tullius was unacquainted with the virtue of true friendship, since he was completely unaware of its beginning and end, Christ."[65]

---

62. Igitur cum sacra Scriptura dulcesceret, et parum illud scientiae quod mihi mundus tradiderat, earum comparatione vilesceret, occurrebant animo quae de amicitia in praefato libello legeram, et iam mirabar quod non mihi more solito sapiebant. *SA* Prologue.4.

63. To be loved and to love. The phrase is not Cicero's, but St. Augustine's, *Confessions*, II, 2, 2.

64. Iam tunc enim nihil quod non dulcissimi nominis Iesu fuisset melle mellitum, nihil quod non sacrarum Scripturarum fuisset sale conditum, meum sibi ex toto rapiebat affectum. *SA* Prologue.5.

65. Constat enim Tullium verae amicitiae ignorasse virtutem; cum eius principium finemque, Christum videlicet, penitus ignoraverit. *SA* I.8.

To "begin in Christ, continue in Christ, and be perfected in Christ,"[66] then, constitutes the defining feature of true,[67] or "spiritual," friendship. This fundamental distinction, what might be conveniently called the "christological difference," has other analogues in Aelred's reworking of Cicero's classical treatise. Thus, over against the rare famous pagan pairs who could meet Tullius's definition of friendship as "mutual harmony in affairs human and divine coupled with benevolence and charity,"[68] Aelred summons up a vision of the early church, replete with "thousands of pairs of friends" and epitomized by the biblical description in Acts 4:32: "And the multitude of believers had but one heart and one soul; neither did anyone say that aught was his own, but all things were common unto them."[69] As will become clear below, the phrase "one heart and one soul" proves to be a biblical leitmotif for Aelred's entire theological outlook. Another such differentiated parallel comes at SA I.13, where Aelred recalls one of Cicero's most elegant praises of friendship: "'Wherefore, friends,' says Tullius, 'though absent are present, though poor are rich, though weak are strong, and—what seems stranger still—though dead are alive.'"[70] Although Aelred cites these words with approval, the implicit contrast with his own recollection of the dead Ivo a few moments before is striking. Of "my most beloved," Aelred muses:

> his constant love and affection are, in fact, always so fresh to my mind, that, though he has gone from this life in body, yet in my spirit (*in meo animo*) he seems never to have died at all. For there (*ibi*) he is ever with me, there (*ibi*) his pious countenance inspires me, there (*ibi*) his charming eyes smile upon me, there (*ibi*) his happy words have such relish for me, that either I seem to have gone to a better land with him or he seems still to be dwelling with me here upon earth.[71]

---

66. In Christo inchoari, et secundum Christum produci, et a Christo perfici. SA I.10.

67. Cf. SA I.45: Amicitia enim spiritalis quam veram dicimus . . . (For spiritual friendship, which we call true . . .).

68. Amicitia est rerum humanarum et divinarum cum benevolentia et caritate consensio. SA I.11. Cf. Cicero, *De am.* 20. Note that when Cicero uses the word *caritas* it lacks entirely the theological content with which it is later invested by Christian authors.

69. SA I.28–29.

70. Quo circa amici, ut ait Tullius, et absentes adsunt sibi, et egentes abundant, et imbecilles valent; et, quod difficilius dictum est, mortui vivunt. SA II.13. Cf. Cicero, *De am.* 23.

71. Equidem carissimi mei recordatio, immo continuus amplexus et affectus, ita mihi semper recens est; ut, licet ex humanis exemptus, conditioni satis dederit, in meo

Theologizing Friendship

The echo of Cicero's "though dead are alive" is conspicuous. Yet the pagan, from the Christian point of view, can intend at best a metaphorical living after death—where a man's virtue lives on, so does he "live." Aelred's sentiment concerning Ivo, on the other hand, has a quite different cast. His assertion does not pertain merely to imagination or memory. Rather, Aelred here articulates his personal experience of the dogma of the communion of saints. Ivo is alive and well and relating to Aelred—among various possible modes no doubt the most conscious and direct being Aelred's memory of actual conversation with him when he was alive on earth. In a more concise and unequivocal testimony concerning two other friends, in the closing pages of his treatise, Aelred states: "I recall now two friends, who, although they have passed from this present life, nevertheless live to me and always will so live."[72] Consequently, the metaphysics of friendship is subtly transposed from the metaphorical presence in absence of the pagans to a real presence in absence in Christian ontology, a presence only possible in Christ, and only knowable in the light of Christian revelation.

The Johannine Character of Aelred's Theology of Friendship

That spiritual friends (whether two, or three, or the entire communion of saints) have but one heart and one soul (Acts 4:32) finds its most characteristic Aelredian expression in what may at first seem a peculiar emphasis on the sharing of secrets (*secreta*).[73] Aelred's psychological insight, no doubt testimony to much personal experience, that the private exchange of confidences typifies relationships of deep trust and intimacy, has an important theological analogue, deriving from St. John's theology of revelation. Indeed, the profoundly christological character of spiritual friendship itself has a distinctly Johannine flavor in Aelred's thought. Recalling John 15:15, Aelred points out that Jesus explicitly links his new designation of his disciples—formerly servants—as friends, to his sharing with them his

---

tamen animo numquam videatur obiisse. Ibi enim simper mecum est; ibi mihi religiosus vultus eius elucet; ibi dulces eius arrident oculi; ibi eius iucunda mihi verba sic sapiunt, ut vel ego videar cum eo ad meliora transisse; vel ipse mecum adhuc in his inferioribus conversari. SA II.5.

72. Recordor nunc duorum amicorum meorum, qui licet exempti praesentibus, mihi tamen vivunt, semperque vivent. Ibid., III.119.

73. See, e.g., SA I.32, II.11; SC I.28.79, the biblical example of Jonathan and David at III.29.71, and especially III.39.110. On the betrayal of secrets as demonstrating the antithesis of true friendship, see SA III.22, 25, 27, 44, etc.

own knowledge of the Father, a knowledge essentially secret (and radically unknowable to humanity) prior to the Son's revelation of it.[74] To bolster his argument, Aelred adduces a passage from St. Ambrose, in which the Doctor of Milan formulates true friendship in terms of the same passage from John: "If [a friend] is true, he pours forth his soul just as the Lord Jesus poured forth the mysteries of the Father."[75] Thus, the goal of spiritual friendship, the perfect union of will and ideas (affection and reason), epitomized by the mutual sharing of secrets, finds its warrant in the biblical doctrine of the Incarnation—in terms, moreover, of a specifically Johannine Christology.

The centrality of Johannine theology is apparent throughout *SA*, becoming more pronounced as the dialogue evolves. Another important text receives attention in the first book, when Ivo raises the question whether he should "say of friendship what John, the friend of Jesus, says of charity: 'God is friendship.'"[76] To this proposal, Aelred gives qualified assent, as we have already noted. His conclusion, in keeping with sentiments expressed elsewhere, gives rise to Katherine TePas's criticism that Aelred seems at times to confuse the two loves—terrestrial friendship, however exalted, on the one hand, supernatural charity on the other—which at other times he wishes to distinguish.[77] On balance, the criticism is probably overblown; however, see both our section on the trinitarian character of friendship, and the conclusion of this chapter, below.

The third key Johannine text cited by Aelred is John 15:13: "Greater love has no man than this, that a man lay down his life for his friends."[78] Considering the treatise as a whole, the difference between Aelred's treatment of this passage and his use of the passage two verses later (15:15), noted above, is striking. In the first book, he adduces John 15:13 as his first great christologically defined criterion for true spiritual friendship.[79] Yet in Book Two, after again proposing the passage as the measure of "how far love between friends should extend," he concedes readily to one of his

---

74. Ibid. III.83. Note that Jesus' revelation of the Father coincides with the Son's own self-revelation, the tension between identity and distinction of the respective contents of these two revelations comprising *the* signal theological problematic of St. John's Gospel.

75. *Si verus est, effundit animum suum, sicut effundebat mysteria Patris Dominus Iesus.* Ibid.

76. Ibid., 65. Cf. 1 Jn. 4:16.

77. TePas, "*Amor, Amicitia,* and *Miscercordia,*" 257–61.

78. See *SA* I.30, II.33.

79. Ibid., I.30.

interlocutors that "the wicked or pagans [may] take such joy in the mutual harmony of evil and wickedness that they are willing to die for one another."[80] Needless to say, Aelred can only concur in denying that such associates in evil "have reached the zenith of friendship,"[81] at the same time implicitly undermining the usefulness of John 15:13 as a criterion for assessing true friendship. Granted, the relationship between wicked associates *ipso facto* fails to satisfy the requirements of true friendship, inasmuch as the constituents of the association are not themselves individually good. Nevertheless, one may wonder whether the easy concession is partly accounted for in terms of historical accident, a peculiar consequence of Aelred's monastic innocence, as it were. Aelred was a monk, not a martyr. The sacrifices which routinely imposed themselves on members of a religious order in the twelfth century tended to be less extreme than the willing forfeiture of one's bodily life for a fellow. On the other hand, Aelred had already long ago and in no uncertain terms "given up his life" for his monastic friends by his very act of submitting to the strict obedience of the Cistercian order. Any interior recognition of this spiritual dying to self as an evangelical sacrifice, however joyfully embraced, might tend somewhat to mute the dramatic power of Christ's words interpreted in the most literal sense.

In fact, the category of self-disclosure seems to be more fundamental for Aelred than that of self-sacrifice for determining the parameters of spiritual friendship. In any case, Aelred's reluctance to defend John 15:13 in the long run clears the way for the ever expanding vistas which begin to open out from his resounding endorsement of the subsequent criterion of self-revelation found in John 15:15: "No longer do I call you servants, for the servant does not know what his master is doing; but I have called you friends, for all that I have heard from the Father I have made known to you." Upon the foundation of this verse, Aelred builds his case that

> friendship is a stage bordering upon that perfection which consists in the love and knowledge of God, so that man from being a friend of his fellow-man becomes the friend of God, according to the words of the Savior in the Gospel: "I will not now call you servants, but my friends."[82]

80. Ibid., II.35.
81. Ibid.
82. Quidam gradus est amicitia vicinus perfectioni, quae in Dei dilectione et cognitione consistit; ut homo ex amico hominis Dei efficiatur amicus, secundum illud Salvatoris in evangelio: *Iam non dicam vos servos, sed amicos meos.* Ibid., II.14.

Although Aelred outlines his project in terms of an attempt to determine the nature, fruition and excellence, and means of preservation of true friendship in this life,[83] the most striking contribution of his work comes arguably with his vision of this passage from the "bordering stage" of actual spiritual friendship—already attained and even mature—to the "perfection" of life in Glory, where supremely friendly communion will finally be realized. To this eschatological dimension of spiritual friendship we shall turn shortly. But in order to understand the whole breadth of Aelred's theology of friendship, we must first consider his doctrine of the three Sabbaths, elaborated in *SC*.

Aelred's Doctrine of the Three Sabbaths

In some ways the crowning achievement and most original element of Aelred's *SC* is his doctrine of the three Sabbaths. About this doctrine Squire says: "it was from brooding upon Augustine's *De Genesi ad litteram* that Aelred arrived at a valuable, original insight. At least there appears to be no other patristic or medieval writer who explores these matters quite in Aelred's way."[84] In effect, Aelred's feat is to locate a fairly succinct, yet thorough, account of Christian anthropology within the structuring metaphor of the correlative Old Testament ideas of the Sabbath and the seventh day of creation.

The pinnacle of God's creation is man, whom He created in His own image and likeness on the sixth day. Endowed with free will, Adam was capable with God's grace of continuing to love God without fail, but he was also capable of diverting his love to a lesser good. Having fallen through such a diverted love, man lost God's likeness, becoming instead "like the beasts that perish" (Ps. 49:20).[85] As for God's image, consisting essentially of reason and free will, this was not lost with the Fall. It became distorted, however, in its trinitarian character: memory becoming subject to forgetfulness, understanding to error, will or love to self-centeredness.[86] By a certain fitting symmetry, just as it is our love that is diverted from its proper object to lesser goods, it is by the transformation of this love into charity

---

83. Ibid., Prologue.7.

84. Squire, *Aelred of Rievaulx*, 39; cf. n. 14.

85. See *SC* I.4.10–11. The whole Cistercian pastoral theology of the *regio dissimilitudinis* is built on such accounts as this, thoroughly patristic in flavor and original content.

86. Ibid., I.4.12.

that the restoration of God's likeness in us is accomplished and the work of healing the image set in motion.[87] Aelred's appeal to another key Johannine text at precisely this point is striking: "I give you a new commandment" (John 13:34). The new commandment, unstated by Aelred here, is "that you love one another," implying clearly that graced human love for one another ("as I—Christ—have loved you" is the necessary qualifying clause that completes the verse) is in itself supernaturally transformative of the sinner. Thus, according to Aelred, "charity raises our soul up to that for which it was created; but self-centeredness degrades it to what it was sinking towards of its own accord."[88]

Breaking spontaneously into prayer, Aelred addresses the Lord with the words: "Those who love you, rest in you. And there is true rest, true tranquillity, true peace, a true sabbath for the mind."[89] This is a thoroughly Augustinian insight, and yet it is just here that Aelred's thought takes one of its most distinctive flights above and beyond Augustine.[90] As Squire observes, once more touting Aelred's originality, "although a mystical interpretation of the sabbath as such occurs frequently in Augustine, and in other patristic writers too, none offers a systematic presentation of the related notions accumulated in this Old Testament book"[91]—namely, Genesis.

In the pivotal nineteenth chapter of book one of the *SC*, Aelred lays the foundation for his theology of the three sabbaths through a traditional exegesis of the Genesis account of the seven days of creation, with particular attention to the sixth and seventh days. Recalling that the seventh day, unlike the previous six, has no morning or evening, Aelred argues that this seventh or sabbath day, God's rest from His creative activity of the week, "is His eternity, because it is nothing other than his divinity."[92] Expounding further on the text's relegation of God's rest entirely to the seventh day,

---

87. Ibid., I.8.24.

88. *Animam itaque nostrum ad id ad quod facta est, caritas sublevat; ad id vero, ad quod illa sponte defluxit, permit cupiditas.* Ibid., I.8.26.

89. *Qui enim diligunt te, requiescunt in te: et ibi vera requies, vera tranquillitas, vera pax, verum mentis sabbatum.* Ibid., I.18.52.

90. In their various ways Hallier, and especially Squire and Bouyer, clearly recognize Aelred's originality over against Augustine. See Hallier, *The Monastic Theology of Aelred of Rievaulx*, 52; Squire, *Aelred of Rievaulx*, 39, 42–43; Bouyer, *The Cistercian Heritage*, 147, 158.

91. Squire, *Aelred of Rievaulx*, 39.

92. *Ergo requies eius, aeternitas eius, quod non est aliud quam divinitas eius. SC* I.19.55.

The Theological Account of Friendship in Aelred of Rievaulx

Aelred asserts that "his rest is not described as being in any creature, that you may know precisely that he needs none of them, is self-sufficient in everything, and created nothing to meet his own needs, but everything to satisfy his overflowing charity."[93] And what is this charity, for which and through which alone God has created all things? It is itself His rest:

> Charity alone is His changeless and eternal rest, his eternal and changeless tranquillity, His eternal and changeless Sabbath.... For His charity is His very will and also His very goodness, and all this is nothing but His being. Indeed for Him this is to be always resting, that is, always existing, in His ever gracious charity, in His ever peaceful will and in His ever abounding goodness.[94]

Bouyer calls Aelred's identification of Sabbath rest with divine charity "one of the rare metaphysical *dicta* in his work."[95] Yet Aelred is not content with a merely unitarian—or Jewish—metaphysics: in the following chapter he presses on to uncover the trinitarian dimensions of sabbath. Specifying the charity already identified with God's rest as the love between the Father and the Son, he further points out that this divine mutual love is substantial, constituting the person of the Holy Spirit:

> This mutual delight of Father and Son is the gentlest love, the pleasing embrace, and the most blessed charity by which the Father reposes in His Son and the Son in His Father. This imperturbable rest, genuine peace, eternal calm, incomparable goodness, and indivisible unity is surely the unity of both, or rather, that in which each possesses the unity, sweetness, kindness, and joy we call the [Holy] Spirit.[96]

---

93. Idcirco non in aliqua creatura requies eius describitur, ut scias nullius indigentem, sed sibi in omnibus sufficientem, nec creasse aliquid, ut suae consuleret egestati, sed ut satisfaceret suae plenissimae caritati. Ibid.

94. [Caritas] sola incommutabilis et aeterna requies eius, aeterna et incommutabilis tranquillitas eius, aeternum et incommutabile Sabbatum eius.... Caritas enim eius, ipsa est voluntas eius, ipsa est et bonitas eius: nec hoc totum aliud quam esse eius. Hoc est enim ei in sua dulcissima caritate, in sua placidissima voluntate, in sua abundantissima bonitate, semper quiescere, quod semper est esse. Ibid., I.19.56.

95. Bouyer, *The Cistercian Heritage*, 135.

96. Haec mutua Patris Filiique dilectio amor suavissimus, gratus complexus, caritas beatissima, qua Pater in Filio, Filius repausat in Patre: haec plane, haec utriusque imperturbabilis requies, sincera pax, aeterna tranquillitas, incomparabilis bonitas, unitas indivisibilis; hoc utriusque unum, immo in quo uterque unum, dulce, suave, iucundum, sanctum dicimus Spiritum. *SC*, I.20.57.

Aelred proceeds then to recognize the connaturality of rest for all creatures: all of creation is disposed by its Creator to beauty, tranquillity, and peace.[97] Yet the highest creature, man, can only rest when his rational soul attains happiness, and true happiness cannot be attained through any other creature, but only through God Himself, Who is love. As so often, a central theological assertion is presented here in christological terms:

> Now let us heed the Sabbath himself: *Take my yoke upon you and learn from me, because I am meek and humble of heart and you will find rest for your souls.*[98] Look! Here is rest, tranquillity, and a sabbath. *And you will find rest for your souls, for my yoke is easy and my burden light.*[99] Yes, his yoke is easy and his burden light; therefore you will find rest for your souls. This yoke does not oppress but unites; this burden has wings, not weight. This yoke is charity. This burden is brotherly love. Here one rests, here one celebrates a sabbath, here one is free from servile works.[100]

With his theological foundation now carefully prepared, Aelred proceeds to align the three sabbaths—the seventh day of the week, the seventh year, and the jubilee or fiftieth year (the year following a sabbath of sabbath-years)—with "the state of charity in the will in respect of its three principal objects, self, neighbor, and God."[101] Of the first sabbath—rest in the properly ordered love of self—we need only note that for Aelred, while this love is both inevitable according to nature and indispensable as the measure for love of others according to revelation (cf. Matt 22:39),[102] nevertheless it is to be carefully circumscribed and monitored, lest it degenerate into mere cupidity. In anticipation of our treatment of the theology of Thomas Aquinas, it is worth noting that Aelred's description of this sabbath could be described, analogically, as a kind of friendship with oneself. According

---

97. See ibid., I.21.

98. Mt. 11:29.

99. Mt. 11:29–30.

100. Iam ipsum Sabbatum audiamus: *Tollite iugum meum super vos, et discite a me, quia mitis sum et humilis corde, et invenietis requiem animabus vestris.* Ecce requies, ecce tranquillitas, ecce Sabbatum. *Et invenietis requiem animabus vestris. Iugum enim meum suave est, et onus meum leve.* Prorsus iugum istud suave est, et onus leve, ideo invenietis requiem animabus vestris. Iugum istud non premit, sed unit; onus istud pennas habet, non pondus. Iugum istud caritas est, onus istud fraterna dilectio est. Hic requiescitur, hic sabbatizatur, hic a servilibus operibus vacatur. SC, I.27.78.

101. Squire, *Aelred of Rievaulx*, 39. See SC III.1.1–6.19.

102. See SC III.2.3.

to Aelred, proper love of oneself manifests itself as inner harmony in a man, wherein we find in accord "the entire throng of his thoughts, words, and deeds, like a most well-ordered and most peaceful family."[103] Such a description is certainly cognate with, if not identical to, the characterization of friendship as union of wills. However, any notion of literal friendship with oneself would make little sense to Aelred, and no such sentiment finds expression in his writing.

As the sabbath of years far exceeds in magnitude the sabbath of days, by a similar degree does the sabbath of fraternal charity excel that of charity towards oneself. Aelred's language here is splendid, invoking again the programmatic phrase from Acts 4:32:

> Just as only one day is set aside for the first sabbath—it is evident that it is one because it consists of tranquillity of one's own conscience—so it is not without reason that an entire year is devoted to this sabbath. Just as a year is made up of many days, so also in the fire of charity one heart and soul are molten from many souls.[104]

At this point, too, Aelred brings to bear one of his favorite passages from the Psalter, as authoritative and poetic support for the importance of this second sabbath: "Behold, how good and how pleasant it is when brothers dwell in unity."[105] Notwithstanding Aelred's exuberant praise of this kind of love, it is crucial to recognize that fraternal charity is by no means perfectly coterminous with spiritual friendship. Rather, the asymmetry observed with charity in general obtains here as well: though on the one hand spiritual friendship cannot exist without fraternal charity, on the other hand, one can certainly love one's brother—and is bound to do so—whether or not this relationship should ever attain to the heights of true friendship. In fact, it is the love of *enemies* "which constitutes the summit of fraternal charity." A curious transformation can take place, however, in the rare person who reaches that spiritual plateau upon which he manages to love and to forgive his enemy. Letting go at last of his anger and no doubt of his own

---

103. Et instar ordinatissimae ac pacatissimae cuiusdam familiae, omnis cogitationum, sermonum, operumque turba. Ibid., III.3.6.

104. Sicut autem primo illi Sabbato unus tantum dies dedicatur, quia videlicet singulare est, quod in propriae cuiusque conscientiae tranquillitate consistit, ita non immerito huic annus integer consecratur; quia, sicut ex multis diebus annus efficitur, ita ex multis animabus unum cor, et una anima caritatis igne conflatur. Ibid., III.4.8. The verb *conflatur*, from *conflare*, means to kindle or ignite, or to melt down, as with metals.

105. Ecce quam bonum et quam iucundum, habitare fratres in unum. Ps 132:1; cf. *SC* III.4.8.

sin, "himself forgiving and loving, he is forgiven and loved. From being a slave, he becomes not only a freeman but even a friend."[106] At the close of the chapter, Aelred writes:

> Therefore a person possessing this virtue [i.e., of charity, particularly towards one's enemies] should be said to celebrate this sabbath especially when he enters into his heart and applies his spirit to the sweetness of brotherly love. Completely surrendered to this most agreeable attachment to those dearest to him, he tastes how good and pleasant it is for brothers to dwell together in unity.[107]

Though he omits the key words here (friend, friendship), Aelred nonetheless suggests strongly that the paradigmatic case, and indeed the pinnacle, of fraternal charity is, after all, spiritual friendship.

Finally, there is the third and greatest sabbath, the jubilee year, consisting in the mystical rest obtained through man's love of God Himself. Once again, Aelred transposes his theological project immediately into the christological register, in terms of the Prologue to St. John's Gospel. In explanation of the relationship between the third and greatest sabbath and the lesser two, between love of God on one hand and love of oneself and one's neighbor on the other, Aelred states that "the love of God inclines us toward and fosters this twin love, because *the Word was made flesh and dwelt among us.*"[108] In the passage that follows, Aelred recommends, and

---

106. Donec ipse dimittens et diligens, dimittatur et diligatur, de servo non modo liber, sed etiam amicus efficiatur. Ibid., III.4.11. An anecdote from Aelred's youth at the Scottish court, recorded in Walter Daniel's *Vita Aelredi*, warrants mention here. A certain knight in attendance at King David's court conceived a virulent and utterly groundless loathing for the young Aelred. One day, the long-nursed hatred boiled over and the knight exploded into streams of slanderous public abuse, in the presence of the king. As Walter Daniel recounts with enthusiasm, Aelred "did not hurl recriminations at the blasphemer, but, with words of pure truth, which deserve enduring record, he met with gentle patience this drunkard in iniquity. 'You say well, excellent knight,' he replied, 'you say well and everything you say is true; for I am sure, you hate lying and love me. Who indeed is worthy to fight for King David, or to serve him as he should be served? I know only too well, and hold myself in deep displeasure, that I am a sinner, and have failed much in my service, not to the king whom I serve on earth, but to the King of Heaven'" (Daniel, *Vita Aelredi*, 93–94). The knight was so stunned by Aelred's magnanimity that he repented and, in the sequel, the two became good friends. See Daniel, *Vita Aelredi*, 95.

107. Hac igitur virtute possessus tunc maxime Sabbatum hoc celebrare dicendum est, cum ingrediens cor suum in fraternae dilectionis dulcedinem intendit animum, et erga carissimos sibi in quemdam suavissimum resolutus affectum, gustat quam bonum et quam iucundum habitare fratres in unum. Ibid., III.4.12.

108. Sciendum quia ad hanc geminam dilectionem Dei nos dilectio movet et

provides an outline for, a detailed imaginative meditation on the life, passion and death of Christ.[109] Such meditation is the surest remedy for both our concupiscence (the realm of self-love) and our disinclination to love our enemies (the realm of love of neighbor). Thus, Aelred provides pastoral advice to his monks and other readers, while at the same time establishing for the "twin love" of the first two sabbaths a single guiding principle: adoration and imitation of Christ's humanity. Elegantly completing his christological thought, Aelred associates the third sabbath, the jubilee year, with "the blissful embraces of the Lord's divinity."[110] Now the soul "goes beyond the veil of the flesh and, entering into that sanctuary where Christ Jesus is spirit before its face, it is thoroughly absorbed by that ineffable light and unaccustomed sweetness."[111] At last Aelred reaches the climax of his sabbath theology, which he summarizes in a lyrical series of triads, each correlated with charity's three sabbath moments:

> For the seventh day is, as it were, the foundation of charity, the seventh year its increase, and the fiftieth year—which comes after seven times seven—its fullness. On each of these there is rest, on each of these there is leisure, on each of these there is a spiritual sabbath. First there is rest in purity of conscience, then in the very pleasant joining together of many minds, and finally in the contemplation of God Himself. On the first sabbath the soul keeps free from fault, on the second from self-centeredness, and on the third from absolutely everything that dissipates it. On the first sabbath the mind tastes how sweet Jesus is in his humanity; on the second it sees how perfect he is in charity, and on the third how sublime in his Godhead. On the first the soul is recollected within itself, on the second it is extended outside itself; on the third it is caught up above itself.[112]

---

promovet, secundum id quod *Verbum caro factum est, et habitavit in nobis* (Jn. 1:14). Ibid., III.5.13.

109. For a provocative and, to this author's mind persuasive, argument that Aelred's style of imaginative meditation on the life of Christ provides *the* original, and almost the sole, basis for St. Ignatius's *Spiritual Exercises*—not to mention St. Bonaventure's *Lignum Vitae!*—see Dutton-Stuckey, "The Cistercian Source," 151–78.

110. [Domini] divinitatis felices . . . amplexus. Ibid., III.6.17.

111. Velamen carnis excedat, intransque in illud sanctuarium, ubi spiritus sit ante faciem suam Christus Iesus, ab illo ineffabili lumine, ab illa inusitata dulcedine penitus absorbeatur. Ibid.

112. Nam septimus dies quasi caritatis est inchoatio, septimus annus promotio, quinquagesimus annus, qui est post septies septem, eius est plenitudo. In singulis requies, in singulis vacatio, in singulis spiritalis quaedam sabbatizatio. Primo requies in puritate

Theologizing Friendship

In Aelred's highly original theology of the three sabbaths we discover what is in many ways the key doctrine in his theology of charity. Thus, the three-tiered rest of the will which Aelred identifies with the activity of charity—rest in self, in neighbor, and in God—constitutes the theological *sine qua non* of spiritual friendship, though, as always, such friendship is not a guaranteed accompaniment to charity, at least not in this life.[113] To see this more clearly, we must return now to the structure of Aelred's two major works, the better to understand the dramatic character of Aelred's theology of friendship.

Aelred's Theology of Friendship is Dramatic

We have already noted in a general way Aelred's use of dramatic narrative elements in the composition of the three dialogues which make up his *SA*. More specifically, Aelred over and over again presents himself, as the chief spokesman of the text, *enacting* friendship. This is particularly pointed at the outset of the first and second dialogues, in Aelred's initial engagements with Ivo and Walter, respectively.[114] In addition, there are adduced from time to time, sometimes by Aelred, sometimes by his interlocutors, examples of friends and friendships in Aelred's own life.[115] The most important of these examples are the two friends recalled by Aelred towards the end of the third dialogue, to which we shall return momentarily.

We have also identified as a significant bridge between Aelred's treatise on charity and his work on spiritual friendship, completed much later, the pivotal final chapter of the first book of *SC*. This text, *SC* I.34, itself constitutes the most striking instance of literary drama, in a work otherwise

---

conscientiae, deinde in multarum mentium dulcissima coniunctione, postremo in ipsius Dei contemplatione. In primo sabbato vacatur a crimine, in secundo a cupiditate, in tertio ab omni prorsus distensione. In primo gustat mens, quam dulcis est Iesus in humanitate; in secundo videt quam perfectus in caritate; in tertio quam sublimis in Deitate. In primo colligitur ad se; in secundo extenditur extra se; in tertio rapitur supra se. Ibid., III.6.19.

113. See "The Communal, Trinitarian and Eschatological Dimensions of Friendship" in chapter 3, below.

114. See *SA* I.1–4, II.1–3, passim.

115. See, e.g., Aelred's "irascible" friend, discussed at III.16–20, and the two friends mentioned in III.67, "that friend of yours across the sea," and "your dearest friend, the old sacristan of Clairvaux," III.67. All of these friends are introduced into the dialogue not by Aelred, but by one of his interlocutors, Walter in the first instance, Gratian in the second.

much less conspicuously, and pervasively, dramatic than the dialogues of *SA*.[116] The chapter, alleged by Aelred himself to be an interruption of his original narrative plan, takes up more than 330 lines in *CCCM*, fully one sixth of the first book of the treatise.

The circumstance that occasions this lengthy interruption is the death of Simon, a young monk to whom Aelred was deeply attached. Certainly Aelred's lament postpones his promised discussion of the threefold concupiscence enumerated in 1 John 2:16. Yet the text ultimately proves to be less of a whimsical interjection than the careful integration into a holistic theological perspective of what no doubt arose first as a spontaneous movement of Aelred's heart and mind towards his recently deceased friend.[117] Formal evidence for this assertion surfaces with the realization that through his lament for Simon, Aelred gives existential expression to a major theme of *SC*, the struggle between attachment (*affectus*) and reason (*ratio*), a theme he will go on to develop in depth in book three, chapters 11 through 29. Another point in support of the integral reading of chapter 34 bears more directly on the theology of friendship. Two chapters earlier, in a discussion of charity as the perfection and consummation of all the virtues,[118] Aelred had described *caritas* as *honesta morum compositio*: "the virtuous harmony of practices." Now, amidst a stream of heartrending protestations of his grief, Aelred calls Simon *compositio morum meorum*: "the harmony/harmonizer of *my* practices." When the two texts, already in close proximity, are deliberately read together—in harmony, as it were—the inescapable effect is the personification of charity in Simon, Aelred's beloved and unquestionably "spiritual" friend: once again, charity and spiritual friendship are seen to converge, this time as a consequence of the dramatic structure of Aelred's text itself.

Aelred's most climactic evocation of the dramatic character of his theology of friendship comes in the closing pages of *SA*, in a long passage

116. A loose comparison to the dialogues of Plato, not to mention, of course, Cicero's ever present *De am.*, is appropriate here.

117. Cf. Dumont, introduction to *The Mirror of Charity*, 61–62; Squire, *Aelred of Rievaulx*, 45–46; Bouyer, *The Cistercian Heritage*, 138–39. TePas is content to describe the chapter as an "interjection": see TePas, "Aelred of Rievaulx," 58. Squire, on the other hand, shows how Aelred deftly epitomizes Simon as the antithesis of the Johannine threefold concupiscence: the concupiscence of the flesh, the concupiscence of the eyes, and the pride of life, or *libido dominandi*, according to Aelred.

118. Just as the seventh day of creation constitutes the completion and fulfillment of the previous six. The biblical-allegorical argument is both deeply patristic and typical of Aelred throughout his writing.

strongly reminiscent of his lament for Simon in *SC*, though significantly more serene in tone. Here, Aelred recalls two friends, the first of whom is probably Simon,[119] thus forging a further link between Aelred's two texts, and thereby between his two principal theological concerns. This time, however, the cherished friend who died in youth is given only brief attention, as if Aelred's recollection must be cut short, just as was the life of the young monk. The dramatic difference between the two remembrances of the same person carries the greatest significance. Before, Aelred struggled to master his affection with reason, only grudgingly admitting that Simon's soul must be happier in heaven than at Aelred's side at Rievaulx. Now, Aelred regards his friend with a mature affection—indeed, with an attachment that, at risk of paradox, has become detached. With the same tone of reasoned affection, though at much greater length, Aelred recalls also another friend, with whom he experienced over many years every stage in the development of true friendship, from selection, through testing, affirmation, and finally perfection.[120] He concludes his reminiscence with the following splendid lines:

> Was it not a foretaste of blessedness thus to love and thus to be loved; thus to help and thus to be helped; and in this way from the sweetness of fraternal charity to wing one's flight aloft to that more sublime splendor of divine love, and by the ladder of charity now to mount to the embrace of Christ Himself; and again to descend to the love of neighbor, there pleasantly to *rest* [my emphasis]? And so, in this friendship of ours, which we have introduced by way of example, if you see aught worthy of imitation, profit by it to advance your own per-fection.[121]

The passage is both quietly sabbatical (*viz.* rest in the love of neighbor) and frankly eschatological (*viz.* a foretaste of blessedness). What is more, it cannot but be read as a deliberate corrective of St. Augustine's condemnatory use of the haunting phrase *amare et amari*, already invoked by Aelred in his

---

119. See, e.g., Aelred of Rievaulx, *Spiritual Friendship*, 126 n. 138. The notes to this text are provided by M. Basil Pennington. For the Latin text, see *SA* III.19.

120. See Ibid., III.119–27.

121. Nonne quaedam beatitudinis portio fuit, sic *amare* et sic *amari*; sic iuvare et sic iuvari; et sic ex fraternae caritatis dulcedine in illum sublimiorem locum dilectionis divinae splendorem altius euolare; et in scala caritatis nunc ad Christi ipsius amplexum conscendere, nunc ad amorem proximi ibi suaviter *repausaturum* descendere? In hac igitur amicitia nostra quam exempli gratia inservimus, si quid cernitis imitandum, ad vestrum id retorquete profectum. Ibid. III.127; my emphasis.

Prologue, where it still retains its Augustinian flavor. Viewed by the great doctor on the whole as grave spiritual dangers, intimate friendships at their best are embraced by Aelred as auxiliaries to sanctification.

The dramatic quality of Aelred's major works, then, is no mere stylistic flourish, either from whim or for heightened rhetorical effect. Rather, it expresses in literary form the underlying dramatic character of the author's themes—specifically, of charity and friendship. Though Hallier, Squire, Dumont and Bouyer all recognize the profoundly existential character of Aelred's theology, none of them develops this insight in terms of the dramatic structure of his major works. Not only Aelred's writing, then, but the whole of his theological enterprise, including preeminently his theology of friendship, must be characterized as both existential and dramatic.[122]

The Communal, Trinitarian, and Eschatological Dimensions of Friendship

A few important aspects of Aelredian friendship, each mentioned in passing above, still remain to be briefly discussed. These are its communal, trinitarian and eschatological dimensions.

Katherine TePas has pointed out, as already noted, that Aelred characterizes life in union with God "more as a great communal celebration of a wedding than as a bridal couple's private embrace."[123] This observation resonates with our own, and that of Hallier, concerning Aelred's doctrine of the divinely created need in man for the help and friendship of others. Several texts may be brought to bear here. First, in the third book of *SC*, Aelred suddenly introduces *mutual* love, in a chapter concerned with love of neighbor. Unlike our love for God, which He does not need, when it comes to human neighbors, because of our "mutual need, we must have

---

122. Another context, beside that of his two major treatises, in which one might expect to find the dramatic character of friendship showcased is that of Aelred's historiographical and hagiographical works. Such an expectation is in some sense satisfied by a close reading of these works, but not ultimately in a way that warrants further comment here. In fact, friendship appears *not* as an extraordinary theme in any of the histories or saints' lives, but rather as a matter-of-fact element of life along with many others: Aelred is thinking about the phenomenon as it occurs, both in his own experience and in his reworking of the histories of Edward and of the material for David's genealogy. The point is that this is not a systematic but rather an organic process, which will be given further shape as Aelred proceeds to focus on friendship as a specific theological theme in both *SC* and more closely still in *SA*. Cf. also n. 292, below.

123. TePas, "Aelred of Rievaulx," 258.

concern for each other's interests."[124] A close though more explicit parallel occurs in a sermon for Pentecost, where Aelred contends,

> consequently God, though he is a sufficient good for Himself, nevertheless extended to the creature the abundance of his goodness, robbing himself and bestowing advantage upon all. But since the rational soul could bestow nothing upon God, there were created many of the same nature, so that in this manner also the likeness of the divine goodness, which pours out upon many, might appear through the mutual exchange of benefits.[125]

Theologically even more explicit is a beautiful passage from a sermon for the Feast of St. Benedict, in which Aelred plainly has his own monastic community in view as he writes:

> Almighty God can immediately bring to perfection anyone he pleases and bestow all the virtues on any one person. But in his caring way of dealing with us he causes each person to need the other and to have in the other what one does not possess in oneself. Thus humility is preserved, charity increased and unity recognized. Therefore each belongs to all and all belong to each.... [126]

Thus, while friendship is never guaranteed to anyone in this life, our need for friends is inscribed in us by God's providential design. Moreover, by our interchange of benefits, we actually reflect God's likeness, in respect of his self-diffusing goodness.

The deeply communitarian character of Aelred's thought raises the obvious further question of the relationship in his theology between friendship and the Trinity. As already noted, TePas has found that "in his extant writings, Aelred never called the three persons in the Trinity friends

---

124. In mutua autem dilectione quoniam mutuo indigemus, necesse est ut nobis invicem consulamus. *SC* III.22.52.

125. Deus, itaque, licet sit sufficiens bonum sibi, abundantiam tamen bonitatis suae extendit reaturam, sibi detrahens et utilitatem omnibus conferens. Sed quia anima rationalis deo nil conferre potuit, creati sunt eiusdem nature plures, ut in hac etiam parte similitudo divinae bonitatis, quae refunderet in multos, mutuis beneficiis appareret. Aelred of Rievaulx, *Sermones inediti B. Aelredi Abbatis Rievallensis*, 108.

126. Posset quidem omnipotens Deus quemcumque vellet ad perfectionem statim promovere et singulis omnes virtutes largiri. Sed pia dispensatione nobiscum agit ut unusquisque alio indigeat et quod in se non habet, hoc in altero habeat, ut sic servetur humilitas, augeatur caritas, unitas cognoscatur. Sunt ergo singula omnium et omnia singulorum... (Aelred of Rievaulx, *Aelredi Rievallensis Sermones I–XLVI, Sermo VIII*, par. 10).

with each other."[127] Having researched the problem according to a strict historical methodology,[128] by conducting an exhaustive inventory of textual evidence, she risks an argument essentially from silence, contending that Aelred "did not dwell very much on [friendship] in terms of the inner workings of the Trinity."[129] Nonetheless, in light of the preceding elucidation of Aelred's understanding of spiritual friendship, it is difficult to see how the Persons of the Holy Trinity could *not* be considered friends in the most rigorous terms. On the contrary: an intimate relationship between persons, grounded in both reason and affection,[130] that begins, continues and ends in Christ,[131] Who is none other than the Incarnate Second Person of the Trinity, could certainly be seen as exemplified supereminently by the relations between the divine Persons. As in the case of Aelred's caution when presented with the proposition "God is friendship," the absence in his writings of references to the relations between the divine Persons as relations of friendship can readily be accounted for in Aelred's own words: "That would be unusual, to be sure, nor does it have the sanction of the Scriptures"[132]—we may well add, "or of Tradition." Nonetheless, Aelred's appropriate disinclination to meddle with dogma need not deter us from seeking valid, theologically interesting descriptions of a reality infinitely vast, and therefore admitting in theory of endless new description. Indeed, such scruples did not entirely deter even Aelred himself from offering the friendliest imaginable description of the trinitarian relations in a passage which bears citing a second time:

> This mutual delight of Father and Son is the gentlest love, the pleasing embrace, and the most blessed charity by which the Father reposes in His Son and the Son in His Father. This imperturbable rest, genuine peace, eternal calm, incomparable goodness, and indivisible unity is surely the unity of both, or rather, that in

---

127. TePas, "Aelred of Rievaulx," 122.

128. In the preface to her dissertation, TePas notes in passing that she has undertaken her work under the rubric of Historical Theology. This is as opposed to Systematic Theology, which maintains a certain distinctive character over against the former discipline, however much the two tend to merge in subject matter, and to a lesser extent even in formal articulation (TePas, "Aelred of Rievaulx," vi).

129. TePas, "Aelred of Rievaulx," 122.

130. Cf. pg. 58 n. 59, above.

131. Cf. pg. 61 n. 66, above.

132. Inusitatum quidem hoc, nec ex Scripturis habet auctoritatem. *SA* I.70.

which each possesses the unity, sweetness, kindness, and joy we call the [Holy] Spirit.[133]

Thus, just as Aelredian friendship has a communal character in the anthropological realm, it is seen to have a parallel trinitarian expression in the theological domain.

These two dimensions of Aelred's doctrine of spiritual friendship, the communal and the trinitarian, converge at last in what may fairly be termed an eschatology of friendship. In effect, Aelred describes the gradual transition from true terrestrial spiritual friendship to participation in the inner life of the Most Blessed Trinity, in terms of subsequent analogical anticipations of trinitarian *perichoresis*, which may be defined concisely as the profound interpenetration of persons without consequent loss of personal identity.[134] Aelred's creative presentation and elaboration of this doctrine is made the more striking by the fact that he does not himself use this word, once given theological credibility by St. Gregory of Nazianzus and St. John Damascene. The concept is nonetheless indisputably present in Aelred's writing and highly applicable in our project of elucidating his theology of friendship.

In the analysis which follows, it is important to understand that the application of this analogy—we may call it the perichoretic analogy—entails no confusion of Creator and creation. Aelred gives no evidence of any tendency to confuse spiritual union—a union of wills (also termed a moral union)—between man and man or man and God, with either the hypostatic union or the union among the divine Persons.[135] Moreover, we shall assume that any analogue to trinitarian perichoresis entails personal interpenetration in precisely such a way as always to preserve the distinction between the persons involved: as with the three divine Persons, so, *mutatis mutandis*, with our human participation in the inner life of the

---

133. SC I.20.57. For the Latin text, see n. 96, above (p. 67). We may note here as well, *pace* Aelred himself, that the Johannine name for the Holy Spirit, *paracletus*, often translated "Helper," has undeniable overtones of friendliness, albeit in an economic, rather than an immanent trinitarian context.

134. In the single case of the *perichoresis* enjoyed by Christ's two natures, the definition must be modified accordingly: interpenetration of *natures*, without confusion, as defined by the Council of Chalcedon.

135. In Bernard, the distinction is made explicit in terms of the contrast between an ontological union, or "union of nature," between Father and Word on the one hand, and a "unity of spirit between God and the soul" on the other: cf. SA, 75, n. 23. Aelred himself simply does not give any formulations which would cause suspicion.

Trinity in glory; so also with the creaturely perichoresis of the communion of saints, made possible and constantly sustained by the Holy Spirit. Furthermore, personal communions are perichoretic according to their own proper mode, as it were. Thus, in the Trinity, the perichoresis of Persons is *essential*—which cannot be true of any lesser perichoresis, including that which obtains between Christ's two natures. And clearly the perichoretic character of the communion of saints is metaphysically far inferior to its intra-christological (hypostatic) analogue.

At the most mundane level, Aelred attests even to a certain material expression of the perichoresis among friends, discovered in the sharing of material goods: "... they expend *themselves* and their goods for one another in such a way, etc." (my emphasis).[136] One might also compare with this point the mutual physical and spiritual self-giving of the marital act, par excellence. It is noteworthy that while Aelred does not explicitly make such a connection here, nevertheless his example is of Boaz and Ruth, though in terms of Boaz's material charity prior to their marital union.[137] Aelred evidently makes no conscious connection at this point to the kind of mutual interpenetration of persons characteristic of marriage. In his first book, however, he matter-of-factly identifies marriage as a species of friendship and characterizes this special friendship as one the constitutive parties of which are "collateral" and "equal."

From such material and humanly composite perichoreses, Aelred passes on to more strictly spiritual expressions, slowly revealing a kind of bridge from this-worldly sympathy or empathy to the joyous companionship among one's fellow citizens of the heavenly Jerusalem. Thus, "a friend ought... to think of his friend's fault as his own."[138] No doubt "to think of what is one's friend's as one's own" remains an assertion explicitly of the epistemic order. Yet its logical extrapolation in the order of grace is the perichoresis of the communion of saints. In a convenient summary of all of the perichoretic adumbrations thus far discussed, Aelred declares exultantly: "Therefore in friendship, which is the perfect gift of nature and grace alike, let the lofty descend, the lowly ascend; the rich be in want, the poor become rich; and thus let each communicate his condition to the other, so that equality may be the result."[139] In two passages already cited

---

136. Sic se sibi suaque impendant, etc. SA III.99. Cf. *Sermo VIII*, par. 10.
137. Cf. SA III.100.
138. Debet... amicus... vitium [amici] suum putare. Ibid., III.107.
139. Itaque in amicitia quae naturae simul et gratiae optimum donum est, sublimis

at a different point in our argument, Aelred bears existential testimony to his deep personal conviction of the metaphysical sturdiness of this perichoretic bridge, able to span death itself and join together friends on either side. Of Ivo, he muses:

> though he has gone from this life in body, yet in my spirit he seems never to have died at all. For there he is ever with me, . . . there his happy words have such relish for me, that either I seem to have gone to a better land with him or he seems still to be dwelling with me here upon earth.[140]

As noted in the previous context, Aelred's sentiment must be read as his personal experience of the dogma of the communion of saints. Ivo is *alive*, in heaven, and relating to Aelred, however rarefied the experience of that relationship must inevitably be. Concerning two other friends, Aelred states matter-of-factly: "I recall now two friends, who, although they have passed from this present life, nevertheless live to me and always will so live."[141]

Throughout Aelred's upward-spiraling meditation on the passage from spiritual friendship to participation in the inner trinitarian life, the person of Jesus Christ remains always pivotal. Thus, for example: "[various adjunct qualities of friendship] take their beginning from Christ, advance through Christ, and are perfected in Christ."[142] Again, "our Lord and Savior himself has written for us the formula of true friendship, when he said: 'You shall love your neighbor as yourself.'"[143] Aelred's enthusiasm for Johannine Christology has already been considered. And in an early anticipation of his climactic concluding passages, Aelred places Psalm 132:1—"Behold

---

descendat, humilis ascendat; dives egeat, pauper ditescat; et ita unusquisque alteri suam conditionem communicet ut fiat aequalitas. Ibid., III.91.

140. [Ut,] licet ex humanis exemptus, conditioni satis dederit, in meo tamen animo numquam videatur obiisse. Ibi enim semper mecum est; . . . ibi eius iucunda mihi verba sic sapiunt, ut vel ego videar cum eo ad meliora transisse; vel ipse mecum adhuc in his inferioribus conversari. Ibid., II.5.

141. Recordor nunc duorum amicorum meorum, qui licet exempti praesentibus, mihi tamen vivunt, semperque vivent. Ibid., III.119.

142. Quae omnia a Christo inchoantur, per Christum promoventur, in Christo perficiuntur. Ibid., II.20.

143. Ipse Dominum ac Salvator noster verae nobis amicitiae formam praescripsit: *Diliges*, inquiens, *proximum tuum sicut te ipsum*. Ibid., III.69.

how good and how pleasant it is for brethren to dwell together in unity"—at the very center of a passionate reflection on the kiss of Christ and its sweetness.[144]

It is hardly surprising, then, that it is Christ who provides the ultimate transition from holy friendship to union with God, via the prayer of each friend for the other. Such prayer,

> in the remembrance of a friend, is the more efficacious in proportion as it is more lovingly sent to God, with tears which either fear excites or affection awakens or sorrow evokes. And thus a friend praying to Christ on behalf of his friend, and for his friend's sake desiring to be heard by Christ, directs his attention with love and longing to Christ; then it sometimes happens that quickly and imperceptibly *the one love passes over into the other*, and coming, as it were, into close contact with the sweetness of Christ himself, the friend begins to taste his sweetness and to experience his charm [my emphasis].[145]

Mounting towards his splendid climax, Aelred once more invokes Psalm 132:1 as his governing thesis: "How good and how pleasant it is for brothers to dwell together in unity"—and what a dwelling together!

> How advantageous it is then to grieve for one another, to toil for one another, to bear one another's burdens, while each considers it sweet to forget himself for the sake of the other, to prefer the will of the other to his own, to minister to the other's needs rather than one's own, to oppose and expose one's self to misfortunes![146]

Aelred leads us from this final reprise of what Christian friendship in this life can be, through the organic yet supernatural relationship between such friendship and prayer, and on to a christological perichoresis—not

---

144. Ecce quam bonum et quam iucundum, habitare fratres in unum. Ibid., II.26. The passage on the kiss runs from II.21 through II.27.

145. In amici memoria tanto efficacius, quanto affectuosius ad Deum emittitur, profluentibus lacrimis, quas vel timor excutit, vel affectus elicit, vel dolor educit. Ita pro amico orans Christum, et pro amico volens exaudiri a Christo, ipsum diligenter et desideranter intendit; cum subito et insensibiliter aliquando affectus in affectum transiens, et quasi e vicino ipsius Christi dulcedinem tangens, incipit gustare quam dulcis est, et sentire quam suavis est. Ibid., III.133.

146. Quam utile tunc dolere pro invicem, laborare pro invicem, onera sua portare invicem, cum unusquisque pro altero semetipsum neglegere dulce habet; alterius voluntatem suae praeferre, illius necessitati magi quam suae ipsius occurrere; adversis semet opponere et exponere. Ibid., III.132.

hypostatic, in this case, but one which comes about among true friends in Christ's company[147] via prayer. Thence, at long last, he brings us to a vision of glorified friendship, in which the good particular friendships of this life overflow "upon all"—in an image strongly suggestive of our participation in the Pseudo-Dionysian self-suffusing Love and Goodness—"and by all [will be] outpoured upon God, and God shall be all in all."[148]

AELRED'S FRIENDLY EXEGESIS

We must finally make an inquiry, however limited, into Aelred's relationship to Scripture. The point here is not to anatomize the content of his exegetical works: friendship is never a major theme there in the way that it is in the two major treatises with which this chapter has been largely occupied. Mention has already been made of passages relevant to the theology of friendship found in two sermons, on Pentecost and on the Feast of St. Benedict. Such passages, in a substantial homiletical corpus, are few and far between.[149] Rather, the question here is much more a matter of form. In addition to Aelred's typical exegetical approach in his preaching, we will consider the way he uses Scripture in two other important exegetical works, *De Iesu puero duodenni,* and *Oratio pastoralis,* revisiting SC summarily as well, in order to illuminate a certain congruence between his relationship to the sacred text and his understanding of true, or spiritual friendship.

Iesu puero was written in the mid-1150s, midway between SC and SA, and therefore at roughly the halfway point in his twenty-five year-long writing career. Aelred composed this spiritual reflection on Jesus at the age of twelve specifically at the request of Ivo, undoubtedly the same monk who had engaged Aelred in discussion a decade earlier, in the first dialogue of SA. This fact already renders the work a personal undertaking, in a way

---

147. Cf. Aelred's allusion at the very outset of book one to Jesus' promise, "When two or three are gathered together in my name, I will be in the midst of them" (Matt 18:20) (ibid., I.1).

148. Cum haec amicitia ad quam hic paucos admittimus, transfundetur in omnes, et ab omnibus refundetur in Deum, cum *Deus fuerit omnia in omnibus.* Ibid., III.134. Cf. 1 Cor. 15:28.

149. Thus: "Outside of his treatise on friendship and of portions within his first work, *Speculum caritatis,* Aelred rarely mentioned friendship. His hagiographies, histories, sermons, prayers and other works speak much of love, but not that much of friendship love" (TePas, "*Amor, Amicitia,* and *Misericordia,*" 249). This assessment is thoroughly confirmed by my own investigations.

quite different from what it would have been had Aelred merely determined one Lent to write a meditation on Luke 2:41–52, either as an act of private penance, or even for the spiritual edification of his community as a whole. Thus, instead of an "I" soliloquizing, or even addressing a plural "you," we have here a text structured from the outset within what Martin Buber famously referred to as an "I/Thou" relationship. Furthermore, Aelred shifts the direction of his speech, frequently and somewhat spontaneously, from Ivo to Christ Himself, back to Ivo, then to the Jews, to St. Joseph, and back to Ivo again.[150] This peculiar style of ever-shifting second person address undoubtedly echoes the Psalmist, who ricochets back and forth in his address to Israel, to God, and back again to Israel.[151] By employing such an unstable form of address, Aelred, like the Psalmist, effectively reproduces on the silent page the texture, even something of the experience, of actual speech. Furthermore, Aelred's engagement with each new addressee is intimately personal—again, like the Psalmist. This is true even when Aelred addresses the Jews. Though the general tone is that of diatribe, there remains an undeniable undertone of invitation to those who have, without any serious doubt, from the perspective of a twelfth-century churchman, spurned the New Covenant along with its bearer: "So 'come back, woman of Sunam, come back,' come back to Jerusalem and you will find him."[152] Thus, Aelred invokes the Song of Songs (6:12), recognizing in Israel the wayward bride, whose Bridegroom and Friend is Yahweh Himself.

The whole second part of *Iesu puero* comprises an extended allegory of Lk. 2:41–52, in much the same way that Aelred's theology of the three sabbaths in *SC* constitutes a detailed allegorizing of Gen 1:1—2:3 and Lev 23:3 and 25:3–4, 8 and 10. In both cases Aelred engages in a thoroughly patristic exercise, with what at the time was a uniquely Cistercian emphasis on affective meditation on Christ in his human nature.[153] Such warm meditation savors strongly of personal friendship, of the sort embodied by the relationship between Bride and Bridegroom in the Song of Songs, cited

---

150. See, e.g., the shift from par. 1 to par. 2, then the explicitly renewed address to Ivo at par. 11. At par. 14f. Aelred addresses the Jews, at par. 17, St. Joseph, then returns resoundingly at par. 19 to Ivo.

151. See, e.g., Ps. 20, with its dramatic shift in the final verse, or Ps. 135, where the psalmist in turn addresses Israel, Egypt, the Lord, then Israel again.

152. *Revertere, itaque, revertere Sunamitis*, revertere in Ierusalem et invenies. *Iesu puero* 15.

153. We recall here *SC* III.5, where Aelred urges precisely the kind of meditation on the life of Christ exemplified in *Iesu puero*.

frequently throughout *Iesu puero*. Indeed, its *symbolic* character, in addition to its capacity for *narrative* expression in extended application, give to allegory a fundamentally *relational* cast. This relational quality, in turn, renders this mode of Scriptural engagement inevitably far more personal than the so-called prooftext, wherein a biblical text is cited entirely out of context, usually to shore up a dogmatic proposition. It is not coincidence, therefore, that the theologian of friendship as a rule prefers allegory to prooftext. When Aelred does employ the latter approach to biblical revelation, however, he tends to do so in ways that integrate the relevant biblical passages seamlessly and even organically into his whole argument. We have seen this in his incorporation of major Johannine texts into his argument for the christological character of spiritual friendship.[154] We might also choose, almost at random, any number of passages from Aelred's sermons, for example, Sermon Fourteen, For the Nativity of John the Baptist, where Aelred interweaves his reflection from beginning to end with the finest threads of the Gospels, the Psalms, St. Paul and the Pentateuch.[155] Such texts as these, along with his skillful uses of allegory, evoked Dumont's observation, recorded above, that "Aelred's scriptural argumentation is remarkable enough to be considered unique, both in its scope and in its precision."[156] We would only add that Aelred's precision is never achieved at the price of impersonal abstraction from the biblical text's authors, human or divine.

Finally, we have O. past., a long prayer written toward the end of Aelred's life, with abbots specially in mind.[157] The prayer consists of an elegant tapestry of biblical texts, lovingly woven into the most intimate,

---

154. See the section "The Johannine Character of Aelred's Theology of Friendship" in chapter 2, above. By way of anticipation, we may also note that the schoolmen quite deliberately eschewed such extended, sustained allegories, in favor of increasing attention to the literal sense of the biblical text. Already we can see the momentum shifting in Hugh of St. Victor, in the mid-twelfth century. By the mid-thirteenth century, a sea-change has taken place. This shift in emphasis from the allegorical to the literal sense of Scripture is too well-documented by the likes of Jean Leclercq and Henri de Lubac to warrant extended citation. See Leclercq, *The Love of Learning* and Lubac, *Exégèse médiévale*.

155. See *CCCM* IIA, *Sermo XIV, in toto*.

156. See n. 93, above (p. 37). Dumont's phrase "scriptural argumentation" is a fortuitous one and might well be employed to characterize monastic theologizing in general, over against the distinctly rationalist (specifically Aristotelian) method of argumentation employed by St. Thomas and the other thirteenth-century schoolmen. See the section "Biblical versus Non-Biblical" in chapter 4, below.

157. Propria praelatorum maxime abbatum. *CCCM* I, *O. past.*, tit.

tender appeal to Jesus—to the Good Shepherd, from a shepherd who is not good.[158] Here Aelred imparts to his readers—no doubt especially to those who read in order to pray his prayer—an intense awareness of the identification of the Word as revealed in Scripture with the Word Incarnate. Thus, the "Inspector of my heart" of Proverbs 24:12 is the same Lord to whom Aelred now protests "that there is nothing in my soul that I would hide from you."[159] And recalling Solomon's request of Jahweh for the wisdom to govern the Jewish people, Aelred continues, "at that time you had not met the Cross, nor shown your people that amazing love."[160] In his pastoral prayer, then, Aelred effortlessly bridges the metaphysical gap, widening at the dawn of modernity into a chasm, between reader and text. Here, and generally in Aelred's reading of Scripture, friendship with the text ought not to be construed as mere metaphor, for the text is the living Word, upon whose breast the beloved disciple once reclined, with whom Aelred was wont to speak every day, whispering his secrets to his dearest friend.

Conclusion: Aelred's Monastic Theology of Friendship

Over the course of his literary work, though most especially in *SC* and *SA*, Aelred of Rievaulx articulates a profound spiritual vision of holy friendship and its eschatological telos, in the idiom of medieval monastic theology. This idiom, at the hands of the Cistercian abbot, is neither argumentative nor systematic; suffused with the prayer of the monastic choir, it evinces the author's own innocence and purity of heart. Alongside the many passages already adduced from Aelred's works, one will suffice to summarize both Aelred's vision and our interpretation, taken from Aelred's closing recollections of the most excellent friendship of his own experience:

---

158. O bone pastor, iste non bonus pastor. Ibid., 1.

159. Tu enim scis, o inspector cordis mei, quia nihil est in anima meaquod vellem later oculos tuos. Ibid., 5. Note here as well Aelred's signal criterion of friendship, the ability to share one's deepest secrets, according to the Johannine paradigm of the mutual self-revelation of Father and Son.

160. Postulavit aliquando quidam antiquorum sapientiam dari sibi, ut sciret regere populum tuum. Rex enim erat, et placuit sermo in oculis tuis, et exaudisti vocem eius, *et necdum in cruce obieras, necdum illam miram caritatem ostenderas populo tuo.* Ibid., 6. Cf. 2 Chr. 1:10.

> In this way love increased between us, affection glowed the warmer and charity was strengthened, until we attained that stage at which we had but one mind and one soul to will and not to will alike, and at which our love was devoid of fear. . . . There was no pretense between us . . . , no concealment, but everything open and above board; for I deemed my heart in a fashion his, and his mine, and he felt in like manner towards me.[161]

In a remarkable way, then, the potent intellectual legacy of patristic thought, the thought of the likes of Gregory Nazianzen or the Damascene, has found an organic, perhaps even unwitting, expression in Aelred's work.[162]

No disparagement is intended in calling both Aelred and his work innocent, or even "somewhat naive,"[163] theologically speaking. The truth is that Aelred *lived* his theology in the daily routine of a twelfth-century monk and abbot. In this connection, one may note Jean Leclercq's insight that "[the monks] created an environment which made the appearance of a 'theology,' which was the work of one of their own, both possible and necessary."[164] In answer to such needs, Aelred crafted his *SC*, as well as his dialogues on spiritual friendship. The outcome in each case was a work which "contained a theology intended for a monastic audience for whom it had been conceived and composed"[165]—a "monastic theology" of genuine merit, however literally innocent, or unknowing, when compared to the *Summae* of ensuing ages.

Two consequences of this theological innocence may be briefly noted here. First, Aelred may well not be perfectly consistent, as Katherine Te-Pas contends, both in her dissertation and in an article published shortly

---

161. Ita inter nos amor crevit, concalvit affectus, caritas roborabatur, donec ad id ventum est, ut esset nobis *cor unum et anima una*, idem velle et idem nolle, essetque hic amor timoris vacuus. . . . Nihil inter nos simulatum . . . nullus angulus, sed omnia nuda et aperta; qui meum pectus quodammodo suum putarem, et eius meum, ipseque similiter. SA III.124–25.

162. We may even be tempted to see in the grand sweep of Aelred's account of spiritual friendship an exquisite, albeit preliminary, articulation of Western sanctification and Eastern theosis in perichoretic terms. However, the exploration of such implications of Aelred's thought goes far beyond the scope of the current project.

163. So Charles Dumont terms Aelred's articulation of one of his key ideas, his distinction between charity and friendship (Dumont, "Aelred of Rievaulx's *Spiritual Friendship*," 193).

164. Leclercq, *The Love of Learning*, 191.

165. Ibid.

The Theological Account of Friendship in Aelred of Rievaulx

afterward.[166] Yet, to ask this medieval abbot for a kind of analytical, even linear, consistency is perhaps to ask the wrong question. Aelred is neither a controversialist who must, like the Cappadocians or St. Augustine, meet an aggressive intellectual opponent point for point, nor is he a systematician, self-consciously concerned to preserve the strict internal and discursive coherence of a comprehensive account of the dogmas of the faith. He is a monk writing for monks, in a milieu in which the poetry of the Psalms and the rhythm of prayer and physical labor suffuse the mind and heart of all. Second, Aelred is capable of generating a modest yet authentically creative piece of theology while maintaining complete humility, perhaps even unaware that he is doing so. He weaves this theology in utmost simplicity from sundry elements of the living tradition of the Church: from both Testaments, from the great Western fathers, especially St. Augustine, even occasionally from such a great contemporary as St. Bernard. At the same time, he absorbs and enriches with the light of revelation one of the select fruits of the Greco-Roman philosophical tradition, Cicero's *De am*.

On the other hand, we venture to propose that Aelred has in fact given us the tools necessary to respond on his behalf to TePas's critique. In the closing pages of *SA*, Aelred provides an extended glimpse of his notion of beatitude in terms of friendship that has become truly universal. He points out that the closer we come to friendship universalized, the happier we are. The startling thrust of Aelred's idea is that the communal life in heaven is no mere exchange of a generalized—and by implication dumbed-down—charity; it is, rather, the exaltation of friendship in all its utter particularity along every conceivable axis! Consequently, while we may provisionally concede what appears to be occasional confusion between the two notions on Aelred's part, this "confusion" undoubtedly derives precisely from the otherworldliness—or just plain holiness—of his perspective. Thus, in a perichoretic foretaste of heaven, Aelred avers, "I felt indeed my spirit transfused into all and the affection of all to have passed into me."[167] To the extent that Aelred confuses or conflates the particular love of spiritual friendship with charity in all its universal breadth and depth, he does so out of the astonishing certitude of his "conviction of things not seen."[168] It is a certitude that almost tastes the reality of the universalized particular friendship

---

166. TePas, "*Amor, Amicitia*, and *Misericordia*," 249–63.

167. Sentiebam quippe meum spiritum transfusum in omnibus, et in me omnium transmigrasse affectum. *SA* III.82.

168. Cf. Heb 11:1.

enjoyed by the whole communion of saints participating eternally in the perichoretic inner life of the Blessed Trinity. Ultimately, then, Aelred's eschatological vision serves to resolve not only the confusion pointed out by TePas, but the tension articulated by Brian McGuire, in section of chapter 2 above on McGuire, as well.

A final comment regarding the way this English Cistercian monk used his sources will lead us on to our own concluding words. In the plainest terms, Aelred's use of Cicero is consistent with the regulated Christian humanism that pervaded twelfth-century Europe and his use of Scripture is quite compatible with the notion, attested by Leclercq, of "a prolongation of patristic theology."[169] Furthermore, Aelred's use of autobiographical material confirms the more general observation that the texts with which we are confronted here are the work of a genuinely holy man, unconcerned to create a system or defend a position under attack.[170] Indeed, the lucidity and simplicity—the "sweetness," to use one of his own favorite words—of Aelred's writing evokes an overwhelming sense of transparency to the purity of heart of the author himself.

Such purity of heart, though Aelred never names it explicitly, would seem almost indispensable to his ideal of spiritual friendship, the most fundamental characterization of which proves to be the "union of will and ideas"[171] between the persons in question. The more one's soul is purged of the "avarice and envy, . . . contentions, emulations, hates and suspicions"[172] introduced through the fall, the more capable one becomes of true friendship. In keeping with the spirit of early Cistercianism, Aelred probably had little doubt that monastic community constituted the ideal environment for encouraging such purgation, and consequently rendering possible the coming into being and subsequent growth of holy friendships. Whether monk or layman, however, ultimately only hearts thoroughly purified will be able to sustain the most perfect friendships, in which each person gradually, by full consent, makes himself totally transparent—as far as possible in this life, at any rate—to his friend.

169. Leclercq, *The Love of Learning*, 191.

170. In fact, SC was written at the behest of Saint Bernard, who did indeed desire a literary weapon for defense of Cistercian austerity against critics both within and outside the order. Nevertheless, both Aelred's tone and the very scope of the work, which far exceeds the bounds of the argument concerning religious discipline, bespeak a cast of mind that is anything but polemical.

171. Communio voluntatum et consiliorum. This is my own paraphrase, derived by converting the negative criterion found at SA I.59.

172. Avaritia invidiaque . . . contentiones, aemulationes, odia, suspiciones. Ibid., I.58.

3

The Theological Account of Friendship in Thomas Aquinas

Contemporary Scholarship

Rousselot's "Problem of Love" and Vansteenberghe's "Amitié"

In parallel with chapter 2, we will begin our presentation of Thomas Aquinas's theology of friendship with a brief survey of some of the most important contributions by contemporary scholars. It should be noted that in the background of the current discussion stand two influential works from the first half of the twentieth century: the Jesuit Pierre Rousselot's *Pour l'histoire du problème de l'amour au moyen âge* (1907/08)[1], and G. Vansteenberghe's thirty-column article "Amitié," in the *Dictionnaire de Spiritualité* (1937).[2] The former work purports to present St. Thomas's account as the ultimate medieval solution to "the problem of love" (i.e., Is truly selfless love possible for man?), though whether Rousselot's is in fact an entirely correct interpretation of Thomas's position has been disputed.[3] The latter

---

1. Rousselot, *The Problem of Love in the Middle Ages*. Rousselot's text received ecclesial *imprimatur* the previous year.

2. Vansteenberghe, "Amitié," cols. 500–29.

3. Vansteenberghe, for example, appears to be in fundamental agreement with Rousselot's stark pitting of Thomas's account against the "ecstatic conception" encountered in the writings of some of the Victorines, Cistercians, and Franciscan schoolmen (see Rousselot, *The Problem of Love in the Middle Ages*, 79). Thus, he observes in "Amitié" that "cette 'conception extatique' de l'amitié, pour reprendre l'expression employée par le P. Rousselot à propos de l'amour, n'est pas celle de saint Thomas" (col. 506). David

work, a thorough, evenhanded historical survey of the meaning of friendship in the Christian tradition, not only has St. Thomas's basic insights and arguments at its core, but reflects throughout an essentially Thomistic outlook. Notwithstanding their significance as provocative catalysts to the modern reexamination of the topic, these works have on the whole been superseded by the late twentieth and early twenty-first century contributions of Guy Mansini, Paul Wadell, David Gallagher, and Christopher Malloy. In this introductory section of chapter 3, we will summarily evaluate the contributions of each of these thinkers, concluding with some more macroscopic observations by the great Dominican Jean-Pierre Torrell.

Guy Mansini

In 1995, Guy Mansini, OSB, published two penetrating articles directly pertinent to the topic of Aquinas's theology of friendship: "*Similitudo, Communicatio*, and the Friendship of Charity in Aquinas" and "*Duplex Amor* and the Structure of Love in Aquinas," both in *Thomistica*.[4] One of Mansini's most significant contributions is to show through careful textual work exactly how, and how closely, St. Thomas relies on Aristotle in developing his own understanding of Christian love. Thus, at the outset of "*Similitudo*," he writes:

> One of St. Thomas's most successful theological innovations was to identify the charity poured forth into our hearts through the Holy Spirit (Rom. 5:5), the love by which we are children of God (1 Jn. 3:1), with friendship, the mutual benevolence of the virtuous, flowering in intimacy, as discussed by Aristotle in Books 8 and 9 of the *NE*.[5]

In this article, Mansini attempts to show how Thomas translates Aristotle's notion of the friend as "another self" into an understanding of *similitudo*—likeness—extensive and flexible enough to span the *analogia entis* between God and man. The tension between love of self and love of God is ultimately seen to be resolved in terms of a likeness of the part to its whole, or of the

---

Gallagher, on the other hand, in "Desire for Beatitude" contends that Rousselot has not "sufficiently recognized the central role of the distinction between *amor concupiscentiae* and *amor amicitiae*" (2). Guy Mansini and Christopher Malloy would undoubtedly agree with Gallagher.

4. Mansini, "*Similitudo*," 137–96.
5. Ibid., 1.

particular to the universal good.⁶ In the second article, Mansini elucidates another fundamental dichotomy in Thomas's account, that between *amor concupiscentiae* and *amor amicitiae*, and again, the importance of Aristotle is paramount. Through more close textual work, Mansini traces the history of this pivotal distinction: from William of Auxerre's initial effort to carve out a third kind of love—a "natural love"—between St. Augustine's *uti* (use) and *frui* (enjoyment), through Philip the Chancellor's corrections of William, and finally to a meticulous elucidation of the development of the distinction in St. Thomas's own thought, from the *Sentences* commentary, through the Exposition of Dionysius's *De divinis nominibus*, and finally arriving at his most compact and mature account in the Secunda Pars of the *Summa theologiae*. Once more, Mansini finds *similitudo* to have a crucial impact on Thomas's final implementation of the distinction between the two loves as one of the cornerstones of his moral theology.⁷ Regarding Thomas's multiple explications of the distinction throughout his work, Mansini concludes:

> Fundamentally, the various explanations serve to give philosophic, ultimately ontological, intelligibility to the phenomenality of love, the distinction between self- and other-regarding loves first captured in the Aristotelian division of friendship.⁸

Paul Wadell

Whereas Mansini comes at his topic as a textual scholar and a metaphysician, Paul Wadell has made a mark on the discussion of St. Thomas's theology of friendship chiefly from the perspective of the moral theologian, arguing forcefully that friendship is the interpretive key to understanding Aquinas's whole moral theological project.⁹ In *Friendship and the Moral Life*, Wadell provides a pithy outline of the great problem of the perceived conflict (referred to in chapter 2, above) between agapic love as "the love

---

6. Ibid., 23–25.
7. Mansini, "*Duplex Amor*," 184–87.
8. Ibid., 196.
9. In *Friends of God*, for example, Wadell argues that "if one understands what Thomas means by charity as friendship with God and how that functions as something of a metaphor for the Christian moral life, then not only will his account of the virtues be better appreciated, but it will also be clear why what he says about the virtues cannot be separated from what he says about the passions and the Gifts" (1).

proper to Christianity" and the love of friendship.[10] Wadell argues that the way out of the dilemma is a recognition of narratives: the narrative within or by which a particular friendship "is formed," as well as the "Christian narrative" as a whole, which qualifies a friendship in peculiar ways, thereby making it capable of taking on an agapic shape or formulation.[11] Wadell proceeds here with critical but sensitive treatments of Kierkegaard and Anders Nygren[12], followed by more sympathetic treatments of Augustine, Aelred of Rievaulx, and finally of Karl Barth.[13]

Wadell's basic answer to Kierkegaard is as follows:

> [B]oth philia and agape are secondary categories which take their meaning not in terms of one another, but in terms of the God in whom love is perfectly displayed. Once it is acknowledged that both Christian friendship and agape originate in the same love, not only are they reconcilable, they are also inseparable.[14]

He goes on to say that "to speak of Christian love as one in which 'God is the middle term'"—as does the later Kierkegaard—"is not to dismiss friendship, but to locate it in a different narrative, to place it in the Christian story of men and women seeking God."[15] In general, Wadell is concerned to show that agape (charity) and philia (friendship) are not intrinsically at odds—against Kierkegaard, Nygren, and Gilbert Meilaender.[16] Ultimately, Wadell justifies his claim by his reading of Aquinas. Moreover, like Mansini, Wadell traces carefully Aquinas's reading of Aristotle. Indeed, a good deal of his basic argumentation derives from his delineation of the basic Aristotelian criteria for friendship, as he finds them presented by Thomas in the Secunda Pars of the *ST*.[17]

---

10. Wadell, *Friendship and the Moral Life*, 71.

11. Ibid., 73.

12. Nygren's strongly Lutheran position, reminiscent of the stark "either-or" dichotomies of Kierkegaard and of Luther himself, already provides the major foil for Rousselot's Catholic account at the beginning of the century.

13. Ibid., 74–119.

14. Ibid., 83.

15. Ibid.

16. Ibid., 102.

17. See Wadell, *Friends of God*, 3. For a detailed discussion of these criteria, see the section "Love, Friendship and Charity" in our own presentation of St. Thomas's thought, below.

The Theological Account of Friendship in Thomas Aquinas

David Gallagher

In the late 1990s, David Gallagher published two articles, both profoundly concerned with the relation between love of self and love of the other according to St. Thomas.[18] As with Mansini, a proper grasp of the distinction between *amor amicitiae* and *amor concupiscentiae* is deemed paramount to understanding Aquinas's whole enterprise. In the first article, "Desire for Beatitude and Love of Friendship in Thomas Aquinas," Gallagher's point of departure is a careful presentation of Thomas's Aristotelian psychology. He observes that every being's appetite inclines it naturally towards its own perfection, and that the will, the intellectual appetite of rational creatures, inclines those creatures naturally to beatitude or happiness: the fulfillment or perfection of every rational being.[19] He proceeds to show how every other desire must ultimately reduce to this primal desire. The problem, then, is whether—and how—it is possible for one to love another, even if the other in question is God, for that other's own sake. According to Gallagher, Thomas's basic answer is that the rational being, angelic or human, is capable of recognizing another as in some sense an "extension" of the self, in such a way that love of that—subsistent, personal—extension initially comes into being as an expression of self-love.[20] The key Thomistic notion for understanding how this extension comes about is *unity/union*.[21] In connection to the problem of the two loves, the two most important instances of unity are likeness (*similitudo*), in the case of a rational creature's love for another rational creature,[22] and the relation of a part to the whole to which it belongs, in the case of the rational creature's love of God.[23] In his second essay, "Thomas Aquinas on Self-Love as the Basis for Love of Others," Gallagher does not alter or add appreciably to his earlier conclusions. Rather, he attempts to clarify some of Thomas's central concepts and relationships as introduced in the previous article. Thus, he continues to elaborate on the Thomistic meanings of *union* and *similitudo* and their relationship to each other. He also explicates the relationship of part to whole as the meta-

---

18. Gallagher, "Desire for Beatitude," 1–45; Gallagher, "Thomas Aquinas on Self-Love," 23–44.
19. Gallagher, "Desire for Beatitude," 1.
20. Ibid., 20–34.
21. Ibid., 20–24.
22. Ibid., 30.
23. Ibid., 34.

physical underpinning of the relation between one's own and the common good, which latter relationship proves to be congruent with man's love of friendship for God.

Christopher Malloy

In 2001, Christopher Malloy defended his doctoral dissertation, entitled "Love of God for His own Sake and Love of Beatitude: Heavenly Charity according to Thomas Aquinas," at The Catholic University of America. Although the ultimate goal of the dissertation is not an exposition of Thomas's theology of friendship *per se*, such an exposition is an indispensable element of Malloy's project. In fact, Malloy provides what his contemporaries will likely come to consider by far the most thorough, penetrating and accurate account to date of this central feature of St. Thomas's theological enterprise. In preparation for laying out his own argument, Malloy begins his dissertation with detailed critiques of the accounts of "the problem of love" in St. Thomas offered by several scholars of the latter half of the twentieth century—among them Paul Wadell and David Gallagher. His fairly harsh criticism of Wadell's position derives mainly from his observation that Wadell tends "to blur the distinction between love of beatitude and love of God," or even, more or less synonymously, "to equate love of self with love of God."[24] With Gallagher, however, Malloy finds himself substantially sympathetic. As a framework for his own approach, he only slightly emends Gallagher's fourfold schema of possible relationships between love of self and love of others to include a fifth, whereby "the love of God inclines a man to love himself."[25] Furthermore, he finds Gallagher's fundamental analysis of

---

24. Malloy, "Love of God," 37. Later, Malloy also says that Wadell "identifies charity with beatitude" (69). Malloy's criticism of Wadell may perhaps be somewhat tempered by noting that Malloy proceeds, much in the mode of both Mansini and Gallagher, as a strict metaphysician, concerned to explicate in the most rigorous terms possible the rich philosophical theology embedded in St. Thomas's thought. Wadell, on the other hand, as has already been observed, reads Thomas through the eyes of a moral theologian, who, without forfeiting academic rigor, is nevertheless concerned most of all to make the insights of the Common Doctor maximally accessible to Christian readers in their quest for holiness. Consequently, Wadell's interpretation of Thomas may be seen as on the whole both valid and valuable, notwithstanding Malloy's quite legitimate demand for greater precision if we are to progress in our understanding of the fine points of St. Thomas's thought.

25. Malloy, "Love of God," 23.

Thomas's thought largely satisfactory—far more so than any of the other writers he considers.[26]

Malloy's own interpretation of St. Thomas's understanding of heavenly charity depends upon his careful explication of the relationship in Aquinas's thought between *amor amicitiae* and *amor concupiscentiae*. At this point in his argument, Malloy does not differ drastically from Gallagher, or from Mansini, inasmuch as all three writers recognize clearly that for Thomas the two loves cannot simply be lined up in neat, mutually exclusive correspondence with love of other and love of self, respectively. Rather, in light of his careful reading and expounding of Aristotle's *NE*, Thomas contends that *every* rational love involves *both* a love of friendship *and* a love of concupiscence.[27] How these two loves operate conjointly within the human soul will be a key element of our own presentation of St. Thomas's theology, below. Malloy finally situates his meticulously calibrated delineation of the relations between these two loves within the much grander sweep of St. Thomas's eschatological vision, concluding magnificently:

> [God] is loved as the very principle and end of the proper good of the human lover. God and man are united in the order of being, as cause and effect. There is no ontological alienation to be overcome that would demand a denial of self-love and the enactment of a disinterested love. The very love that seeks God above all things and for His own sake enkindles the lover's ardent wish to see his beloved: 'from the love of God, the lover ardently pines to gaze upon His beauty.'[28]

---

26. See ibd., 74: "Only David Gallagher sufficiently explores how self-love inclines a man, in the order of generation, to love God more than himself, etc." As for shortcomings in Gallagher's account, Malloy mentions a failure to acknowledge "that Aquinas sometimes uses the terms love of friendship and love concupiscence in imprecise senses" (74 n. 138). Guy Mansini, however, treats these imprecisions in minute detail in his "*Duplex Amor.*" Though Malloy refers several times to Mansini's work when he comes to engage this question more closely in his own analysis (see 147 n. 25; 149 n. 31; 151 n. 37), we may perhaps reasonably ask why Mansini does not qualify for more substantial treatment of the sort received by Wadell or Gallagher.

27. Thus Malloy argues that, although St. Thomas's thought on the subject matured gradually, eventually "he taught love of concupiscence as simply one aspect of every act of rational love, which always also includes a love of friendship" (Malloy, "Love of God," 157).

28. Malloy, "Love of God," 377. The concluding quotation is Malloy's translation of *ST* 2-2.180.1, *corp*.

Theologizing Friendship

It would appear, then, that Malloy puts the Thomistic understanding of friendship at the service of other, and broader, conclusions. We shall see, however, that even a discussion such as our own, attempting as it does to confine itself to Thomas's theology of friendship *proper*, gravitates inexorably towards the heavenly Jerusalem.[29]

Jean-Pierre Torrell

In *Saint Thomas Aquinas, Volume 2: Spiritual Master*, Jean-Pierre Torrell entitles one of the later chapters of his great work "Without Friends, Who Would Want to Live?", a title he draws from Thomas's commentary on Book VIII of Aristotle's *NE*.[30] One of the greatest values of Torrell's reflections is to remind the reader of the breadth of Thomas's theological and spiritual vision and the myriad ways the Thomistic theme of friendship inevitably commingles and sets off reverberations with other ideas, both Thomas's own and those of the Church's Tradition at large. Torrell points out that Thomas's theological interpretation of the Aristotelian notion of friendship evokes the themes of *societas*, *communicatio*, *habitus*, and *inclinatio*. In turn, these themes bring in their wake whole spheres of intellectual discourse, including secular politics and economics, as well as marriage, natural and divine law, and ecclesiology. The chief benefit of Torrell's survey for our own project is to remind us that a true and profound understanding of what at first might seem a fairly localized theme within St. Thomas's prodigious corpus will in fact have vast implications: not only does friendship inform the discipline of theology as a whole, but also such related disciplines as philosophy, psychology, political science and economics, as well as such institutions as the family, the Church, the university and the state—not to speak of the interactions among these disciplines and institutions.

THOMAS'S SOURCES

Scripture and the Fathers

As with Aelred, we must comment briefly on Thomas's sources, and again, the main point for our purposes is to see how typical Thomas was of his

---

29. In this important respect, among others to be discussed in our final chapter, Thomas's account clearly resonates with that of Aelred.
30. Torrell, *Saint Thomas Aquinas*, 276–308.

own ethos. If Aelred epitomizes the twelfth century monastic author in his use of the sources at his disposal, so Thomas exemplifies thirteenth century scholastic usage. Thus, Thomas still shares with Aelred the great medieval patrimony of all educated churchmen: the Bible. Moreover, he was content with the Vulgate translation he owned,[31] so that the Scriptural text with which he was familiar was the same read not only by the sweep of his thirteenth century fellow schoolmen, but also by their twelfth century predecessors, both academic and monastic. In broad terms, he shares, too, the patristic legacy so crucial to Aelred's perspective, not excepting the overwhelming dominance of the writings of St. Augustine. The most significant difference reflected in Thomas's use of the Fathers is breadth of scope: whereas Aelred was more or less content to steep himself in the readings of the great Western Fathers[32]—and principally their major and most frequently read works, at that—St. Thomas read every patristic text he could possibly get his hands on. Thus, Thomas seems to have read not just widely, but exhaustively, in the Fathers of the West, as well as all available Latin translations of the Greek Fathers. In the latter case, the works at Thomas's disposal increased substantially during his lifetime, especially through the translating activities of William of Moerbeke. Moreover, by the early 1260s, Thomas had discovered translations of the *acta* and *gesta* of the early councils.[33] Of particular importance to his understanding of love and charity, and therefore, at least by extension, of friendship, was Thomas's familiarity with the work of the Pseudo-Dionysius, translated from Greek several centuries earlier by John Scotus Erigena.[34] In general, though Thomas often surpassed his peers in the breadth and depth of his patristic reading, his approach was fundamentally that of the great schools of Paris and Oxford: read everything and everyone, distilling from this vast wealth of sources what is most true and good.[35] When all is said and done, however, the importance of St. Augustine for St. Thomas's thought is unrivaled among his Christian sources.

---

31. Cf. Weisheipl, *Friar Thomas*, 164.

32. For minor qualifications of this assessment, see our section on Aelred's sources, chapter 2.

33. See Weisheipl, *Friar Thomas*, 164–65.

34. Ibid., 173–74.

35. On the same principle, we should remember that Thomas was also deeply conversant with the great medieval Islamic scholars, Avicenna and Averroes, as well as with the works of the medieval Jewish thinker, Moses ben-Maimon.

Theologizing Friendship

Aristotle

Though the humanist renaissance of the eleventh and twelfth centuries still made itself felt through a general familiarity with the Roman rhetorical tradition, the major pagan source for St. Thomas, as for so many of his mid-thirteenth-century contemporaries, was Aristotle. Whereas a century before, only a few of Aristotle's works, and even parts of works, had become available to Western Christendom, the thirteenth century witnessed the rapid reception and translation of the entire Aristotelian corpus, thanks again in some significant part to the labors of William of Moerbeke. In a very few years, St. Thomas commented on the major works, leaving many other commentaries incomplete at his early death. Beyond the commentaries themselves, Aristotle's influence is evident throughout Thomas's theological enterprise, steadily increasing in proportion to other sources, from *Sent.*, through *SCG* and Disputed Questions, and finally culminating in *ST*.[36] As will be seen below, Aristotle's impact on Thomas's theology of friendship is foundational. We may also note here in passing the striking contrast between, on the one hand, St. Thomas's thoroughgoing (albeit ingenious) integration of Aristotle's thought into his own, and, on the other hand, Aelred's openly conflicted relation to Cicero.

Modern Authors and Contemporaries

In accordance with the principle enunciated two paragraphs above, St. Thomas also cultivated a thorough familiarity with the writing of the "modern" thinkers of the several preceding centuries—including especially St. Anselm, Abelard, Hugh of St. Victor, and St. Bernard[37]—as well as the thought of his contemporaries, not least of these his own teacher, St. Albert, and the great Franciscan, St. Bonaventure. If we consider his own early Benedictine formation and an evident devotion to the Cistercians, it is reasonable to ask whether Thomas knew the works of Aelred of Rievaulx. Given the importance of the concept of friendship for Thomas's theological enterprise, it is worthy of note that he evidences no familiarity, explicit or otherwise, with Aelred's thought. James McEvoy notes that Thomas does

---

36. For a thoughtful discussion of Thomas's use of Aristotle and some of the motivations behind this use, see Weisheipl, *Friar Thomas*, 272–85.

37. Thomas cites Bernard, among other places, in a *Sed contra* within his account of the theological virtue of charity, to which we shall shortly turn. See *ST* 2-2.27.6, *Sed contra*.

not even quote Cicero's *De am.*, let alone the writings of Aelred.[38] Commenting on McEvoy's observation, Torrell offers the plausible explanation that "Thomas may not have known the latter figure owing to the shift in interest caused by the widespread introduction of Aristotle in the thirteenth century."[39] In sum, Thomas's reading can be said to have been virtually comprehensive, both diachronically and synchronically, to the extent such comprehension was possible in his time, the fundamental constraint having been one not of choice but of simple availability.

Thomas's Synthesis and Original Position

Texts on Friendship

A prefatory word needs to be said concerning the major texts of Thomas to be considered in the following presentation of his theology of friendship. Whereas in Aelred's case the choice of his two major theological treatises is obvious, almost from the titles alone, no such readymade criterion offers itself when we turn to the Thomistic corpus. Thomas composed no special treatise devoted to the subject of spiritual friendship, nor even, strictly speaking, to the topic of charity.[40] Nevertheless, there are five major contexts in which friendship might be expected to constitute a significant category in Thomas's thought: (1) in *Eth.*, books 8 and 9; (2) in *DDN*; (3) in *Iohannis*, in connection with the passage from Christ's last discourse that includes his references to friendship at John 15:13 and 15:15; (4) and (5) in Thomas's two most comprehensive theological works, the two *Summae*. For our purposes, it is unnecessary to delve into *Eth.*, for the following straightforward reason: here Thomas, seeking to maintain a strictly philosophical perspective, carefully confines his treatment of friendship to the natural plane, prescinding entirely from matters of divine revelation.[41] But in a dis-

---

38. McEvoy, "Amitié, attirance et amour chez S. Thomas d'Aquin," 399.

39. Torrell, *Spiritual Master*, 277.

40. Even conceding some validity to the anachronistic habit of designating thematically unified parts of the *Summa* as "treatises," the closest one comes to a treatise on charity is the so-called treatise on the theological virtues in the *Secunda Secundae*, of which the questions on charity comprise a substantial part.

41. There is a long-running debate over whether Thomas's commentaries on Aristotle in general, and his commentary on the *NE* in particular, ought to be classified as philosophical or theological works. A number of weighty authorities in fact incline to the latter position, including Joseph Owens, R. A. Gauthier, Mark Jordan, and Jean-Pierre Torrell.

cussion of the Christian theology of friendship, especially in comparison with a twelfth-century monastic writer like Aelred, such a bracketing of the supernatural is precisely not what is called for. Moreover, Thomas has incorporated Aristotle's insights from the natural order into his theological accounts, so that close analysis of the *Ethics* commentary becomes largely redundant.

DDN is effectively a discourse on the subject of love and, as the name of Dionysius's work suggests, is not limited to the natural realm. The commentary, then, is relevant in principle and in fact some of Thomas's most original insights regarding love make their first appearance in this context. Here again, however, Thomas imports the most crucial of these insights directly into his later discussion in the *Secunda Pars*, frequently citing the *DDN* in support of his now thoroughly polished argument.

In his running commentary on the Gospel of John, the *Lectura super Iohannem*, Thomas treats of Christ's two explicit references to friendship as a matter of course. Two comments seem to be necessary here. First, in his third lecture on John 15, Thomas recognizes the parallel between the sharing of secrets as a *signum* of [natural] friendship and Christ's renaming his disciples *amici* on the basis of his disclosure to them of *quaecumque audivi a patre meo*.[42] Here, Thomas approaches one of Aelred's central insights.[43] Yet while he clearly sees its importance for John's theological vision, he does not develop the idea elsewhere, either in connection to his definition of charity in terms of friendship or otherwise. The second observation to be made pertains to genre, as well as to Thomas's theological enterprise considered as a whole. It must be said, then, that the few pithy theological

---

Nevertheless, we find persuasive the arguments to the contrary presented by James C. Doig in his recent work, *Aquinas's Philosophical Commentary on the "Ethics": A Historical Perspective*. For an overview of Doig's argument, see his introduction, XI-XVII. In the even more specific case of the commentaries on books 8 and 9, where friendship is the stated topic, it is surely enough to quote Thomas from midway through his commentary on book 8. There he writes: "If the persons are far apart, like men from God, then the friendship we are discussing does not survive" (Aquinas, *Commentary on the Nicomachean Ethics*,VIII. Lecture VII: C 1635). While critics may still dispute whether Thomas interprets Aristotle theologically *in spite of himself*, his conscious intention here seems abundantly clear: only when abstracting completely from the context of Christian revelation can Thomas describe friendship between man and God as intrinsically impossible.

42. See *Iohannis*, 15 (3). Cf. *SCG* IV, 21 (5) and (7).

43. For an interesting discussion of Thomas's exposition of friendship in *Iohannis*, including passing reference to Aelred and the monastic engagement of the Stoic tradition, see Young, *The Politics of Praise*, 108-13.

insights concerning friendship to be found in Thomas's commentary on John are *ad hoc*. This is as much to be expected of a biblical commentary as of a philosophical one. Given Thomas's genius and the extraordinary comprehension and coherence of his thought, it is not unreasonable to incorporate occasional comments found in isolation into a wider synthesis of what he has to say about that theme *per se*. Nevertheless, such patchworks are always somewhat artificial and must be undertaken with caution. In the particular instance in question, Thomas's thinking on friendship in *Iohannis*, however broadly congruent with his theology of friendship as a whole, remains *ad hoc* and thus peripheral to our assessment of his overall account.

In the case of *SCG*, several points may be briefly made. First, *SCG* was completed (probably around 1264) more than five years before *Eth.* was begun (1271),[44] when Thomas would have been especially preoccupied with working out the implications of Aristotle's notion of friendship for his own theological enterprise. In fact, a survey of the work confirms the insignificance *on the whole* of friendship as an explicit theme. Only three exceptions call for particular remark. In Book III, chapters 95 and 96, while discussing the value of prayer, Thomas recalls the classical notion of friendship as characterized by lover and beloved willing the same thing. Thomas's reference is to Sallust, not to Aristotle, and though the thought is consistent with that of *ST*, it is not at all developed. Rather, here and in the following chapter, the classical description of friendship is imported briefly to help explain the relation of divine providence to human free desiring of good or evil things. Thanks to Thomas's systematic proclivities, the basic insight that "on the basis of friendship God grants the wishes of those who are holy"[45] gets thoroughly integrated into his later masterpiece, *ST*. In the second text of concern, Book IV, chapters 21 and 22, the fundamental perspective is once more entirely congruent with the more comprehensive account of the later *ST*. Nevertheless, the development is sufficient and the formulation distinctive enough to warrant some further comment in section "Thomas's Theology of Friendship is 'Transcendent'" in chapter 3, below, as well as in comparison to Aelred's thought, in our final chapter. The third passage,

---

44. For a recent and authoritative assessment of scholarly opinion on the dates of Thomas's major works, see Torrell, *Saint Thomas Aquinas*. For the relative dates of the *SCG* and the commentary on the *Ethics*, cf. esp. 102, 227–28.

45. *SCG* III, 96.

from Book IV, chapter 54, also requires brief remark in the section just named.

In the final analysis, for the purposes of presenting a precise and thorough account of Thomas's best theological thinking about friendship, we will be best served to focus our attention on Thomas's most condensed and refined, because most mature, discussion, beginning, roughly, at Question 25, Article 2 and continuing through Question 28 of the *Prima Secundae*, then resuming at Question 23 and proceeding through Question 27 of the *Secunda Secundae*. We will begin by remarking briefly on the formal structure of Thomas's argument, proceeding in the subsequent sections to elucidate in detail the major terms, premises, conclusions, and implications of that argument.

Prima Secundae and Secunda Secundae

St. Thomas presents his most refined thinking on friendship squarely within the bounds of the *Secunda Pars* of *ST*—at the heart, that is, of his moral theological enterprise.[46] The discussion is comprised of two moments, as it were, one in the *Prima Secundae*, the other in the *Secunda Secundae*. Having identified *amor* as the first of the concupiscible passions at *ST* 1–2.25.2, Thomas briefly introduces the notion of *amicitia* at 1–2.26.3, within the wider context of his exposition of love and its prominent place among the passions of the soul. The following article is entirely devoted to the question "Whether love is fittingly divided into love of friendship and love of concupiscence?"[47] In Question 27, Thomas takes up the important matter of the relationship between *similitudo* and friendship. Then, in Question 28, several further terms important for a thorough understanding of *amor* are discussed, namely *unio* (article 1), *mutua inhaesio* (article 2) and *extasis* (article 3). Finally, in Questions 23 through 27 of the *Secunda Secundae*,

---

46. We recall here Paul Wadell's insistence on the centrality of charity, with its intimate ties to friendship in St. Thomas's thought, to Aquinas's moral theology as a whole.

47. Utrum amor convenienter dividatur in amorem amicitiae et amorem concupiscentiae. *ST* 1–2.26.4. I have generally followed the Dominican translation published by Benziger Brothers, Inc. in 1948. All variants are my own, unless otherwise noted. St. Thomas's Latin does not generally present great problems for translation, as is well known. Thus, when I differ from the Dominican translation, it will in most cases be a matter of style or slight nuance; always I aim for the most literal translation I can discover, ideally maintaining even word order as far as possible, short of doing grave violence to idiomatic English.

Thomas gives a sustained discourse on the theological virtue of charity, for which the point of departure is a definition of charity in terms of friendship, at *ST* 2–2.23.1.

We are tempted to seek parallels between this basic pattern in Thomas's thought and the relation between Aelred's two major works on love and friendship, *SC* and *SA*. For the most part, this comparison must wait for our fourth chapter, but we may make the following summary observations: Setting aside the many important formal differences between the scholastic *quaestio* and a proper discourse or treatise of the sort plainly represented by Aelred's *SC*, when we consider the latter work alongside the questions from the *Secunda Secundae*, we have before us two careful treatments of the theological virtue of charity, one of them monastic, the other scholastic, each concerned to draw out, among other things, relations between *caritas* and *amicitia*. In the case of the other pole, so to speak, of each author's discussion of friendship, however, no such clear correlation obtains. Aelred's *SA* is a treatise in dialogue form on spiritual friendship. Thomas's discussion of *amor* in the *Prima Secundae*, though it engages friendship as an important category for understanding the operations of the human soul, is in the end more about psychology than it is about the very specific activity of Christian friendship. Furthermore, the relations between the two poles of each author's discussion of love are mirror images of each other, at least as far as the location of each one's particular treatment of *caritas* is concerned: Aelred's *SC* comes first; Thomas's questions on charity, only after his initial exposition of love.[48] In our final chapter, we shall assess in more detail what is to be made of the two authors' respective orderings of their ideas and of the relative emphases placed on various elements of each one's thought.

Love and Friendship

As noted above, Thomas's most complete and profound theological account of friendship can be construed as beginning with his designation of *amor* as the chief of the concupiscible passions, at *ST* 1–2.25.2. There, he defines

---

48. In addition to all these considerations, we must also not lose sight of the fact that the two texts by Aelred are envisioned and executed as two distinct works, notwithstanding the conviction of Louis Bouyer that they ought to be read as of-a-piece. In the case of Thomas's texts, on the other hand, the questions on love and those on charity have both been carefully placed within the framework of the *Secunda Pars*, which, in turn, has its precise place within the grand design of *ST* as a whole.

love as the "aptitude or proportion of the appetite to good,"[49] or even more pithily, as "complacency in good."[50] In the same article, in response to an objection citing *De divinis nominibus* as an authority, Thomas begins to explicate the key notion of *unio amati ad amantem*.[51] Distinguishing between *unio realis* and *unio affectiva*, Thomas argues that "real" union obtains when the lover is actually joined to the object of his love. In the absence of the beloved object, the lover, precisely in virtue of his *aptitudo*, or *proportio*, or *inclinatio* towards that object, experiences "already" (*iam*) a kind of participatory union with it, a union Thomas characterizes as "affective."[52] Whereas the first kind of union pertains to joy or pleasure, the second kind anticipates, and indeed provokes, desire.[53]

In the opening article of the pivotal following question, Thomas continues to elucidate *amor* in terms of *appetitus*,[54] arguing that for every basic kind of appetite there is a corresponding kind of love. To the natural appetite corresponds a natural love, to the sensitive appetite a sensitive love, and to the intellectual or rational appetite—also called the *will*—an intellectual or rational love. Further, Thomas explains that while all appetites follow upon an apprehension of a desirable object, such apprehension may occur either *in* the subject or in another. In the case of the last two appetites and their corresponding loves, the apprehension takes place in the subject

---

49. aptitudo sive proportio appetitus ad bonum. *ST* 1-2.25.2, *corp*.

50. complacentia boni. Ibid.

51. Ibid., *ad* 2. It should be noted that Thomas persistently engages and qualifies Pseudo-Dionysius's position, especially from *DDN*, iv, throughout questions 25 to 27. Thus, cf. *ST* 1-2.25.2, Obj. 2 and Reply; 26.1, Obj. 3 and Reply; 26.2, Obj. 1 and Replies to both Obj. 1 and Obj. 2; 26.3, Obj. 1 and *Sed contra* and the Replies to each; 27.1, Obj. 3 and Reply; 28.1, *Sed contra*; 28.3, *Sed contra*; 28.4, *Sed contra*; 28.5, *Sed contra*; 28.6, *Sed contra*; in Thomas's discussion of charity in *Secunda Secundae* the conversation with Dionysius continues, though with somewhat less intensity: cf. 2-2.24.2, Obj. 1 and Reply; 25.7, Obj. 3 and Reply; 25.11, Obj. 1 and Reply; 27.4, *corp*.; 27.5, Obj. 2 and general Reply to the Objections.

52. Alia autem est unio affectiva, secundum scilicet quod aliquid habet aptitudinem vel proportionem, prout scilicet ex hoc quod aliquid habet aptitudinem ad alterum et inclinationem, iam participat aliquid eius. Ibid.

53. Here, then, Thomas follows St. Augustine in dividing the passion of love exhaustively, according to the two possible modes of its object, present and absent: when the object is present, love moves the lover to enjoy it; when absent, to desire it. Thus: Sed contra est quod Augustinus dicit in XIV *De Civit. Dei* [Cap. 7, 9], quod omnes passiones ex amore causantur; "amor" enim "inhians habere quod amatur, cupiditas est; id autem habens, eoque fruens, laetitia est." Ibid.

54. cum utriusque obiectum sit bonum. *ST* 1-2.26.1, *corp*.

itself: the sensitive appetite is dominated by necessity—completely, in the case of irrational animals, or "partaking somewhat of liberty in men"[55]; the rational appetite or will, on the other hand, follows the same or a comparable apprehension "according to free choice."[56] In the case of the natural appetite, on the other hand, the relevant apprehension belongs not to those things desiring what "is fitting to them according to their nature,"[57] but rather to the one who brought their nature into being: God. In his splendid reply to the third objection, Thomas reminds us of the Aristotelian doctrine that the lower modes of a soul's existence are not supplanted by, but rather taken up into, the higher modes, so that

> Natural love is not only in the powers of the vegetative soul, but in all the soul's powers, and also in all parts of the body, and universally in all things: For, as Dionysius says (*DDN*, iv), "The beautiful and the good are lovable to all"; since each thing has a connaturality to that which is fitting to itself according to its nature.[58]

Thus, Thomas demonstrates that man can love that which is good for him, including God Himself, in two ways: both naturally, or necessarily, and also freely.

In *ST* 1–2.26.2, Thomas adds an important qualification to what it means to call *amor* a passion, arguing that it is "*properly* so called according as it is in the concupiscible faculty; in a wider and extended sense according as it is in the will."[59] He also reiterates and clarifies his argument from 25.2 *ad* 2 concerning the important relationship between *amor* and *unio*.[60] All of this is preparatory to the two subsequent all-important articles, set under the respective headings: "Whether Love Is the Same as Dilection?"[61]

---

55. in hominibus aliquid libertatis participat. Ibid.

56. secundum liberum iudicium. Ibid.

57. quod eis convenit secundum suam naturam. Ibid.

58. Dicendum quod amor naturalis non solum est in viribus animae vegetativae, sed in omnibus potentiis animae, et etiam in omnibus partibus corporis, et universaliter in omnibus rebus; quia, ut Dionysius dicit, iv cap. *De Div. Nom.*: "Omnibus est pulchrum et bonum amabile"; cum unaquaeque res habeat connaturalitem ad id quod est sibi conveniens secundum suam naturam. *ST* 1–2.26.1, *ad* 3. My translation.

59. proprie quidem, secundum quod est inconcupiscibili; communiter autem, et extenso nomine, secundum quod est in voluntate. *ST* 1–2.26.2, *corp.*

60. See ibid., *ad* 2.

61. Utrum amor sit idem quod dilectio. *ST* 1–2.26.3.

and "Whether Love Is Fittingly Divided into Love of Friendship and Love of Concupiscence?"[62]

In *ST* 1–2.26.3, Thomas introduces the word *amicitia* for the first time in the context of his treatment of the passion of love, seemingly almost in passing. At the same time, not coincidentally, *caritas* also comes into play in a serious way for the first time. The main point of the article is to show how the general notion of love can be specified in various ways—as *amicitia*, *dilectio*, or *caritas*—and to begin to work out how each of these more particular terms is related to its genus. Beyond the note that, according to Aristotle, *est quasi habitus*, *amicitia* is left momentarily to the side. *Dilectio* is explained as love that involves *choice* (*electio*) and described as residing "only in the will, and in the rational nature alone."[63] Dilection, then, is nothing else than intellectual or rational love. Lastly, while carefully reserving his definition of charity for the questions devoted to the theological virtues, Thomas is content at this juncture in his argument merely to describe *caritas* as "a certain perfection of love,"[64] inasmuch as it recognizes the beloved as "of great price."[65]

Finally, in the fourth article of Question 26, Thomas begins his finely wrought explanation of friendship and how it relates to rational human love. The argument hinges on Thomas's close reading of Aristotle's assertion in the *Rhetoric* that "to love is to wish good to someone." From this pithy formulation, Thomas educes that

> the movement of love has a twofold tendency: towards the good which a man wishes to someone—to himself or to another—and towards that to which he wishes some good. Accordingly, man has love of concupiscence towards the good that he wishes to another, and love of friendship towards him to whom he wishes good.[66]

Moreover, he contends that the two modes of loving are related logically "as prior and posterior," inasmuch as what is loved with the love of friendship is

---

62. Cf. n. 47, above (p. 102).

63. in voluntate tantum, et est in sola rationali natura. *ST* 1–2.26.3, *corp*.

64. perfectionem quandam amoris. Ibid.

65. A recognition, thinks Thomas in Isidorean fashion, evident in the Greek word itself, which echoes the Latin *carus*, meaning dear.

66. motus amoris in duo tendit, scilicet in bonum quod quis vult alicui, vel sibi, vel alii; et in illud cui vult bonum. Ad illud ergo bonum quod quis vult alteri, habetur amor concupiscentiae; ad illud autem cui aliquis vult bonum, habetur amor amicitiae. *ST* 1–2.26.4, *corp*.

loved simply and for itself, whereas what is loved with the love of concupiscence is loved *"for another."* From this already somewhat abstract description of human love, Thomas proceeds immediately to reduce his argument to even more radically metaphysical terms: *ens, esse* and *bonum*. Given the convertibility of *bonum* and *ens*, he argues that, just as there are two modes of being, being *simpliciter* (being *simply*)—predicated of that which has *esse* (existence)—and being *secundum quid* (*relative* being)—predicated of that which exists in another[67]—so, the good has the same two modalities: *simpliciter* when a thing has its own goodness, *secundum quid* when it is only the good of another. Correlatively, that love of something which consists in wishing its good is love *simpliciter*, while the love of a good wished for another is love *secundum quid*.

Giving full weight, as Thomas certainly does, to Aristotle's words in the *Rhetoric*, we find that we are working with a strict definition of *amare*— "to love." Among various implications of such a reading for Thomas, the following is paramount: *every* act of love involves a double motion, one towards the relative good a man wishes for someone—"to himself or to another"—another towards the one for whom he wishes that good. Thus, the idea that love of concupiscence and love of friendship are each freestanding ways of loving, the former self-oriented, the latter oriented towards another, is not the final, mature account of St. Thomas.[68] Instead, Thomas asserts that every rational human love has a dual aspect. Moreover, the "friendly" element of an act of love need not even be directed to someone other than the lover himself, as Thomas explicitly states. What is necessary is only that the object of this friendship love be a rational being: a human, angelic, or divine person. As Thomas points out in the *Sed contra*, again citing Aristotle for support, the love a man may have for wine is not a love of friendship.[69] Rendering Thomas's thought somewhat more concretely: when a man does love wine, without particular reference to another, in fact he is loving the wine concupiscently, as the good he wishes for himself, while the wishing of the wine for himself constitutes an act of love of friendship for

---

67. Substantial being or accidental being, respectively, to use the Aristotelian categories on which Thomas depends.

68. In *"Duplex Amor,"* Mansini meticulously examines the development in Thomas's thought from this early position, as articulated in *Sent.*, to his mature position in *ST*. The point is ably made by David Gallagher as well, in "Desire for Beatitude," 13–18. Cf. also Malloy, "Love of God," 146–56.

69. Similarly, Thomas later explains that one cannot love irrational creatures with the love of friendship. See *ST* 2-2.25.3.

himself. Alternatively, whenever one loves another person with a love of friendship, one inevitably wishes that person to have good things, whether material or spiritual.[70] Such material and spiritual goods are then, necessarily, loved concupiscently, or *relatively*, in relation to the person for whom they are wished. Finally, in his reply to the third objection, in explanation of Aristotle's delineation of three kinds of friendship, Thomas remarks that friendship based on use or pleasure is not friendship in the strictest sense, inasmuch as the good wished for the friend is further referred to one's own good, in the form of one's own pleasure or use. Only in the case of friendship founded upon goodness or virtue does the lover's wish for his friend's good terminate in the friend.[71] How such a friendship is possible, Thomas works out principally through his doctrines of *similitudo* and *unio*, in the third article of Question 27 and the first article of Question 28, respectively.

We have already seen, in our discussion of David Gallagher's work, the centrality in Thomas's scholastic psychology of the natural appetite: the desire in every natural thing for its own perfect good, a desire that takes the form in the rational soul of desire for beatitude. We should also recall that, according to Thomas, this primary drive for one's own perfection grounds all other desires. Therefore we ought surely to ask at this point: Is not every love for another person in the end just one more concupiscent love, ultimately revealed as terminating not in the other, but in oneself, constituting in some way one's own good, much like the love for wine?[72] Thomas begins his answer to this question by explaining the relation of *similitudo* to friendship, in Question 27, article 3, where he asks: "Whether Likeness is a Cause of Love?"[73] Here Thomas states that both actual and potential likeness cause love, the former, love of friendship, the latter, love of concupiscence. For Thomas, to say that two things, or people, are "actually" alike is as if to say that they have a single form, like humanity, or whiteness. Moreover, as a result of their having, as it were (*quasi*), one form "they are in some way *one* in that form." Because of their oneness, in humanity, or whiteness, or

---

70. Thus, Gallagher: "So too, one cannot speak of loving someone with a love of friendship without implying the presence of a love for what is good for that person" ("Desire for Beatitude," 14).

71. See *ST* 1–2.26.4, *ad* 3.

72. Anders Nygren in fact misinterprets St. Thomas as holding precisely this position, as Malloy points out, 176. Malloy also believes that Wadell makes a similar error, notwithstanding his efforts to affirm a genuine love of the other for the other's own sake. See Malloy, "Love of God," 43, 45.

73. Utrum similitudo sit causa amoris. *ST* 1–2.27.3.

membership in the bricklayers' guild, "the affection of one tends toward the other, as to a one-with-himself, and he wishes good to him as to himself." Such affection and the consequent disposition of benevolence belong to the love of friendship. The love of concupiscence, on the other hand, can be seen to be grounded in a potential likeness, wherein the lover, desiring his own act, loves that which he recognizes as "like" himself, inasmuch as it possesses in actuality a form he has in potency. Thus, the poor man loves money. Furthermore, friendships of usefulness and pleasure can also be seen to consist in such a love caused by potential likeness: the likeness, that is, of some actual form in another, to the same form in potency in the lover himself. Thus, the useful or pleasant friend is beloved not for himself, but for the sake of the quality he possesses (material or otherwise), one which the lover desires for his own perfection.[74]

In the opening article of the following question, Question 28, Thomas develops the point that being alike makes two in some way *one*, in whatever form they have in common. Having asserted that *aliqui duo . . . , quasi habentes unam formam, sunt quodammodo* unum *in forma illa*, Thomas now explicates the two types of union possible between lover and beloved, reiterating and expounding on a point already made briefly at *ST* 1–2.25.2, *ad* 2. From that earlier discussion, we recall that *real* union obtains in the event of the beloved's actual conjunction with, or presence to, the lover. Such union is the effect of love particularly sought by the lover, for the joy or pleasure it provides. In the case of *affective* union, on the other hand, Thomas is interested in how the unity obtaining between lover and beloved in the affection of the lover is apprehended or understood by that lover.

---

74. The main body of Thomas's argument, omitting the final paragraph, reads as follows: Dicendum quod similitudo, proprie loquendo, est causa amoris. Sed considerandum est quod similitudo inter aliqua potest attendi dupliciter. Uno modo, ex hoc quod utrumque habet idem in actu; sicut duo habentes albedinem, dicuntur similes. Alio modo, ex hoc quod unum habet in potentia et in quadam inclinatione illud quod aliud habet in actu; sicut si dicamus quod corpus grave existens extra suum locum habet similitudinem cum corpore gravi in suo loco existenti. Vel etia secundum quod potentia habet similitudinem ad actum ipsum; nam in ipsa potentia quodammodo est actus.

Primus ergo similitudinis modus causat amorem amicitiae, seu benevolentiae. Ex hoc enim quod aliqui duo sunt similes, quasi habentes unam formam, sunt quodammodo unum in forma illa; sicut duo homines sunt unum in specie humanitatis, et duo albi in albedine. Et ideo affectus unius tendit in alterum, sicut in unum sibi, et vult ei bonum sicut et sibi. Sed secundus modus similitudinis causat amorem concupiscentiae, vel amicitiam utilis seu delectabilis. Quia unicuique existenti in potentia, inquantum huiusmodi, inest appetitus sui actus, et in eius consecutione delectatur, si sit sentiens et cognoscens. *ST* 1–2.27.3, *corp*.

When one loves a thing concupiscently, it is evident that he perceives it as belonging to his well-being.[75] When one loves another with the love of friendship, however, "he wills good to him even as he wills good to himself," thereby showing, says Thomas, that "he apprehends him as another self, inasmuch, namely, as he wills good to him as even to his very self."[76] Thus, Thomas invokes Aristotle's famous description of a friend as "a man's other self" as the fundamental explanatory principle of genuine friendship love. As David Gallagher correctly explains,[77] it is only through such an apprehension that man can genuinely love another, since all loves must ultimately be grounded in the primal love of one's own perfection. Nevertheless, this does not entail a mere collapse of the other into the self: having apprehended the other *as* another self—the as (*ut*) is crucial here, bearing almost the sense of the English "like"—the lover is enabled genuinely to will a good to that other that does not clandestinely return or redound to himself: this is the basis of the explanation of love of another "for the other's own sake," whether that other be human, angelic or divine.[78]

Two other important effects of love named by Thomas in Question 28 are mutual inhesion, or indwelling (*inhaesio*), discussed in article 2, and ecstasy (*extasis*), treated in article 3.[79] In some sense, the two effects can be seen as flip sides of the same coin. The main function of these two articles is to spell out in detail the various perspectives from which the unitive relation between lover and beloved can be viewed, especially with respect to the notion of the friend as another self. Thus, in article 2, Thomas describes

---

75. Cum enim aliquis amat aliquid quasi concupiscens illud, apprehendit illud quasi pertinens ad suum bene esse. ST 1–2.28.1, *corp*.

76. cum aliquis amat aliquem amore amicitiae, vult ei bonum sicut et sibi vult bonum; unde apprehendit eum ut alterum se, inquantum scilicet vult ei bonum sicut et sibi ipsi. Ibid. Besides real and affective union, Thomas notes also a third kind, substantial union. This is union in the highest degree, consisting in ontological identity, or union with oneself. See *ST* 1–2.28.1, *ad* 2. Thomas returns to this point in the questions on charity, when he asks, "Whether a Man Ought to Love Himself out of Charity?" at *ST* 2–2.25.4.

77. Gallagher appeals to the notion of an "extension of self-love" to articulate Thomas's understanding of the love of friendship. See Gallagher, "Desire for Beatitude," 20–34.

78. Indeed, Gallagher terms "the paradox of *amor amicitiae*" the fact that "the motion to overcome otherness, the affective union, does not merely leave the ontological otherness intact but actually depends upon it. I can love the other as myself only if the other is not myself" ("Desire for Beatitude," 26).

79. Gallagher's discussion of the way the two notions are related in Thomas's account is informative. See ibid., 23–27.

how the beloved can be understood as inhering or dwelling "in" the lover and the lover "in" the beloved, with respect both to apprehension[80] and to appetite.[81] Then, in article 3, he goes on to explain how the lover can be said to be "ecstatic"—"placed outside himself"[82]—in virtue of his love for the beloved, and again, in terms of both knowing and desiring. The most important point for our purposes comes in the concluding lines of the *Respondeo* of article 3. In yet another contrast between the two kinds of love, Thomas argues that the ecstasy resulting from love of concupiscence is only *secundum quid*, inasmuch as the extrinsic good that would provisionally draw the lover outside of himself is in its turn drawn *into* the lover, precisely because he wants that good *for himself*. In love of friendship, on the other hand, "one's affection goes out from oneself *simpliciter*, for he wishes and does good to his friend as accomplishing his care and provision for the sake of the friend himself."[83]

Love, Friendship, and Charity

We may remark that everything said so far could equally well be situated towards the outset of a comprehensive treatise on moral philosophy or philosophical ethics. Yet Thomas places these insights at the heart of his theological masterpiece, *ST*. Turning now to the *Secunda Secundae*, we shall see how Thomas's carefully constructed account of love in the realm of natural psychology has prepared the way for his exposition of supernatural charity.

---

80. Intellect, in the case of rational love.

81. Will, in the case of rational love. Thomas's appeal to the First Epistle of John in the *Sed contra* of article 2 should also be noted. The relevance and character of Thomas's appeals to St. John will be taken up in two sections in this chapter: "Thomas's Theology of Friendship is 'Transcendent'" and "Thomas's Aristotelian Framework."

82. extra se ponitur. *ST* 1–2.28.3, *corp.*

83. Sed secundum extasim [i.e., secundum vim appetitivam] facit amor directe; simpliciter quidem amor amicitiae; amor autem concupiscentiae non simpliciter, sed secundum quid. Nam in amore concupiscentiae quodammodo fertur amans extra seipsum, inquantum scilicet non contentus gaudere de bono quod habet, quaerit frui aliquo extra se. Sed quia illud extrinsecum bonum quaerit sibi habere, non exit simpliciter extra se, sed talis affectio in fine infra ipsum concluditur. Sed in amore amicitiae affectus alicuius simpliciter exit extra se, quia vult amico bonum, et operatur bonum quasi gerens curam et providentiam ipsius propter ipsum amicum. *ST* 1–2.28.3, *corp.*

Theologizing Friendship

In the very first article of his opening question on the theological virtue of charity, Thomas asks: "Whether Charity is Friendship?"[84] The citation that gives rise to the question is of the highest authority: the Lord's own words in the Gospel of John: "I will not now call you servants . . . but My friends" (John 15:15). In his *Respondeo*, however, Thomas proceeds with an argument not fundamentally from Scripture, but from his interpretation of Aristotle. Characteristically building on and qualifying what has gone before, Thomas notes that friendship seems to be one species of love, namely, a love accompanied by benevolence, whereby "we love someone so that we wish good to him."[85] Conversely, when the thing loved is not that to which we wish a good, but rather is that good itself, wished by us for ourselves (like wine, or a horse), this type of love is love of concupiscence:[86] a love characterized precisely as non-benevolent. Distinguishing the love of friendship from the love of concupiscence, however, does not adequately specify friendship, and so Thomas adds that such a love must be "mutual," since, literally, "the friend is a friend *to* a friend."[87] Furthermore, Thomas asserts that such mutual well-wishing, or benevolence, is founded on a *communicatio* of some sort.[88] The final step in the argument consists in the observation that there is, indeed, a communication of man with God, in that "He communicates his beatitude to us," and that the love founded on this particular divine-human communication is what we call charity. If, then, the love grounded in such communication is rightly understood to be a love of friendship, then charity is properly recognized as "a certain friendship of man for God."[89] The only biblical citation Thomas offers in the

---

84. Utrum caritas sit amicitia. *ST* 2–2.23.1.

85. Dicendum quod secundum Philosophum in VIII *Eth.*, non quilibet amor habet rationem amicitiae, sed amor qui est cum benevolentia; quando scilicet sic amamus aliquem ut ei bonum velimus. 2–2.23.1, *corp*. Cf. *ST* 1–2.26.3, *corp*. and 1–2.26.4, *corp*.

86. Si autem rebus amatis non bonum velimus, sed ipsum eorum bonum nobis velimus, sicut dicimur amare vinum aut equum aut aliquid huiusmodi, non est amor amicitiae, sed cuiusdam concupiscentiae. *ST* 2–2.23.1, *corp*.

87. Sed nec benevolentia sufficit ad rationem amicitiae, sed requiritur quaedam mutua amatio, quia amicus est amico amicus. Ibid.

88. Benevolence, reciprocity or mutuality, and shared good are the three Aristotelian criteria of true friendship remarked by Paul Wadell as constituting the core of Thomas's description of friendship. See Wadell, *Friends of God*, 31–36.

89. Talis autem mutua benevolentia fundatur super aliquam communicationem. Cum ergo sit aliqua communicatio hominis ad Deum secundum quod nobis suam beatitudinem communicat, super hanc communicationem oportet aliquam amicitiam fundari. . . . Amor autem super hanc communicationem fundatus est caritas. Unde

body of his response attempts to bring together the two notions of communication and friendship, in an echo of the Johannine passage cited in the *Sed contra*. Thus, where St. Paul writes "God is faithful: by Whom you are called unto the fellowship of His Son" (1 Cor 1:9), Thomas interprets *societas* as equivalent to *amicitia* and the words *vocati estis* as an expression of *communicatio*. Having heard, or read, Thomas's *Respondeo* in full, we are now attuned to the resonance between the Pauline passage and St. John's *dicam vos ... amicos meos*: in each case, a divine calling to, or communication of, friendship, articulated by an apostolic *auctoritas*.[90]

In the following article, Thomas makes a significant correction of the position of Peter Lombard, who held that charity "is not something created in the soul, but is itself the Holy Spirit, inhabiting the mind," or more precisely, that charity's "movement is from the Holy Spirit, not from some mediating habit."[91] If such were the case, Thomas argues, the human act of charity would not be free. Therefore, with the advent of grace in the soul, some *habitus* must come into existence there, created by God to mediate between the Holy Spirit and the human mind. Thus the will, disposed by the supernatural, created *habit* of charity, performs freely the *act* of charity towards oneself or another rational being. Nevertheless, in reply to an objection citing St. Augustine, Thomas concedes that "The divine essence is charity," inasmuch as God is love (cf. 1 John 4:8), and consequently the created virtue of charity in the (human or angelic) soul is "a certain

---

manifestum est quod caritas amicitia quaedam est hominis ad Deum. Ibid. In this critical part of Thomas's argument, an unstated and indispensable assumption should be noted, namely, that this *communicatio* between man and God involves *mutua benevolentia*, otherwise, friendship does not obtain, according to what has preceded. No doubt God's communication of his beatitude counts for his benevolence towards us, but what of our benevolence towards God? The omission is the more striking when we consider closely Thomas's concluding definition of charity, which, read literally, inverts the stress, calling charity not God's love for us, as might seem to accord better with the communication just described, but rather, our love for God!

90. In the following section we will take up the important question of the particular place of Christ in these and other citations, and in Thomas's argument as a whole.

91. According to Thomas's recapitulation, the Lombard contends "quod caritas non est aliquid creatum in anima, sed est ipse Spiritus Sanctus mentem inhabitans. Nec est sua intentio quod iste motus dilectionis quo Deum diligimus sit ipse Spiritus Sanctus, sed quod iste motus dilectionis est a Spiritu Sancto non mediante aliquo habitu, sicut a Spiritu Sancto sunt alii actus virtuosi mediantibus habitibus aliarum virtutum, puta fidei aut spei aut alicuius alterius virtutis. Et hoc dicebat propter excellentiam caritatis." *ST* 2-2.23.2, *corp*.

participation of divine charity."[92] We may note, too, although *amicitia* does not come up explicitly in the article, that if the divine essence is charity and charity is a kind of friendship, then the divine essence must be a kind of friendship. To this point we shall return in the section entitled "The Communal, Trinitarian and Eschatological Dimensions of Friendship," below.

For the purposes of this general presentation of Thomas's account of charity and its relationship to love and friendship, especially in service of our comparison with the thought of Aelred of Rievaulx, the most interesting matters still to be considered pertain broadly to the question of charity's object. More specifically, how does Thomas apply the category of friendship to the charitable love of self, of God and of neighbor, including enemies?[93]

We have already noted that *amor amicitiae*, for Thomas, can be directed either to oneself or to another person, the defining feature of such love being its orientation to a person *per se*, whereas the love of either a non-personal thing or of a person as a means to one's own use or pleasure constitutes *amor concupiscentiae*. In the context of *ST* 1–2.26.4, however, such loves were examined with respect to the activity of the soul in the natural order. Now, in the context of his investigation of the supernatural virtues, Thomas inquires "Whether a man ought to love himself out of charity?"[94] Recalling again that charity is a kind of friendship, he proceeds by distinguishing charity considered according to the common notion of friendship from charity properly so-called. According to the common meaning of friendship, Thomas, expanding on his earlier discussions of union, observes that a man cannot accurately be said to be his own friend, inasmuch as friendship implies union, and since a man's unitedness (lit.: *unitas*) to himself is greater than his union with any other, he has with himself not friendship, but something more than friendship. Therefore, "just as unity is the principle of union, so the love by which someone loves himself is the form and root of friendship."[95] Concerning charity *proper*, on the other hand, Thomas reasons as follows: according to its proper *ratio*, charity is friendship of man for God principally, and *consequently* for the things of God, "among which is even the man himself who has charity." Therefore,

---

92. quaedam participatio divinae caritatis. *ST* 2–2.23.2, *ad* 1.

93. How these various loves are ordered to one another, and the significance of this ordering, will be treated in the section "The Order of Charity" later in this chapter.

94. Utrum homo debeat seipsum ex caritate diligere. *ST* 2–2.25.4.

95. Unde sicut unitas est principium unionis, ita amor quo quis diligit seipsum, est forma et radix amicitiae. *ST* 2–2.25.4, *corp*.

"among other things which he loves out of charity as things pertaining to God, he also loves himself out of charity."[96] Drawing together the two poles of Thomas's answer, we see that the reason for a man's love of himself is not that he is his own friend: in ordinary terms, friendship entails a lesser union than that of ontological identity, and so man's self-love on the natural plane is in fact more fundamental than, albeit analogous to, ordinary love of friendship. Nevertheless, a man ought properly to love himself out of charity, inasmuch as he knows himself to belong to God and as such to be a proper secondary object of the love he directs primarily to God in the friendship of charity.

As the preceding argument suggests, man's charitable love for God proves to be the ontological foundation for all other charitable loves. Thus, just as our charitable love for ourselves ought to proceed from the fact of our belonging to God, so our charitable love for our neighbor is an expression of our love for the One to whom he belongs. Specifically, "it is this we ought to love in our neighbor: that he is *in* God."[97] We can see, then, that our charitable love of ourselves and of our neighbor operates on the same general grounds: in both cases the object of our love is loved properly "under the aspect of God," and indeed, as Thomas argues in the opening article of Question 25, by the same act *specifically (specie)*, whereby we love God.[98] But does this principle apply to every neighbor, including the one who is our enemy? In order to answer this question, Thomas makes a threefold distinction. First of all, he rules out as perverse and in fact repugnant to charity the idea that one ought to love his enemy *qua* enemy, since this would mean loving what is evil in another.[99] In a second sense, Thomas

---

96. Alio modo possumus loqui de caritate secundum propriam rationem ipsius, prout scilicet est amicita hominis ad Deum principaliter, et ex consequenti ad ea quae sunt Dei. Inter quae etiam est ipse homo qui caritatem habet. Et sic inter cetera quae ex caritate diligit quasi ad Deum pertinentia, etiam seipsum ex caritate diligit. *ST* 2-2.25.4, *corp.*

97. hoc enim debemus in proximo diligere, ut in Deo sit. *ST* 2-2.25.1, *corp.* Thomas has already provided a version of the argument at *ST* 2-2.23.1, *ad* 2, where he observes of friendship that it can extend "ad aliquem respectu alterius personae, sicut si aliquis habet amicitiam ad aliquem hominem, ratione eius diligit omnes ad illum hominem pertinentes, sive filios sive servos sive qualitercumque ei attinentes."

98. Ratio autem diligendi proximum Deus est; hoc enim debemus in proximo diligere, ut in Deo sit. Unde manifestum est quod idem specie actus est quo diligitur Deus, et quo diligitur proximus. *ST* 2-2.25.1, *corp.*

99. dilectio inimicorum tripliciter potest considerari. Uno modo, ut inimici diligantur inquantum sunt inimici. Et hoc est perversum et caritati repugnans, quia hoc est

argues that, inasmuch as one's enemy is also generically his neighbor, he ought to love him as such and for the same reason. In other words, the charitable love owed universally to our neighbors in consequence of their belonging to the formal object of our charity (namely, God), does not exclude our enemies.[100] Lastly, Thomas considers in what sense one "may be moved in a special motion of love towards an enemy." He rejects the idea that this might be required *absolutely* (*absolute*) by charity, for the same reason that charity cannot require us to love every single man individually: our creatureliness, our finitude in time and space, makes such actual universal love impossible for us. Nevertheless, says Thomas, charity does demand a preparedness of mind to love each enemy individually, "should the necessity occur." That someone may even love his enemies actually and gratuitously, "for God's sake—this pertains to charity's perfection."[101]

If the proper formal object of charity is God and God alone, while all other rational beings, be they angelic or human, are loved with a love of charity precisely *qua* belonging to the primary object of charity, then it may also be observed that only God is properly loved for his own sake. Whereas our friendship for God entails that we love ourselves and our neighbors for the sake of the One to Whom we and they belong, God belongs to no one else: as the final, formal and efficient cause of all creation, God is capable of being loved without further reference to any other being. Though Thomas grants that there is also a legitimate sense in which we love God because of the rewards we hope for or the punishments we fear, such love remains a concupiscent love, subtly reducing our friendship with God to one of use or pleasure, even when the goal in question is as exalted as eternal beatitude. From such imperfect love for God, Thomas assures us one can progress to love of God for his own sake, comparing this transition to a human

---

diligere malum alterius. *ST* 2-2.25.8, *corp*.

100. Alio modo potest accipi dilectio inimicorum quantum ad naturam, scilicet in universali. Et sic dilectio inimicorum est de necessitate caritatis, ut scilicet aliquis diligens Deum et proximum ab illa generalitate dilectionis proximi inimicos suos non excludat. Ibid.

101. Tertio potest considerari dilectio inimicorum in speciali, ut scilicet aliquis in speciali moveatur motu dilectionis ad inimicum. Et istud non est de necessitate caritatis absolute, quia nec etiam moveri motu dilectionis in speciali ad quoslibet homines singulariter est de necessitate caritatis, quia hoc esset impossibile. Est tamen de necessitate caritatis secundum praeparationem animi, ut scilicet homo habeat animum paratum ad hoc quod in singulari inimicum diligeret si necessitas occurreret.

Sed quod absque articulo necessitatis homo etiam hoc actu impleat ut diligat inimicum propter Deum, hoc pertinet ad perfectionem caritatis. Ibid.

friendship, in which, "once we have begun to love, we no longer love the friend on account of [his] benefices, but on account of his virtue."[102] A final point calls for clarification here: If only God can be truly loved for his own sake, how are we to understand Thomas's original explanation of love of friendship in the *Prima Secundae* as love of another simply and for himself, or for his own sake, with no stipulation that this only applies in the case of the *divine* other? The answer ultimately reduces to different frames of reference: *simply speaking, amor amicitiae* does entail love of another rational being for his own sake, such that that love terminates in the beloved friend. Yet the most perfect love of one's human (or, in principle, angelic) friend is in fact one which is the expression—a kind of overflow, as it were—of charity, one's love of friendship for God. Thus, with Thomas, we can legitimately say that a true love of friendship for God includes, subordinated to and expressive of this primary love, the love of his rational creatures, *for their own sakes*.

In the comparatively short sections that follow, we must address a few aspects of Thomas's account that extend in one direction or another beyond the scope of the main features of his position, presented above. At the same time, certain important implications of his theology will also begin to become apparent, many of which will be discussed in more detail in our final chapter.

Thomas's Theology of Friendship is "Transcendent"

By this section's title three main points are intended, two of which are more easily put negatively, in terms of each one's relative opposition to the third. First, it must be said that, notwithstanding his point of departure from natural psychology, in his account of charity as the friendship of man for God, Thomas pays relatively little attention to the relationship between Christian friends. Although later, in his extensive treatment of the virtues, he deals briefly under the rubric of justice with the virtue of affability (*affabilitas*, which sometimes gets translated as "friendliness") and its opposing vices,[103] Thomas offers no sustained theological treatment of the topic of "spiritual friendship," or the like. Given his definition of charity as man's friendship *for God*, this is neither surprising nor necessarily a deficiency in his overall

---

102. postquam iam amare incepimus, non propter illa beneficia amemus amicum, sed propter eius virtutem. ST 2-2.27.3, *corp*. Cf. also ST 2-2.24.9, *corp*.

103. See ST 2-2.114-16.

account: in Thomas's magisterial opinion, the perspective from which best to understand charity, and therefore friendship under its supernatural aspect, may be clearly identified as "from above."

Second, given that such a God's-eye view admits theoretically of different options for theological exposition, Thomas conspicuously does not choose the christological. The most blatant evidence of this point is Thomas's peculiar placement of the two most puissant christological references to friendship in the Gospels, both spoken by Jesus himself in chapter 15 of the Gospel of John. We have already noted the citation of John 15:15, at the very outset of Thomas's long discussion of the theological virtue of charity.[104] What is noteworthy beyond the citation itself, however, is Thomas's placement of it in the *Sed contra*. The *Sed contra* plays a curious role within the scholastic *quaestio* in general, a point to which we shall return below. It is sufficient here to remark that while Thomas clearly recognizes Jesus' words as the most authoritative possible endorsement of the position he wishes to defend and explain, at the same time, he brackets them off entirely from the rest of his argument. Even more peripheral is his placement of John 15:13—"Greater love than this no man hath, that a man lay down his life for his friends." Thomas relegates Christ's identification of the forfeiture of one's own life as the highest form of friendship to a question on the relative order to be observed between love of one's neighbor and love of one's own body.[105] Moreover, he sets the quotation neither in his *Respondeo*, nor in the *Sed contra*, nor even in a reply to an objection, but in the third *objection*, thereby enshrining it within an opposing position, and one of secondary relevance, at that! Beyond the bounds of the *Secunda Pars*, it is all the more striking that friendship plays no significant role whatsoever in Thomas's systematic Christology, presented in the *Tertia Pars*—either in its dogmatic or historical components (*ST* 3.1–26 and 3.27–59, respectively).[106]

104. See *ST* 2-2.23.1, *Sed contra*.

105. See *ST* 2-2.26.5, *Obj*. 3.

106. Indeed, it hardly even appears. In a rare reference in the opening question, Thomas describes the Incarnation *not* as embodying Christ's friendship with us, but rather as the remedy given by God to men, in virtue of his friendship with them. See *ST* 3.1.5, *ad* 1. We may note once more that even this reference appears only in an objection and its corresponding reply. In a later historical question concerning "Christ's way of association" (*de modo conversationis Christi*), in answer to a question "Whether it was fitting for Christ to circulate among men" (*Utrum conveniens fuerit Christum inter homines conversari*), no reference to *amicitia* occurs. Nor does either of the great Dominical references to friendship from John 15 appear, either in the questions on the Passion, or elsewhere.

Here it must be admitted in passing that *SCG* contains one, brief, lapidary formulation of the theology of friendship in brazenly christological terms: the passage from Book IV, chapter 54, alluded to above.[107] There, Thomas contends that:

> since friendship consists in a certain equality, those things that are greatly unequal do not seem able to be coupled in friendship. Therefore, that friendship between man and God might be more familiar, it was expedient for man that God become man, since even by nature man is man's friend: so thus, 'while we know God visibly, we may be rapt to love of things invisible.'[108]

Such a line of theological reasoning is quite consistent with Jesus' farewell discourse in the Gospel of John. Nevertheless, standing as the passage does in splendid isolation, it seems to be something like the exception that proves the rule of the main lines of Saint Thomas's thought. In general, Thomas does not think of friendship in predominantly christological terms, any more than he tends to focus on Christ's character as *friend* of the Christian soul.

In lieu of any consistent christological emphasis, Thomas instead opts decisively in favor of a perspective on friendship that is theological in the strict sense. This is our third and positive reason for designating Thomas's theology of friendship as "transcendent." In *ST* 2-2.23.2, discussed above, as well as in *SCG*, Book IV, chapters 21 and 22,[109] Thomas's argumentation indicates a strong affinity between charity and the Third Person of the Trinity. We have seen that Peter Lombard thought charity in the soul *was*

---

107. See the section "Texts on Friendship" earlier in this chapter.

108. cum amicitia in quadam aequalitate consistat, ea quae multum inaequalia sunt, in amicitia copulari non posse videntur. Ad hoc igitur quod familiarior amicitia esset inter hominem et Deum, expediens fuit homini quod Deus fieret homo, quia etiam naturaliter homo homini amicus est: ut sic, dum visibiliter Deum cognoscimus, in invisibilium amorem rapiamur. *SCG* IV, 54 (6). Thomas's concluding words here are quoted from the Preface of the Mass of the Nativity of our Lord and of Corpus Christi.

109. We have already noted in passing (see "Texts on Friendship" earlier in this chapter, especially n. 357, above) Thomas's recognition at *SCG* IV, 21 (5) and (7) of the sharing of secrets as a mark of friendship. Though the reference is indeed to John 15:15, the stress is not on Christ's own action here, so much as on the Holy Spirit's agency in "establishing us as friends of God." This is in keeping with the theme of the chapter as a whole. Furthermore, as will be argued immediately below, the God with whom friendship is thus established is conceived by Thomas—both here and elsewhere—as God *in His Essence*, rather than as one or more of the divine Persons.

the Holy Spirit,[110] and while Thomas rejects such a strict identification, he himself affirms in the *Prima Pars* that "*amor*, taken personally, is a proper name of the Third Divine Person."[111] Moreover, in the chapters of *SCG* just mentioned, Thomas says that "by the Holy Spirit we are constituted friends of God."[112] In the same article in which he redresses the Lombardian position, however, he acknowledges that "the Divine Essence Itself is charity," thereby implying that the divine attribute of charity need not necessarily be appropriated to any one of the three Persons.[113] In fact, when the whole sweep of his discussion of charity is taken into consideration, this last position appears to dominate Thomas's perspective regarding man's friendship with God. No doubt Thomas's thought in this regard may be perceived as constrained by his concern to expound biblical revelation, where the most significant passages from both Testaments, recalled throughout the questions on charity, speak of God or the Lord, with no further explicit trinitarian or christological specification. In any case, from the opening article of Question 23 to the final article of Question 27 of the *Secunda Secundae*, Thomas expresses no particular interest in delineating the charitable love of friendship as it might be directed particularly to the Father, the Son or the Holy Spirit, but rather, as it moves men and angels towards God in his Essence.[114]

Thomas's Aristotelian Framework

If, as just proposed, Scripture yields a set of parameters for the theological language Thomas employs in his account of charity as friendship with God, Aristotle provides a framework more radically determinative for the direction and development of Thomas's thought on the subject. The point

---

110. *ST* 2-2.23.2, *corp.*

111. secundum quod [nomen amoris] personaliter sumitur, est proprium nomen Spiritus Sancti. *ST* 1.37.1, *corp.*

112. per Spiritum Sanctum amici Dei constituimur. *SCG* IV, 21 (4). Phrases almost identical to this recur several more times in these two chapters: see 21 (5) and (8) and 22 (3) and (4).

113. For Thomas's discussion of appropriation of essential names to the divine Persons, see *ST* 1.39.7. In connection with the argument here, see especially *ad* 1, where Thomas's argument implicitly justifies the position he later concedes in *ST* 2-2.23.2, *ad* 1.

114. See, e.g., *ST* 2-2.23.1, *corp.*, 2-2.27.8, *corp.*, *et passim*.

has been ably demonstrated by Mansini,[115] Wadell,[116] and Gallagher,[117] not only in terms of Thomas's direct textual dependence on Aristotle, but also and more profoundly in terms of an actual genealogical continuity between the two authors' thought. Thomas's appeals to Aristotle abound throughout his treatment of love as a passion in the *Prima Secundae*. Paramount among these is the citation from *Rhetoric* ii, 4, in the *Respondeo* of *ST* 1-2.26.4: "To love is to wish good to someone." As has already been discussed at length above, this single line provides Thomas with a thoroughly adequate foundation for his seminal distinction between *amor concupiscentiae* and *amor amicitiae*. Another critical passage, also impacting his account profoundly, is *Ethics* ix, 4, alluded to by Thomas at *ST* 1-2.28.1, *corp.*: "Hence a friend is called a man's *other self*. . . ."[118] Turning to the *Secunda Secundae*, we find the pivotal eighth book of Aristotle's *NE* cited in all three of the objections of the opening article of the first question on the theological virtue of charity.[119] Thus, Thomas heralds his clear decision to frame his theological discussion of love according to guidelines suggested by the philosophical account of Aristotle. To drive the point home, Thomas begins his own magnificent *Respondeo* to the same article with Aristotle's pithy description of friendship, from the same book of *NE*, as "the love which is together with benevolence, when, namely, we thus love someone, so that we wish good to him."[120] Further significant appeals are made at *ST* 2-2.23.3, *corp.*, 2-2.23.4, *ad* 1 and *ad* 2, 2-2.23.5, *corp.*, 2-2.23.6, *ad* 1, and so on, throughout the discussion. Particularly noteworthy is Thomas's quotation of *NE* in his *Respondeo* of *ST* 2-2.25.4: "friendly relations towards the other come from those towards oneself."[121]

In contrast to the centrality of Aristotle's perspective, it must be noted that the biblical references, copious though they are, convey more a sense of ad hoc support, than one of bearing intrinsically on Thomas's argumentation. This is most conspicuous in regard to the Johannine passages cited,

---

115. See, e.g., Mansini, "*Similitudo*," 1–6 and Mansini, "*Duplex Amor*," 155–56, 180–85, 188, etc.

116. See, e.g., Wadell, *Friends of God*, 5–15.

117. See, e.g., Gallagher, "Desire for Beatitude," 2, 3, 14, 27, 33, etc. and Gallagher, "Thomas Aquinas on Self-Love," 23–24, 34, etc.

118. inde est quod amicus dicitur esse "alter ipse."

119. See *ST* 2-2.23.1, *ad* 1, 2, and 3.

120. amor qui est cum benevolentia; quando scilicet sic amamus aliquem ut ei bonum velimus.

121. amicabilia quae sunt ad alterum veniunt ex his quae sunt ad seipsum.

given the thematic significance in John's Gospel of the two influential references to friendship in John 15, a significance already noted above, both in this chapter and in our chapter on Aelred's thought. Indeed, St. John's writings have a less prominent place even than those of St. Paul, not to speak of the works and thought of Aristotle. In sum, we contend that the deep-structure of Thomas's theological account of friendship is profoundly Aristotelian, albeit in a highly Christianized form—so much so that the biblical witness to which Thomas also appeals inevitably seems somewhat marginalized. To the relative merits and deficiencies of this aspect of Thomas's presentation, we shall return in our final chapter.

The Order of Charity

One of the questions for which Thomas, in the midst of his treatment of supernatural charity, relies on Aristotle for the foundation of his answer, is "Whether there is order in charity?"[122] From the *Metaphysics*, Thomas cites the Philosopher's observation that "*before and after* is said with respect to the relation to some principle," adding that *order* is merely a word for things being before or after. Recalling that "the love of charity tends to God as to the principle of happiness," Thomas completes the syllogism, arguing that charity entails some kind of order, "according to the relation to the first principle of that [charitable] love, which is God."[123] We discussed at some length above the various possible objects of the love of charity: ourselves, God and our neighbor, including our enemies. In *ST* 2-2.26, Thomas devotes thirteen articles to sorting out the proper relative order among the various loves demanded by charity. Here Thomas confirms what we have already shown above: that what our friendship with God constitutes first of all is a love of God that grounds and exceeds all other loves. In turn, this preeminent love of friendship for God himself spills over, as it were, into love for rational creatures, in virtue of their likeness to God. In *ST* 2-2.26.3, Thomas explains this likeness fundamentally as that between whole and

---

122. Utrum in caritate sit ordo. *ST* 2-2.26.1.

123. sicut Philosophus dicit in V *Metaph.*, "prius et posterius dicitur secundum relationem ad aliquod principium." Ordo autem includit in se aliquem modum prioris et posterioris. Unde oportet quod ubicumque est aliquod principium, sit etiam aliquis ordo. Dictum autem est supra quod dilectio caritatis tendit in Deum sicut in principium beatitudinis, in cuius communicatione amicitia caritatis fundatur. Et ideo oportet quod in his quae ex caritate diliguntur attendatur aliquis ordo secundum relationem ad primum principium huius dilectionis, quod est Deus. Ibid.

part. According to this perspective, the individual human (or angelic) person constitutes a part of the universality of creation and, recognizing God as the common good of all, loves that common good more than his own particular good, and consequently loves God more than himself.[124]

Having established the priority in charity of love of God over love of all rational creatures, both oneself and one's neighbor,[125] Thomas now turns to the question of which, among rational creatures, a man ought to love most. To the critical question of whether one ought to love oneself more than one's neighbor, Thomas has recourse again to the important metaphysical notion of *union* and its degrees. Whereas a man loves God as the principle of good and himself as *participating* in that good, his love for his neighbor can only be in virtue of the neighbor's *association* with himself in that same good, in which they both participate. As a result, a man's love of himself exceeds his love of his neighbor just as his self-unity (ontological identity) exceeds his union-by-association with another in participation of the divine good.

Finally, Thomas devotes the remaining articles of *ST* 2–2.26 to questions of the relative priorities in our charitable obligations among neighbors, varying as they do in their degrees of distance from us and in moral stature. For the most part, the details of this analysis are sufficiently peripheral that they need not be enumerated in this presentation. The most noteworthy point is the fact that a neighbor's proximity to oneself tends on the whole to outweigh the measure of his virtue in determining the proper relative degree of our caritative love for him.[126] In our final chapter, we shall explore the resonances, as well as some significant differences, between Thomas's and Aelred's accounts of the order of charity, and between the ways they convey their respective positions.

Thomas's Science of Friendship

We have discussed above Thomas's structuring of his mature presentation of the theology of friendship within the context of the *Secunda Pars*. Here,

---

124. David Gallagher has frequent recourse to this aspect of Thomas's position, pointing out that its most detailed elucidation is to be found in Thomas's commentary on Dionysius's *De divinis nominibus*. See Gallagher, "Desire for Beatitude," especially, 34–38.

125. The latter point is evident from our discussion of charity's object, above. See *ST* 2–2.25.1 and 26.2.

126. See *ST* 2–2.26.6–12, especially articles 6 and 7.

formal decisions as to the order of his presentation are dictated largely by the internal logic of the content he wishes to explicate: as grace builds on nature, so the account of love as a natural passion of the human soul precedes and prepares the way for the exposition of love under the aspect of supernatural charity, defined as man's friendship for God. Conversely, however, certain formalities of St. Thomas's theological methodology subtly impact the material content they are intended to articulate. Of paramount significance in this regard is Thomas's conviction that theology is a science, a conviction he proclaims and carefully defends in the opening question of his theological masterpiece, *ST*.[127] A comparable presupposition fundamentally determines the form of the *quaestio* itself. Developed by the schools as a way to treat broad topics methodically by breaking them down into ever-smaller subdivisions, the *quaestio*, and within it, the *articulus* and *obiectio*, correspond respectively to increasing degrees of specificity, vis-à-vis the immediate question at hand. At the same time, as the number of articles or objections grows, their relative importance tends to decrease. Moreover, the same presumption of theology's scientific character informs the way Thomas typically chooses to situate authoritative voices from the Tradition: quotations from Scripture as well as many citations of Augustine and others of the Fathers, particularly Dionysius, often appear in the *Sed contras*, where, as has been noted, they are preemptively bracketed to a real degree from the argument itself. Otherwise, they tend to provide the main subject matter of the objections, which Thomas either corrects or qualifies with his own strictly rational argumentation.

The same underlying assumption of the scientific character of theology as a discipline entails necessarily that whatever falls under the purview of theology can and ought also to be treated scientifically, including friendship. For St. Thomas, *amicitia* as a formal category, whether considered by way of preamble under its natural psychological aspect, or more perfectly as the genus of which supernatural charity constitutes the highest species, ultimately warrants investigation as belonging to the scientific discipline of theology. Thomas aims, then, to think scientifically about friendship. Viewed in this way, as we have attempted to demonstrate above, friendship is, in the final analysis, an airtight scientific concept: no wiggle-room is allowed for interpretation about what precisely constitutes such a specification of the soul's affections, under either natural or supernatural auspices. Moreover, a *concept*, in the Aristotelian-Thomistic account, strictly

---

127. See *ST* 1.1, especially articles 2, 3, and 7.

speaking, pertains only to *universals*: since change and particularity cannot be genuinely known, the concept of *amicitia* inevitably seems to assume a certain immobility, or stasis, thereby militating directly, however subtly, against more fluid or dynamic expressions of the phenomena that come into play under the rubric of friendship.[128] By the same token, Thomas's account inevitably excludes any poetic or romantic notions of friendship—not so much because they necessarily enshroud theological error, but because they may prove unhelpful, or worse, confusing in the sober pursuit of one's own theological education and concomitant spiritual progress.[129] Furthermore, as with all other topics treated according to the same methodological presuppositions, Thomas consistently abstracts as far as possible from personal experience in his effort to provide an accurate theological account of love, friendship and charity. Notwithstanding St. Thomas's insistence that the principles of the science of theology are precisely the revealed truths of the Catholic faith, his project is to expound these truths with the maximum degree of scientific detachment, and to neutralize as far as possible any explicit personal involvement with his subject matter: the "I" in *ST*, although in no way inconsistent with what we know of the life of Thomas Aquinas, nevertheless speaks formally, objectively, as the mouthpiece of a thoroughly purified human Reason, albeit one illuminated by divine grace. In our fourth and final chapter, we shall assess the benefits and limitations of such a scientific treatment—of friendship as a theological *topos* and, by extension, of theology in general.

The Communal, Trinitarian, and Eschatological Dimensions of Friendship

Three more dimensions of friendship, theologically considered, must be briefly addressed as having some relevance to St. Thomas's account: the

---

128. In our final chapter, we shall consider, for example, Thomas's engagement of the biblical notion of "enemy," as compared to Aelred's very different treatment. In the latter's vision, a dynamism is discovered within this notion that seems to be lacking from Thomas's perspective.

129. It must always be remembered that Thomas composed the *Summa* "for the instruction of beginners" (*ad eruditionem incipientium*. *ST* 1, *Prooemium*), by which was intended mostly seminarians and young clerics, who would then have been responsible for digesting this exhaustive exposition of sacred doctrine, expressed so "briefly and clearly" (*breviter ac dilucide*, ibid.) by St. Thomas, before passing it on to the masses, especially via preaching and the sacrament of reconciliation.

communal, the trinitarian, and the eschatological. Among the wider implications of St. Thomas's theology of *amicitia*, as Torrell has observed, a communal or communitarian extension of the concept can be seen to be at work in discussions of politics, of the Church, and ultimately of the Communion of Saints.¹³⁰ Nonetheless, it would be difficult to maintain the position that Thomas in his theological account identifies an *intrinsically* communal component of friendship, one at least that goes beyond the dyadic criterion of mutual benevolence between two friends. That is to say: while fully endorsing the Aristotelian position that man is by nature social, Thomas's theological description of friendship concerns itself much more with the relationship between one man and another, or between one man and God, than it does with the relationship between a man and the community around him. Even Thomas's discussion of the likeness between part and whole appeals to the relationship between an individual citizen and the city as metaphorically analogous to the faithful Christian's relationship to a *single* being, God, who constitutes the common good of which he is a part: the actual character of the individual's relationship to the collectivity of his fellow men, Christian or otherwise, does not come into question. For Thomas then, in the final analysis, the communal aspect of friendship remains more of an occasional, albeit important, *implication* of his basic doctrine than a primary element of that doctrine itself.¹³¹

Granted this inclination to focus throughout his theological treatment of friendship on elucidating the graced love relationship between *two* persons (whether two men, or one man and God, or, analogously, a man's charitable love for himself), perhaps it should not be surprising that we find in his account no formally articulated doctrine of *amicitia* among the community of divine Persons.¹³² Yet we have noted Thomas's admission

---

130. See the section on "Jean-Pierre Torrell" earlier in this chapter.

131. A striking confirmation of this point comes well before Thomas concentrates his attention on the psychology of friendship specifically. Near the very outset of the *Prima Secundae*, in his treatment of *beatitudo* in general, Thomas argues unequivocally that "si loquamur de felicitate praesentis vitae . . . felix indiget amicis. . . . *Sed si loquamur de perfecta beatitudine quae erit in patria, non requiritur societas amicorum de necessitate ad beatitudinem, quia homo habet totam plenitudinem suae perfectionis in Deo.*" ST 1–2.4.8, *corp.* In his reply to the third objection of the same article, Thomas drives the point home, insisting that "si esset una sola anima fruens Deo, beata esset, non habens proximum quem diligeret. Sed supposito proximo, sequitur dilectio eius ex perfecta dilectione Dei. Unde *quasi concomitanter* se habet amicitia ad perfectam beatitudinem." ST 1–2.4.8, *ad* 3.

132. *Pace* Paul Wadell, who insists that such a doctrine is part and parcel of St.

that God's essence is charity[133] and that therefore, by implication, God is friendship.[134] Consequently, since God is in his very essence triune, both three and one, it would be reasonable to extrapolate the doctrine that the love of friendship has its primary analogate in the relations among the Persons of the Trinity. Nevertheless, Thomas does not put forward such a formulation, either in his detailed discussion of the trinitarian relations in the *Prima Pars*,[135] or in his treatment of the theological virtue of charity. Given his demonstrated tendency, and ability, to render explicit all that he finds theologically indispensable in the Tradition, we are inclined to count his reticence here as indicative of a real omission in his own perspective,[136] while readily conceding that such a doctrine is implicit within his theological enterprise.

If communal and trinitarian notions do not figure centrally in Thomas's theological doctrine of charity as friendship with God, the role of eschatology could hardly be greater. From beginning to end of Questions 23 to 27 of the *Secunda Secundae* and on into Question 28 on joy, Thomas maintains that "the friendship of charity is founded upon the fellowship (*communicatio*) of eternal beatitude."[137] We have seen the importance of

---

Thomas's perspective. Wadell does not attribute to Thomas an idea of friendship shared communally and symmetrically among all three divine Persons, any more than Thomas articulates such a position. Rather, Wadell ascribes to Thomas what amounts to the traditional Augustinian position, whereby the Holy Spirit is identified as the personification of the activity of "the love or friendship between Father and Son. . . ." See Wadell, *Friends of God*, 18-19. The problem is that the equation between *amor* and *amicitia* is never made in the trinitarian context by Thomas himself.

133. *ST* 2-2.23.2, *ad* 1.
134. See "Love, Friendship, and Charity" earlier in this chapter.
135. See *ST* 1.27-43.
136. Whether intentional or due to oversight would be difficult to argue convincingly and would take us too far afield of the current project, which remains the clear presentation of Thomas's fundamental theological doctrine of friendship. A satisfactory explanation would almost certainly include as one element the fact, noticed explicitly by Aelred, of the lack of warrant for the notion *Deus est amicitia* in the Tradition.
137. amicitia caritatis . . . fundatur super communicatione beatitudinis aeternae. *ST* 2-2.25.10, *corp*. Cf. also *ST* 2-2.23.1, *corp*. and *ad* 1; 2-2.23.5, *corp*.; 2-2.24.2, *corp*.; 2-2.25.10, *corp*.; 2-2.25.12, *corp*.; 2-2.26.3, *corp*.; 2-2.26.13, *corp*.; 2-2.28.1, *ad* 3. An intriguing question that cannot be pursued at length here is whether the intrinsic eschatological orientation of supernatural friendship in fact has a teleological analogue within the natural order. One could surely argue, based on Thomas's account, that natural friendship with another *cannot* be explained or justified teleologically for the following simple reason: if love of friendship for another is truly for his own sake and does not clandestinely return to terminate in myself, I seem finally to have no reason at all to love

this Thomistic tenet for the theses of both David Gallagher and Christopher Malloy. Both authors see clearly the centrality of Thomas's recognition that all human loves are oriented fundamentally towards the perfection of the rational soul of the lover, which perfection is happiness. Furthermore, the true form of this happiness is discovered in the light of divine revelation to be eternal beatitude. But the perfection of love is rest, or joy, or "fruition" (*quies, gaudium, fruitio*) in the beloved, which is only accomplished through the actual union resulting from the real presence of the beloved to the lover. Thus, the graced soul *in via* loves God with the charitable love of friendship, yet imperfectly, inasmuch as it is only capable in this life of an affective union.[138] At the same time, the soul hopes for the perfection and fruition of his love in the eternal presence of God in heaven, and this perfection of charity is the soul's perfect happiness. Finally, it may be observed that the *communicatio beatitudinis aeternae* just mentioned must surely be synonymous with the Communion of Saints, thereby linking Thomas's doctrine of the latter with his theological doctrine of friendship. This is true, and entirely in keeping with our assertion earlier in this section regarding the communal aspect of friendship in Thomas's thought: even this most important of communal expressions of charitable friendship remains more an implication of Thomas's doctrine, than a necessary element of the theological notion of friendship *per se*, properly specified in terms of charity, which Thomas defines simply as man's friendship for God.

Thomas's Exegesis: Lectio Utilis?

Finally, we must call attention, albeit in summary fashion, to Thomas's relationship to Scripture, as we did with Aelred in chapter 2. As in Aelred's case, the chief point here is to observe a significant congruity between the peculiar formalities of Thomas's exegetical activity and his theological doctrine

---

the other on such terms. Charity, on the other hand, as friendship for God, provides a real justification for my loving the other for his own sake, namely, his association with me in the participation of God's own good, divine eternal beatitude. At root, this question is an expression of the highly fraught theme of the relation between nature and supernature, to which Henri de Lubac gave new life in the mid-twentieth century with his controversial work *The Mystery of the Supernatural*.

138. The mystical union, even the so-called "abiding union," described by such great mystical doctors as St. Teresa of Avila and St. John of the Cross remain, strictly speaking, only the most exceptional kinds of affective union, inasmuch as they are impermanent in this life.

of friendship. Though *Sacra Scriptura* informs virtually every page of the many thousands St. Thomas wrote in his lifetime, we can do some justice to his mature engagement of the Bible through appeal to a series of sermons composed and given in 1273,[139] barely a year before his death, and to the texts we have been considering in the *Secunda Pars*.

During Lent of 1273, Thomas delivered a series of about fifty-nine sermons to "both students and ordinary faithful" in a parish church in Naples.[140] The sermons were principally doctrinal in nature, and have for that reason typically been identified collectively as "The Catechetical Sermons," or even as "The Catechism of St. Thomas." Many of the sermons deal with one or another specific article of either the Nicene Creed or of the Our Father, or with some point of the Law, Old or New. In his 1953 dissertation on this material James Kraus contends that

> the most striking feature of these doctrinal sermons is St. Thomas's adoption of a special locus of Scripture as 'the' source for most particular articles [of the Creed or *Pater*]. Noteworthy is the fact that this source is far oftener a doctrinal one rather than the historical account for such subjects as Creation, the Incarnation, Ascension, Redemption, etc. Likewise it is almost always the same as his source for the same doctrine in his scientific works.[141]

Along the same lines, Kraus argues that when all 939 Scriptural citations from the series are taken into account, Thomas's "favorite books are the doctrinal ones of both Testaments, Sts. John and Paul in the New, the Sapiential Literature of the Old."[142] Moreover, "the isolated examples of a highly symbolic interpretation prove the rule by their conspicuousness"—the rule, that is, of Thomas's preference for expounding Scripture's literal sense.[143] In other words, at this late point in his career, St. Thomas evidences virtually no allegorical exegesis in his preaching whatsoever.

---

139. The two modern commentaries on these sermons to which we refer below are: Ayo, *The Sermon-Conferences* and Kraus, *The Catechetical Sermons*.

140. Ayo, *The Sermon-Conferences*, 2. Ayo, however, acknowledges at most only twenty-eight sermons in the series, disagreeing with Kraus that the thirty-one sermons on the Law ought to be included among the set given in a single Lent. In any case, there is no dispute about authorship, or about the general time-frame for the composition of all fifty-nine sermons.

141. Kraus, *The Catechetical Sermons*, 24.

142. Ibid., 26.

143. Ibid., 28.

Theologizing Friendship

As Kraus himself notes, similar tendencies can be observed in Thomas's "scientific" theological works, including *ST*. In addition, Thomas's frequent placement of biblical passages within either the *Sed contras* or the objections suggests a preponderance of one of two functions for Scriptural citation in the work: (1) in the objections, Scripture is cited in order to be explained or defended by Thomas on rational grounds, in either his *Respondeo* or in his replies to the objections; (2) in the *Sed contra*, Scripture is cited as an authoritative prooftext for the position he wishes to take, though, as noted above,[144] Thomas typically does not derive his actual theological argumentation from texts cited in the *Sed contra*. In both of these characteristic applications, as with his preaching, Thomas always gives preference to the literal sense of the biblical text. When these several observations are gathered together and envisaged under the single aspect of friendship, we may make the following summary assessment: Thomas reads Scripture as a valuable—or invaluable—tool for understanding God, the primary object of the highest form of friendship. Such understanding as may be gained through careful, prayerful reading of the Scriptures constitutes a good, one that Thomas loves for himself and for his neighbor. Consequently, St. Thomas may be seen as having *amor concupiscentiae* for the Bible, subordinated to the *amor amicitiae* he has for himself and his neighbor. The latter love overflows, in turn, from charity, Thomas's primary *amor amicitiae*, directed to God Himself.

Conclusion: Thomas's Scholastic Theology of Friendship

In his definition of charity as man's friendship for God, we discover a theological formulation simultaneously expressive of Saint Thomas's singular genius and emblematic of one of scholasticism's greatest achievements: the harmonizing of Christian revelation with Aristotelian philosophy. The question whether this harmonization was in fact accomplished through the assimilation of Aristotle to the Bible or vice versa constitutes a leitmotif of the debates among theologians of the Reformation, and even, arguably, of many disputes between Thomists and theologians of other schools today. Though a detailed investigation of this question exceeds the limits of the

---

144. See the sections earlier in this chapter, "Thomas's Aristotelian Framework" and especially "Thomas's Science of Friendship."

current project, we have already suggested that the place of Scripture in Thomas's own account of friendship seems at least to be subtly relativized, if by no means completely undermined, within its thoroughgoing Aristotelian superstructure. On the other hand, as we have also indicated, Thomas's concern to explain and defend the contents of written revelation in rational terms is one of his chief motivations for composing *ST*. Viewed from this perspective the wholesale reception of Aristotle by the West during the thirteenth century was entirely fortuitous, providing Thomas with the superlative tool for accomplishing such a defense.

Undoubtedly some of Thomas's greatest contributions to a Christian theological interpretation of friendship are precisely coterminous with the scholastic character of his account. Thus, his consistent use of terms and the cogency of his treatment of friendship, both internally, under the narrower rubrics of love and charity examined above and, more broadly, as an integral element of a comprehensive and systematic account of Christian belief and practice, are formal tributes to his scholastic training, a fact in no way detracting from the power of his original insight. Indeed, Thomas's theological account of friendship displays all five of the general characteristics of scholastic theology, particularly as contrasted with monastic theology, enumerated in our first chapter.[145] First, notwithstanding Thomas's concern to elucidate Scripture, his account is rendered deliberately in a non-biblical style. He eschews the "scriptural argumentation"[146] so typical of the patristic and monastic traditions, not to speak of these traditions' tendencies to indulge in frequent, even extended, allegorizing of the Bible. Instead, he imports biblical texts, either as authoritative prooftexts or as surds or enigmas needing explanation, into an elaborate argument wholly of his own design, the explicit impetus and formal determinant of which is human rationality, albeit circumscribed by the tenets of credal Christian faith. Second, Thomas consistently favors directness and clarity over any sort of "poetic" expression of the point at hand.[147] Third, in keeping with and in fact underlying these two stylistic aspects of his presentation, Thomas

---

145. See the section "Differences between Monastic and Scholastic Theology: Genre" in chapter 1, above.

146. See the section "Aelred's Friendly Exegesis" in chapter 2, above.

147. Notwithstanding the notoriously prosaic style of Thomas's *quaestio*, however, a tantalizing line of inquiry is suggested by the frequency and indispensability of the word *conveniens* (*convenientia*, etc.) in his theological vocabulary: the ubiquity of the formulation "it is fitting" implies an *aesthetic* character to his theology which has surely been underestimated by his students for more than seven centuries.

strives for the highest degree of scientific neutrality attainable within the limits of human linguistic expression. His constant pursuit of the demonstrable proposition aims at bringing the intellect to rest, and with it, ultimately, the intellectual appetite, or will.[148] Fourth, as a function of the preceding commitment, Thomas maintains a strict personal detachment from his subject matter, as already noted above. The sense of Thomas's personal self-distancing from the text is paradoxically heightened by his magisterial *Respondeo*, delivered formally in the first person, yet at no time making explicit appeal to his own experience: the grammatical first person effectively constitutes more of a *persona* than it does a sign transparent to the psychological person of Thomas Aquinas. Fifth and finally, Thomas's theological account of friendship may be characterized above all as an effort to move men's minds to intellectual conviction through logical demonstration. For all his debt to Saint Augustine, Thomas opts definitively against the Augustinian theological mode, dear to so many monastic authors, of persuasion through a combination of logical argument and rhetorical skill. Instead, Thomas attempts through strictly rational argumentation, albeit from first principles provided by revelation, to validate his taut definition of charity as man's friendship for God. So doing, he fashions one of the most elegant microcosmic pieces of his much more comprehensive theological enterprise, epitomizing at the same time the fundamental theological approach of thirteenth century scholasticism at its acme.

Having now completed our presentation of St. Thomas's account of the theology of friendship, we arrive at the concluding chapter of this dissertation. Here we shall assess the relative merits of the two accounts we have examined, those of Saint Aelred of Rievaulx and of Saint Thomas Aquinas. The conclusions of this analysis will help us to establish in turn certain claims regarding the relative strengths and weaknesses of monastic and scholastic theological approaches in general.

---

148. Whatever protests may be made to the contrary, we maintain that the thoroughgoing systematization of theology inevitably militates against open embrace of the intrinsically erotic character of the Christian theological enterprise. This thesis will be developed further in our final chapter.

4

Aelred and Thomas Compared
Analysis, Conclusions, Final Speculations

The distinct accounts we have presented, along with the conclusions we have already drawn with respect to each of those accounts independently, must now be brought together and evaluated relative to each other. This final task, almost wholly internal,[1] will be accomplished by setting side

---

1. Since Jean Leclercq's death and thereby the completion of his magnificent lifework, no one has stepped forward to carry on a serious, systematic engagement between monastic and scholastic theology, in either historical or speculative terms. As for the specific theological question of friendship, few scholars have even been inclined to bring detailed treatments of *both* Aelred *and* Thomas together in work concerning this theological *topos*. Though Paul Wadell appeals occasionally to Aelred's work within his broader Thomistic account, these appeals, unlike our own, are made largely for purposes of exhibiting resonances between the two accounts. Moreover, Wadell displays no interest in opening a symmetrical dialogue between the two authors. The most important contributor to the modern discussion of the medieval theology of friendship on its own terms may be Richard Egenter, who indeed includes treatments of both Thomas and Aelred in his major work, *Gottesfreundschaft*. However, as his title indicates, along with the scholastic discussion, he is interested not in *monastic* accounts of friendship *qua* monastic, but rather in "mystical" accounts, among which Aelred's has an important place. Thus, concern with the monastic milieu and with how monks do theology *as monks* is somewhat beside the point for Egenter. Furthermore, Egenter's project is driven by a desire to articulate an *inclusive* medieval theological account of friendship. Consequently, he weaves together the contributions of monks, secular clerics and friars into a harmonious whole, rather than thematizing the differences among these accounts— either on their own terms, or as indicative of more fundamental differences between their respective approaches to theological activity. See, especially, his concluding chapter, "Die Gottesfreundschaft auf ihrem Wege durchs 12. und 13. Jahrhundert," 256–90. Finally, a

by side our analyses of the theological accounts of friendship offered by Aelred of Rievaulx and Thomas Aquinas and comparing them, first in terms of content, and then in terms of form. Through this comparative analysis we shall be able to draw certain conclusions about the relative merits of these accounts, and finally to arrive at a vantage point from which it will be possible to assess the implications of these local conclusions for a more far reaching comparison between monastic and scholastic theology.

Content of the Two Accounts Compared

Relations between the Major Texts within Each Account

We will recall from chapter 2[2] that Aelred gives us first a treatise on charity, *SC*, locating friendship in its proper place within the bounds of a more comprehensive account of love according to its supernatural determination, elevated by grace. Subsequently, he offers his briefer work, *SA*, a series of dialogues on the more focused topic of spiritual friendship. Thomas Aquinas, on the other hand, as recounted in chapter 3,[3] begins his most systematic theological account of friendship with an exposition of the passion of love in natural terms, in the *Prima Secundae*. Later, in the *Secunda Secundae*, he completes his account by making friendship the genus of which charity is that peculiar—and most eminent—form specified as "with God." Several observations may be made regarding our authors' very different arrangements of their respective texts.

First, Thomas's account of friendship in the *Secunda Pars* provides an excellent example of the well-known Thomistic thesis that grace builds on nature. Thus, Thomas only unveils, and then unpacks, his magnificent definition of supernatural charity in terms of friendship *after* he has explicated the foundation of his argument on the natural plane. Aelred's account, on the other hand, can be argued to take place entirely, at least in some sense,

---

dissertation by Antonio Pietro, *De la experiencia de la amistad al misterio de la caridad: estudio sobre la evolución histórica de la amistad como analogía teológica desde Elredo de Rieval hasta Santo Tomás de Aquino* (Madrid: Facultad de Teología San Dámaso, 2007), was not available for consideration as of this writing. From the title, Pietro's approach would appear to be somewhat like that of Egenter: inclusive and harmonizing, construing friendship to be a unifying theme, rather than, as per our thesis, one embodying important distinctions between two medieval contexts.

2. See, especially, "*Speculum caritatis* and *De spiritali amicitia*" in chapter 2, above.
3. See, especially, "*Prima Secundae* and *Secunda Secundae*" in chapter 3, above.

Aelred and Thomas Compared

on the supernatural plane, or better: in the manifest light of revelation. It may be correctly observed that Aelred discusses also, for example, friendships that fall short of the ideal of spiritual friendship. Such avenues, however, are never presented as *natural* shortfalls or aberrations. Rather, they are explored only in order to foreground more clearly, by way of contrast, the Christian ideal Aelred is attempting to elucidate.

Second, in view of his theological climax in the *Secunda Secundae*, Thomas's comments on friendship in the context of his discussion of the passion of love in the *Prima Secundae* may be seen at least in some sense as preparatory, or anticipatory, vis-à-vis his later theological development of the notion. In Aelred's presentation, on the other hand, charity is expounded first and in such a way that spiritual friendship tends to appear as the culmination, both in this life and in more exalted terms in the life to come, of the theological virtue and activity of charity. It must be noted that the difference just described is not strictly symmetrical, inasmuch as Thomas prepares for his account of charity as friendship with God *not* with an exposition of spiritual friendship between men, but rather with a careful explanation of natural human psychology. Nevertheless, the symmetrical relation between texts is maintained to a significant extent, inasmuch as the counterpart to each author's principal discussion of supernatural charity is a treatment dealing on the whole with a love relation between human subjects, whether in natural (Thomas) or supernatural (Aelred) terms. Therefore the corresponding *a*symmetry regarding the place of human friendship in the two accounts, between preparation/anticipation on the one hand and culmination on the other, remains interesting.

Third, as noted in our second chapter, both of Aelred's texts were composed at the request of another: in the case of *SC*, his canonical superior, St. Bernard, in the case of *SA*, a young monk from a neighboring abbey loosely under Abbot Aelred's supervision. The important point here is that, no matter Aelred's skill as a writer and theologian, the order of his theological presentation of friendship was to a certain extent imposed upon him from without. In Thomas's account of friendship, on the other hand, the order of all the elements has been meticulously choreographed by the author alone, within the grand sweep of his moral theology, which in turn has its precisely balanced place within the even vaster theological enterprise of *ST*. On many other occasions, Thomas, like Aelred, composed theological or philosophical works at the behest of others, whether superiors, peers, or disciples. In the case of the internal structure of the *Summa*, however, the initiative is all his own. Thomas's systematic theological account of friendship, then, is driven entirely and deliberately by an interior idea, whereas Aelred's ordering of his thought is directly determined, at least in part, by the interests of others. Consequently, the latter author's work has to some degree an arbitrary or accidental character, at least at the junction between his two major works on friendship.

When these three points are considered together, we may inaugurate the work of this concluding chapter by cautiously putting forward the following unifying proposition: Whereas Thomas gives us an account of friendship that highlights the ideal relation between nature and supernature, in which the latter perfects the former, Aelred is somewhat more concerned, at least *prima facie*, to expound friendship in anthropological terms, *yet in the light of grace* (and, somewhat proleptically, *of glory*). Granted the risks of oversimplification, this framing proposition can nonetheless help us to sift through the maze of varying emphases in our two authors' works, with all the incumbent nuances, through the following sections of our analysis.

Relations between [Love,] Friendship and Charity

The brackets in the title of this section recall the fact that, whereas our chapter on Thomas was explicitly occupied with all three of these terms and their interrelations,[4] love—*amor*—was not thematized in the relevant discussion of Aelred's account.[5] We have already noted that for Aelred a considerable semantic overlap obtains among the terms *amor*, *caritas*, and even *dilectio*.[6] The simple fact of the matter is that Aelred is not a systematician and does not attempt to proceed "scientifically" with regard to terminological precision. His largely monastic readership has at least an intuitive grasp of what *amor* is and knows that this broad notion is somewhat better expressed by different words at different times. Knowing his audience, Aelred consequently does not seek technical restrictions on his key terms, so much as to paint a compelling picture of the aspect of Christian life in question, composing and shading various important elements of his account more or less prominently within that overall picture.

---

4. See the sections "Love and Frienship" and "Love, Friendship, and Charity" in chapter 3, above.

5. See the section "Friendship and Charity" in chapter 2, above.

6. See chapter 2, n. 58 (p. 58), above.

In contrast, Thomas's account relies heavily on the precise definition and use of just those terms among which Aelred allows such fluidity. Thus, as we have seen, an exact understanding of *amor* in natural psychological terms is the indispensable raw material from which Thomas, now fixing Aristotle in the bright light of revelation, fashions his splendid notion of *caritas* in terms of *amicitia*. For Thomas, then, friendship is revealed to be the genus of which charity is the most exalted species, differentiated from all other specific instances of friendship in virtue of the qualification "with God."[7] More precisely and explicitly, charity is the friendship *of man* with God. From Thomas's prior delineation and explanation of the two movements of every love, *amor concupiscentiae* and *amor amicitiae*, we know that love of friendship is essentially the wishing of good to someone for his own sake (where concupiscent love is the love experienced toward the good wished for someone). Thus we can say that charity, or man's friendship with God, is in Thomas's view man's love of God for His own sake, founded on the *communicatio* of God's own happiness, in which we are invited to participate.[8]

For Aelred, on the other hand, charity is not conceived as a particular kind of friendship. Rather, Aelred strikingly identifies divine charity with sabbath rest. As he proceeds to expound his original doctrine of the three sabbaths in these terms, Aelred appears to locate [spiritual] friendship most properly within the second sabbath, that of fraternal charity, or rest in one's neighbor. Though he will eventually extend and expand his idea of spiritual friendship significantly in *SA*, it is enough here to observe that from first to last Aelred conceives the theological notion of friendship as subordinate to that of charity, rather than as a more universal category of which charity is a specific instance, in the way that Thomas envisions the relationship. The respective relations among the key terms of our two accounts of friendship thus continue to confirm our provisional schematization of those accounts: whereas Thomas construes charity as the ideal, analogical, supernatural expression of his carefully delineated definition of friendship between the naturally virtuous, Aelred is particularly attentive to graced friendship between men.

---

7. See the section "Love, Friendship, and Charity" in chapter 3, above.
8. See ibid.

Theologizing Friendship

Christological or Transcendent?

When it comes to assessing more precisely the specific *theological* character peculiar to each account, we recall from chapter 2 that Aelred always understands true friendship in the most profoundly christological terms.[9] Thus, spiritual friendship "is begun in Christ, and is advanced according to Christ, and by Christ is perfected."[10] Indeed, what differentiates true friendship from its pale adumbration among virtuous pagans is precisely its Christ-centeredness. Moreover, Christ is the bridge or channel from holy friendship between Christians to union with God, incarnate in none other than Christ himself. For

> a friend praying to Christ on behalf of his friend, and for his friend's sake desiring to be heard by Christ, directs his attention with love and longing to Christ; then it sometimes happens that quickly and imperceptibly the one love passes over into the other, and coming, as it were, into close contact with the sweetness of Christ himself, the friend begins to taste his sweetness and to experience his charm.[11]

In chapter 3, on the other hand, we discovered that Thomas's theological account of friendship, though one as thoroughly caritative at its foundation as that of Aelred, is typically oriented to the indivisible Godhead, notwithstanding occasional christological notes.[12] Thus, while we have remarked on the irregular evidence of christological and even pneumatological dimensions of Thomas's theology of friendship, we maintain that he has on the whole put his unique understanding of the notion of *amicitia* at the disposal of a doctrine of charity more attentive to God in his unitive essence than to any one or another of the Divine Persons.[13]

---

9. See the sections "Spiritual Frienship is Christological" and "The Communal, Trinitarian and Eschatological Dimensions of Friendship" in chapter 2, above.

10. In Christo inchoari, et secundum Christum produci, et a Christo perfici. *SA* I.10 (my translation).

11. pro amico orans Christum, et pro amico volens exaudiri a Christo, ipsum diligenter et desideranter intendit; cum subito et insensibiliter aliquando affectus in affectum transiens, et quasi e vicino ipsius Christi dulcedinem tangens, incipit gustare quam dulcis est, et sentire quam suavis est. *SA* III.133.

12. See the section "Thomas's Theology of Friendship is 'Transcendent'" in chapter 3, above.

13. This is apparent in the economic dimension, too, as evidenced by Thomas's disinclination in the *Tertia Pars* to think of the Incarnation as embodying *Christ's* friendship with men. Instead, he describes it as the remedy provided us by *God*, our divine friend,

Aelred and Thomas Compared

It must be observed that in de-emphasizing the christological, at least in his most mature and systematic theological treatment of friendship, Thomas would appear to undermine somewhat the cogency of that treatment, insofar as the ideal relation between nature and supernature, delineated by Thomas as the friendship of man for God, is surely a relation superlatively mediated by[14] the God-Man, Jesus of Nazareth. Nevertheless, inasmuch as the divine gift of charity that is man's friendship for God gradually moves man all the way from his natural state, through the condition of grace *in via*, and ultimately to union with God in his Essence in glory, the transcendent cast of Thomas's theology remains consistent with the schema proposed above. In Aelred's account, on the other hand, the God-Man is always the friend *par excellence* of every Christian soul, present when two or more Christian friends gather in his name,[15] and accomplishing in and through himself the eventual incorporation of true friendships into the beatified communion of saints. As such, Christ, for Aelred, is himself the light of grace illuminating and transforming friendship shared between virtuous men.

Johannine or Aristotelian?

In chapter 2, we remarked the distinctly Johannine quality of Aelred's theology of friendship.[16] This characterization was based principally upon the centrality to Aelred's account of Christ's two famous references to friendship in the part of his farewell discourse recounted in John 15. We observed that Aelred wrestles with the value of John 15:13, "Greater love has no man than this, that a man lay down his life for his friends," as a criterion for recognizing friendship. Ultimately, however, we discovered that he sets far

---

who is not even specified here as Father. Cf. the section "Thomas's Theology of Friendship is 'Transcendent'" in chapter 3, n. 106 (p. 118).

14. In lieu of "mediated by," it is tempting to go so far as to say "epitomized" or "personified by." Such formulations, however, open up the complex question of whether, and how, the hypostatic union between Christ's divine and human natures might in any legitimate sense be construed as a sort of friendship. Our intuition is that the proposal has the whole weight of Chalcedonian orthodoxy against it, though a nuanced "Nestorian" Christology, of the sort still upheld by the modern-day Church of the East, might accommodate the idea, if only in metaphorical terms.

15. See *SA* I.1.

16. See the section "The Johannine Character of Aelred's Theology of Friendship" in chapter 2, above.

greater store by the sharing of secrets between true friends, a sharing that finds its theological warrant at John 15:15, in Christ's intimate revelation to his disciples of "all that I have heard from the Father." In the fact that it is precisely on the basis of this intimate disclosure[17] that Christ christens his former servants friends we recognize the grounds for Aelred's close association between the mutual sharing of secrets and the perfect union of will and ideas that epitomizes spiritual friendship.

In Thomas's case, on the other hand, we observed the marginalization of these two key Johannine texts within the context of his argument in the *Secunda Pars*.[18] Moreover, his recognition in *Iohannis* of the importance of the theme of the sharing of secrets between friends does not resurface in his systematic account of friendship in the *Summa*. In short, the core of Thomas's theological account of friendship is not constructed along Johannine, or even more broadly, along biblical lines. Rather, we contend that the fundamental framework within which Thomas works out his theology of friendship is the philosophy of Aristotle. This position accords with the research of Guy Mansini, Paul Wadell and David Gallagher.[19]

Neither Aelred's choice nor Thomas's in this connection is surprising, given their respective milieux. On one side, the patristic theology inherited and embraced by the monks of the twelfth century was always most at home in a biblical idiom. In Aelred's particular case, the desire to expound the value and beauty of human friendship when it is centered in Christ inevitably recalled to his mind the prototypical friendship initiated by Christ himself with his disciples, especially as recorded in the Gospel of John. Furthermore, John 15:15 seemed to provide authoritative justification for Aelred's cherished notion that the sharing of secrets is a mark of the most intimate friendship.[20] Thus, the Johannine coloring of Aelred's whole account brings us back continually to his point of departure: human friendship in the light of grace. In the scholastic context, on the other hand, Aristotle was the order of the day in the latter half of the thirteenth century, though certainly Thomas achieved an integration of the Stagyrite's philoso-

---

17. A disclosure inevitably bound up with Christ's own self-disclosure. See chapter 2, n. 49, above (p. 25).

18. See "Thomas's Theology of Friendship is 'Transcendent'" in chapter 3, above.

19. Cf. the section "Thomas's Aristotelian Framework" in chapter 3, above.

20. William Young attributes this association to the monastic appropriation of the Stoic tradition, in which secret-sharing was understood to pertain to the cooperative "cultivation of interior virtue" between friends. See Young, *The Politics of Praise*, 109–10. Cf. also chapter 3, n. 43, above (p. 100).

phy far excelling the efforts of any of his peers. In view of our schematization of Thomas's theology of friendship as the ideal perfecting of nature by supernature, his Aristotelian framework ought to be understood as being illumined and even transformed in some sense by the light and content of revelation. Nevertheless, we cannot ignore the degree to which the biblical witness itself has been bracketed out of the mainstream of Thomas's argumentation, seeming almost to interlope at times, given the *ad hoc* character of its employment.

The Order of Charity

The meaning of charity is central to the theological accounts of friendship of both Aelred and Thomas, notwithstanding the very different ways the two authors explicate the relationship between *amicitia* and *caritas*. In both cases an important element of the theological exposition of charity is the way it determines the proper order of the will's movement of love[21] towards its three chief objects, self, neighbor and God. Accordingly, recalling the relevant sections from chapters 2 and 3,[22] we must now summarize Aelred's doctrine of the three sabbaths, by which he accounts for this caritative hierarchy, along with Thomas's systematic presentation of the order of charity in the *Secunda Secundae*, especially in Question 26. Of particular interest here will be the place of the love of self in each account, as well as the two authors' distinctive treatments of the love of enemies.

In one of the many splendid ejaculations he addresses to God throughout the course of SC, Aelred exclaims: "Those who love you, rest in you. And there is true rest, true tranquillity, true peace, a true sabbath for the mind."[23] Thus, Aelred articulates in general terms his identification of sabbath rest with man's love of God (and ultimately, with God Himself). He then proceeds to parse out this dense theological insight according to the biblical typology of the three sabbaths: the seventh day, the seventh year and the fiftieth or jubilee year. Each of these sabbaths in turn corresponds

---

21. We recall that this particular love, comprising the movement of the rational appetite, is strictly termed *dilectio* by St. Thomas, a term employed by Aelred as well, though with less consistency.

22. See the section "Aelred's Doctrine of the Three Sabbaths" in chapter 2 and "The Order of Charity" in chapter 3, above.

23. SC I.18.52. For the Latin, see chapter 2, n. 89, above (p. 66).

to a different expression of supernatural charity in the graced soul, namely, the love of self, of neighbor, and of God.

Like Thomas, Aelred recognizes the natural primacy of self-love over love of others, as well as its evangelical privilege according to Matthew 22:39, at the same time advising great caution against its tendency to dissolve into cupidity. Granted the dangers, however, a properly cultivated love of self brings with it "purity of conscience" and as such provides the necessary foundation for charity's "increase" in the love of others, symbolized by the seventh, or sabbath year.[24]

In connection with this second sabbath, we noted the peculiar importance for Aelred of two biblical passages: Acts 4:32—"Now the company of those who believed were of one heart and soul, and no one said that any of the things which he possessed was his own, but they had everything in common."—and Psalm 132:1—"Behold, how good and how pleasant it is when brothers dwell in unity." We observed, too, that such fraternal charity is not to be taken as necessarily synonymous with spiritual friendship. Indeed, according to Aelred it is the love of enemies, rather than of friends "which constitutes the summit of fraternal charity." There is, however, this striking caveat in Aelred's understanding of the charitable love of one's enemy: it is possible, thinks Aelred, precisely through one's courageous love and forgiveness of one's enemy, a love that requires giving up one's own anger and sin, to find oneself forgiven and loved in return, whereupon former enemies may actually become friends.[25]

Finally, there is the jubilee year, the sabbath of sabbaths, symbolizing rest in the love of God himself. In pointing out the soul's easiest path to this most desirable of all rests, Aelred again sounds the christological note, prescribing meditation on the life, passion and death of Jesus. The mystical union with the Godhead so attained, in subtle analogy to the Incarnation, constitutes the fulfillment of charity at the same time that it "inclines us toward and fosters" the "twin love" of self and neighbor.[26] Thus, Aelred's order of charity can be said to be dynamic. Developing organically from rest in love of one's own, single, self, through rest in love of many human souls, and arriving at last at perfect rest in God, at the same time, mysteriously, it is the love of God that moves us to love ourselves and others in the first place. It may finally be stated that if charity is true friendship's

---

24. See *SC* III.6.19. Cf. also chapter 2, n. 112 (p. 71).
25. See *SC* III.4.11.
26. See *SC* III.5.13.

necessary, albeit not sufficient, condition, then the stratified sabbath-rest in which charity consists is the *sine qua non* of a mature and vibrant spiritual friendship.

Turning to Thomas's account, we recall the primacy of self-love before all other loves in the natural order. To this extent, Thomas and Aelred are in complete accord. A significant divergence takes place between the two authors, however, when love is considered from the supernatural perspective. In place of the dynamism just observed in Aelred's account, Thomas asserts an ontologically inflexible hierarchy among the soul's movements under the influence of grace.[27] Thus, as we noted in the section "The Order of Charity" in chapter 3, charity, or friendship for God, *is* itself a love of God that grounds and exceeds all other loves, namely, man's loves for his fellow creatures. In metaphysical terms, this love is explained as the part's love for the whole of which it is a part: God is the common good of all and is consequently loved by each of his creatures in virtue of its participation in this common good. Since charity properly elicits love for other rational beings,[28] the only order that remains for Thomas to establish is the priority of man's love for himself over his love for his neighbor. Again, Thomas explains this priority in light of a more fundamental metaphysical distinction. Whereas self-unity, or ontological identity, dictates that one love oneself as *oneself* participating in the divine good, the mere associative unity obtaining between oneself and any other created participant in that original good necessarily entails a love subordinate to the love of self.

There are, however, neighbors and there are neighbors. As with Aelred, the neighbor who is an enemy particularly engages Thomas's attention.[29] Through a series of finely nuanced distinctions, Thomas elucidates different modes by which the will may be disposed lovingly towards one's enemy; three of these modes are legitimate, while another is excluded. Thus, it is perverse to love one's enemy *qua* enemy, since this amounts to loving what is evil in another. One ought, on the other hand, to love one's enemy as belonging to the formal object of charity (God), as much as one ought to love any other neighbor. Furthermore, Thomas says that charity requires more specifically that we be prepared even to love enemies individually, "should the necessity occur." Finally, Thomas contends that the "*actual* and

---

27. See the section "The Order of Charity" in chapter 3, above.

28. and not for irrational ones. See *ST* 2-2.26.

29. See *ST* 2-2.25.8. See also the section "Love, Friendship, and Charity" in chapter 3, above.

gratuitous" love of one's enemies "for God's sake" belongs to the perfection of charity. In this last ascription, Thomas echoes Aelred's opinion that love of enemies "constitutes the summit of fraternal charity." Unlike Aelred, however, Thomas strikingly omits consideration of the possibility that such a love could on occasion transform enemies into friends. It is possible that this difference comprises an instance of the greater rigor in Thomas's terminology inevitably smuggling in a tendency towards *stasis*, thereby militating against the kind of conceptual dynamism congruent with Aelred's more fluid theological language. Whatever the explanation, the enemy remains for Thomas a strictly circumscribed, if highly important, sub-category of the neighbor, whereas for Aelred, the enemy is unveiled as one capable through love and forgiveness of becoming a genuine friend.

In their respective treatments of the ordering of charity, Aelred and Thomas are essentially consistent with our proposed schematization. In accord with the heading itself of Question 26 of the *Secunda Secundae*, Thomas's ordering of charity can only pertain strictly to one side of the nature-supernature divide. Nevertheless, his definition of charity as friendship *for God* implies that the loves at stake in this hierarchy are the perfect analogates of natural loves he has already elucidated in the relevant questions of the *Prima Secundae*. In Aelred's case, the typology of the three sabbaths, though often explicated by appeal to the human relationships of Aelred's own experience, is expounded as precisely coterminous with supernatural charity. Consequently, Aelred is once again seen to be especially preoccupied with anthropology and human psychology *in the light of grace*: human love heaven-bound.

Dramatic or Scientific?

We come now to a comparison between those aspects of the theological presentations of Aelred and Thomas that we characterized as dramatic and scientific, respectively.[30] As we saw in the section entitled "Aelred's Theology of Friendship is Dramatic" in chapter 2, the dramatic character of Aelred's major works proves to be something more than an effective way of grabbing a reader's attention, though it can indeed have that benefit, and may even have been designed in part for that purpose. In fact, what is at some level certainly a stylistic device expresses in literary form the

---

30. See the sections entitled "Aelred's Theology of Friendship is Dramatic" in chapter 2 and "Thomas's Science of Friendship" in chapter 3, above.

genuinely dramatic character of the author's chief themes, specifically, of charity and friendship. Hence, the dialogues between Abbot Aelred and several other monks of his community that make up *SA* not only comprise the forum in which Aelred's notion of spiritual friendship is aired and developed. Rather, these dialogical encounters actually embody glimpses of what virtuous Christian friendship ought to look like. In a similar way, Aelred uses his lament for Simon at the end of book one of *SC* to display his own struggle to regulate his *affectus* for a lost friend with *ratio*, in light of the true dictates of faith, hope and charity. Finally, at the end of *SA*, he recalls again, this time at a much greater chronological remove, his friendship with Simon. With the wisdom of years, this youthful friendship has become the foil, lovely yet lacking in depth, for the mature friendship, described at length, with another monk who has died. In his marvelous, theologically dense peroration, Aelred counts this friendship "a foretaste of blessedness; . . . to wing one's flight aloft to that more sublime splendor of divine love, and by the ladder of charity now to mount to the embrace of Christ Himself; and again to descend to the love of neighbor, there pleasantly to rest."[31] With this literary performance, Aelred mounts simultaneously towards the twofold climax, both dramatic and eschatological, of his theological account of friendship; not coincidentally, it can also be seen as the crowning moment of his whole theological enterprise.

Thomas's theological presentation of friendship, on the other hand, especially in its most cogent and comprehensive form in the *Secunda Pars*, is the antithesis of dramatic. Instead of drama, Thomas offers the most polished expression of scientific inquiry the thirteenth century could muster. In microcosmic articulation of his approach throughout the *Summa*, he integrates cutting-edge research in pagan philosophy into an exhaustive familiarity with the whole Christian Tradition, using the tools of the former to unpack the conclusions embedded in the first principles drawn from the latter. As we noted in the section "Thomas's Science of Friendship" in chapter 3, Thomas's scientific rigor has a significant impact on the content of his theological project, just as the dramatic structure of Aelred's works inevitably conveys the dramatic character of the author's theological ideas. Thus, Aelred's spiritual friendship is as dynamic as his literary style and dramatically oriented to the beatified communion of saints. In the same way, *mutatis mutandis*, true friendship in Thomas's account gradually reveals itself as an airtight scientific concept: the mutual willing by virtuous

---

31. *SA* III.127. For the Latin, see chapter 2, n. 121, above (p. 74).

persons of each other's good, each for the other's own sake. Furthermore, this concept is ultimately subordinated to an equally rigorous account of supernatural charity, in which friendship is unveiled as the underlying genus. In consequence of this mode of presentation, we further observed that the concept of friendship, like all concepts in such an account, tends to harden somewhat, thereby preemptively excluding more fluid or dynamic expressions of the phenomenon betokened in the name.[32] More generally, though concomitantly, we remarked Thomas's disinclination to any poetic or romantic notions of friendship, along with his avoidance of appeals to personal experience. Thomas seeks an accurate and precise theological account of love, friendship and charity and believes that the best mode for obtaining this objective is scientific detachment and the consequent neutralization of any explicit personal involvement.

At this point it becomes possible to raise the following question: *is friendship something more like Aelred's dynamic, dramatic notion, or, rather, more like Thomas's scientific idea?* Correlatively, if we answer in favor of one or the other accounts, to what extent does it matter, if at all, how a theologian articulates or *presents* this idea? To these questions we shall return in the presentation of our own final conclusions, below. We may conclude this section by commenting that both Aelred's dramatic and Thomas's scientific presentations serve admirably to round out the programmatic summaries of their respective accounts, proposed above. Thus, Aelred beautifully depicts the drama of friendship between souls enlightened by grace and redolent with the theological virtues. And Thomas with consummate skill trains his limpid Aristotelian lens on the principles of revelation, in order to chart the transformative course of the human soul from its natural beginnings to its perfection in eternal friendship with God.

The Communal, Trinitarian and Eschatological Dimensions of Friendship

The last part of our comparative analysis strictly confined to the content of our two authors' theological accounts of friendship[33] concerns friendship's

---

32. Such a hardening could serve, for example, to obstruct one's ability to see "enemy" and "friend" not merely as point-neighbors on a static spectrum, but rather as fluid personal descriptors with the phenomenological potential for overlap and conversion within the same spectrum, in the light of grace.

33. The following section on exegesis is not so-restricted, drawing partially on

Aelred and Thomas Compared

communal, trinitarian and eschatological dimensions. We shall proceed by briefly comparing Aelred's and Thomas's contributions regarding each of these dimensions in turn.[34] At the conclusion of the section we shall also comment, as in previous sections, on the ways the two authors do or do not confirm our proposed schemata, in connection with these various aspects of their accounts.

From beginning to end, Aelred's theology of friendship exhibits a profoundly communal dimension, one that is indicative of, among other things, its christological character. This is exemplified in the opening words of SA: "Here we are, you and I, and I hope a third, Christ, is in our midst."[35] Indeed, Christology for Aelred is one of the foundational theological matrices from which the communality of friendship derives. Another is Aelred's distinctive understanding of the doctrine of the divine likeness in man, according to which "there were created many of the same nature, so that in this manner also the likeness of the divine goodness, which pours out upon many, might appear through the mutual exchange of benefits."[36] Moreover, such benefits are not limited to the material order, but include the virtues as well, since God "causes each person to need the other and to have in the other what one does not possess in oneself. Thus humility is preserved, charity increased and unity recognized."[37] Our need for friends, then, is divinely inscribed in our very nature, and when we respond to that need through the generous activity of friendship, we reflect God's likeness, in respect of his self-diffusing goodness. In Thomas's case, on the other hand, we need only recall briefly the absence of evidence in his account of any *intrinsically* communal aspect of friendship, though communitarian extensions of the concept in such spheres as politics and ecclesiology are clearly among the implications of his doctrine.[38] Put simply, Thomas's explicit doctrine of friendship is essentially dyadic, on both the natural and supernatural planes.

---

material from elsewhere besides our main texts in both authors' cases.

34. See sections "The Communal, Trinitarian and Eschatological Dimensions of Friendship" in chapters 2 and 3 above.

35. SA I.1.

36. *Sermones inediti*, 108. For the Latin, see chapter 2, n. 125 (p. 76).

37. CCCM IIA: *Aelredi Rievallensis Sermones I–XLVI, Sermo VIII*, par. 10. For the Latin, see chapter 2, n. 125 (p. 76).

38. See the sections on "Christopher Malloy" and "The Communal, Trinitarian, and Eschatological Dimensions of Friendship" in chapter 3 above.

Theologizing Friendship

The answer to the question of whether Aelred's or Thomas's theology of friendship has a trinitarian expression can be predicted, to an extent, based on their respective interests in friendship's communal dimension, inasmuch as the Trinity may be strictly understood as a community of three Persons. Accordingly, we found stronger evidence of trinitarian thinking in Aelred's theology of friendship than in that of Thomas. In neither case is such a doctrine completely explicit, though Aelred ventures somewhat further in this direction, providing at least one extended trinitarian formulation that plainly evokes friendship among the divine Persons in the most lyrical terms.[39]

Finally, Aelred and Thomas share a deep appreciation of friendship's profoundly eschatological dimension, though the two thinkers express their respective ideas in very different ways, each characteristic of its author's general theological outlook. In Thomas's case, we saw that "the friendship of charity is founded upon the fellowship (*communicatio*) of eternal beatitude."[40] This amounts to an explanation of friendship in the classically scholastic terms of final causality, in which the sharing of eternal happiness constitutes the final cause towards which supernaturally infused *amicitia* (= *caritas*) unerringly moves and thereby receives its essential character. Aelred, on the other hand, gives us nothing less than a finely wrought eschatology of friendship, charting in wonderful detail the transition, always via Christ, from spiritual friendship on earth to participation in the inner trinitarian life in glory. In chapter 2 the section on "The Communal, Trinitarian and Eschatological Dimensions of Friendship," we showed how this transition, for Aelred, embodies subsequent analogical anticipations of trinitarian *perichoresis*. Proceeding from the comparatively limited material and spiritual interpenetration of spiritual friends in this life, through prayer, especially directed to Christ, the friendly soul gradually draws close to "the sweetness of Christ himself." After death, the soul completes this trajectory, coming to rest at last amid the communion of saints, within the inter-Personal life of God.

Recalling the proposed broad schematizations of our two authors' theological treatments of friendship, we may conclude the preceding analysis with a brief assessment of how well Aelred's and Thomas's engagements of the communal, trinitarian and eschatological aspects of friendship fit

---

39. See *SC* I.20.57. See also chapter 2, nn. 96 and 133, above (pp. 67, 78).

40. *ST* 2-2.25.10, *corp.* For the Latin, in addition to a list of similar citations, see chapter 3, n. 123, above (p. 122).

with these schemata. In Thomas's case, of course, there is little to say in the first two instances, given the lack of explicit development of either a communal or trinitarian articulation of his account. As for the eschatological dimension of friendship, Thomas's description of the friendship of charity as founded upon the *communicatio* of eternal beatitude is at least congruent with the framing principle of nature's perfection by supernature, only ratcheted up a notch: as grace perfects nature, so glory perfects what is given in grace. For Aelred, the thematic notion of human friendship in the light of grace is plainly operative in both the communal and eschatological aspects of his theology of friendship. The trinitarian dimension of his account, on the other hand, while it does not contradict our schema, stands as far beyond it as the divine does the human.

Friendly versus Useful Exegesis

Finally, we must briefly compare the exegetical practices of our two authors, as summarized in the relevant sections of chapters 2 and 3. This analysis will round out the comparison of our two authors' accounts at the level of content, at the same time providing a bridge to the questions more strictly concerning form to be taken up in the following part of this chapter.

In our inquiry into Aelred's relationship to Sacred Scripture, we discovered a congruence between this relationship and his understanding of true, or spiritual friendship.[41] Among the key points in our argument was the observation that Aelred, in one of his most sustained biblical exegetical undertakings, *Iesu puero*, addresses biblical personae from the passages with which he is dealing, as well as his reader, in intimately personal terms.[42] Secondly, we remarked Aelred's penchant, in keeping with the patristic legacy he had inherited, for extended allegorizing of biblical texts.[43] In this connection we noted that its *symbolic* character, in addition to its capacity for *narrative* expression in extended application, give allegory a profoundly *relational* cast. Such relationality, moreover, renders allegory more personal than the prooftext, wherein a biblical text is cited entirely out of context,

---

41. See the section "Aelred's Friendly Exegesis" in chapter 2, above.

42. The same tendency is predictably observed in Aelred's long abbatial prayer, *O. past.*, as well as, more sporadically, in *SC* and *SA*.

43. Among the most impressive examples are his treatment of Luke 2:41–52 in *Iesu puero* and the detailed allegorization of Gen 1:1—2:3 and Lev 23:3 and 25:3–4, 8 and 10, as the foundation for his theology of the three sabbaths, in *SC*.

typically to bolster a dogmatic proposition. It was also observed, however, that even Aelred's prooftexts never abstract impersonally from the biblical authors, human or divine. Rather, they are integrated seamlessly and organically into arguments which themselves inevitably proceed in the most concrete and personal terms, always in the first person and often in the mode of direct address, whether to the human reader, or to God himself. Finally, we detected in the background of Aelred's exegetical activity an intense awareness of the identification of the Word as revealed in Scripture with the Word Incarnate.[44] In consequence of this identification, we contend that for Aelred, friendship with the biblical text ought not to be construed as mere metaphor: rather the text *is* the living Word, upon whose breast the beloved disciple once reclined, and with whom Aelred spoke day by day.

Likewise, *mutatis mutandis*, we found the exegetical practice of Thomas Aquinas congruent with his theological doctrine of friendship. Thus, in the section of chapter 3 devoted to this topic,[45] we remarked Thomas's clear preference for citing doctrinal rather than historical texts (both in preaching and in his systematic works). We further noted his avoidance of allegory in favor of exposition of the literal sense. In addition, we commented on his frequent relegation of biblical passages cited in the *Summa* to either the *Sed contras* or the objections. We argued that this stringent circumscription implied one of only two common functions for Scriptural citation in the work: (1) in the objections, Scripture is cited in order to be explained or defended by Thomas on rational grounds, in either his *Respondeo* or in his replies to the objections; (2) in the *Sed contra*, Scripture is cited as an authoritative prooftext for the position he wishes to take.[46] Drawing these several observations together, we proposed that Thomas reads Scripture as an invaluable tool for understanding God, who is the primary object of the highest form of friendship. Since such an understanding as may be gained through prayerful reading of the Scriptures constitutes a good lovable for the lover's own sake and for the sake of others, we contend that St. Thomas exhibits *amor concupiscentiae* for the Bible, subordinated to the *amor amicitiae* he has for himself and his neighbor. To complete the picture, we recall that the

44. The original observation was made particularly with respect to *O. past.*, though the point can readily be generalized.

45. See the section "Thomas's Exegesis: *Lectio utilis?*" above.

46. At the same time being thereby sequestered from Thomas's actual theological argumentation. See our comments in "Thomas's Aristotelian Framework" and "Thomas's Sciecne of Friendship" in chapter 3, above.

source from which this latter love overflows is charity, Thomas's primary *amor amicitiae*, directed to God Himself.

Thomas's relationship to Scripture, then, appears to contrast rather sharply with that of Aelred. A more definitive evaluation, however, of the relative merits of these different fundamental assumptions, is best reserved for inclusion in our final comparative assessment of the two accounts *in toto*. For the time being, it is enough to say that the underlying theological assumptions we have attempted to expose in each author's exegetical practice conform well to the summary schematizations proposed at the outset of this chapter. Practically speaking, this completes our point-by-point comparative analysis of the content of our two authors' theological accounts of friendship.

Form of the Two Accounts Compared

We are now in a position to expand our analysis to include considerations of form. Our procedure will be straightforward, and similar to the one followed in the whole of the section above entitled "Content of the Two Accounts Compared." Thus, we shall again set Aelred's and Thomas's accounts side by side, only this time with an eye to a number of important formal distinctions between those accounts. Our chief aim for this section will be to show how these formal differences exemplify the distinctive ways monks and schoolmen typically pursue their respective theological enterprises *in general*. To carry out this task, we will have frequent recourse to chapter 1, especially to the summary characterizations of the two milieux with which we concluded the first major section of that chapter.[47] We will also appeal to our conclusions from chapters 2 and 3, and, as appropriate, to our findings in the preceding sub-sections of the current chapter.

Biblical versus Non-Biblical

In our close reading of the major texts in which Aelred works out his theology of friendship, we saw how thoroughly his thought is suffused with Scripture, not only at the level of the word, but with respect to the Bible's rich imagery as well. Indeed, Jean Leclercq's ascription of a *style biblique* to monastic theology in general applies admirably to Aelred's writing. That

---

47. See chapter 1 "Dialectics," above.

Theologizing Friendship

the whole theological project of the Abbot of Rievaulx may be aptly characterized as evincing such a biblical style is explained by Leclercq's comment that "monastic speculation is the outgrowth of the practice of monastic life, the living of the spiritual life which is the meditation on Holy Scripture."[48] Through the unceasing practice of *lectio divina*, Aelred's mind and heart came over time to be conformed to the very cadences and vocabulary of the biblical books. This was especially true in regard to the Psalms, though in fact, Aelred could call readily to mind and pen the minutest details of the Gospel narratives, as well as the whole sweep of the Pentateuch, the Davidic and Solomonic histories, the cries of the Prophets and the lush rhapsodies of the Song of Songs. In short, we can hardly resist the impression that Aelred, through exhaustive immersion in the texts of Scripture, managed in a sense to take up imaginative residence within a biblical idiom. The indispensability for the monk of a highly cultivated biblical imagination is further attested by Aelred's own insistence on protracted imaginative meditation, especially on the life of Christ.[49]

In stark contrast, Thomas, as we have seen, eschews "scriptural argumentation" and firmly declines to engage in allegorizing of the biblical text. As crucial as *sacra scriptura* is for his whole theological enterprise, it is strictly relegated to the *object* of that enterprise, while Thomas meticulously proscribes its subjective intrusion into the methods of his inquiry. Somewhat paradoxically, Thomas's concern, like that of the schoolmen in general, to engage the letter of the biblical text seriously on its own terms, entails a simultaneous *dis*engagement from that text as experienced in the full light of faith, namely, as the Living Word of God. Moreover, this disengagement seems to have been understood by Thomas as unavoidable for the successful execution of his project. Embroidering on Beryl Smalley, we might say that to look *at* the text, the schoolmen were convinced one must cease to look *through* it: the biblical lens that generates the biblical style of the Fathers and the monks, almost as a matter of course, must be set aside if one wishes to obtain from the text the fullness of doctrinal truths implicit there.[50] Granted, this wish on the part of the schoolmen arose in the main from the laudable desire to defend the Church and to help her pastors tend

---

48. Leclercq, *The Love of Learning*, 213.

49. See, e.g., the sections entitled "Aelred's Doctrine of the Three Sabbaths," n. 251, and "Aelred's Friendly Exegesis" in chapter 2, above.

50. Cf. Smalley, *The Study of the Bible*, 2. Cf. also the section "Differences between Monastic and Scholastic Theology" in chapter 1, above.

Aelred and Thomas Compared

and feed the Lord's flock. As noted in chapter 3 in the section on "Thomas's Exegesis: *Lectio utilis?*"[51] such "fodder" unquestionably counts as a very great good, willed by the theologian for himself and others. So formulated, the biblical theological enterprise becomes recognizable as an expression of *amor amicitiae* with respect to the persons to whom the good is wished, *amor concupiscentiae* with respect to the text itself. Nevertheless, we may well ask whether this approach to the sacred text does not in the end risk making it something less than it is. Aelred's inclination to identify the revealed with the Incarnate Word is, after all, hardly exceptional, even if he painted the picture in bold strokes. Ultimately, we must consider seriously whether the schoolmen, and even Thomas, in their adroit objectification of the Bible, did not begin to bring about its depersonalization as well.

Beautiful versus Clear

From beginning to end of his major works on charity and friendship, Aelred confirms Jean Leclercq's characterization of monastic theology as typically attentive to aesthetic considerations. Put more simply: *SC* and *SA* are beautiful. This is not merely a judgment regarding their subject matter, but one rendered especially on the *form* deliberately fashioned by Aelred into an ideal vessel for displaying his subject: love—under two different, but overlapping specifications, *caritas* and *amicitia*. What is more, the beauty of Aelred's work is not limited to lyrical paeans to spiritual friendship, though there are many of these. Nor is it confined to biblical theological meditations executed with the fine touch of a latter-day Christian Cicero, of which the extended allegory of the three sabbaths is no doubt the superlative example. Over and above even these superb centerpieces of his works, Aelred offers his readers literary constructions of subtle, yet irresistible charm. Granted, Aelred's aesthetic sensibilities may shine through more conspicuously in the skillfully crafted prologue and three dialogues of *SA*. Yet the patient, carefully balanced unfolding of his theme of *caritas*, the artful incorporation of the prolonged, and even more artful, eulogy to Simon at the end of book one, and the measured building to his splendid climax—all these elements of Aelred's *SC* easily render it the aesthetic rival to its sequel.[52] What

51. See also the section "Friendly versus Useful Exegesis" earlier in this chapter.

52. Though it did not warrant comment in chapter 2, Aelred also gives us in Book II, chapter 23 a wonderful instance of what must have been an anomalous aesthetic even in monastic theology: humor, in a form so exaggerated that it verges on slapstick. The

is certain from both works, not to speak of many others from Aelred's pen, is the intention and effort of the author to make them sensibly attractive to the potential reader.

In Thomas's systematic treatments of friendship and charity, on the other hand, we have seen the consistent preference for directness and clarity over any casual indulgence of literary artistry, poetic, imagistic or otherwise, in his effort to convey the theological or philosophical point at hand.[53] "Stripped of ornamentation and abstract, the scholastic language accepts words originating in a sort of unaesthetic jargon, provided only that they be specific."[54] To this broad generalization by Leclercq, Thomas's theological account of friendship constitutes no exception; rather, it is its epitome: precise terminology, spare grammatical construction, straightforward syntax, all in service of elucidating the truth. Indeed, the steadfast scholastic rejection of all aesthetic accoutrement, a rejection plainly endorsed by St. Thomas, at least in the vast majority of his work,[55] bespeaks a conviction that the truth will be sufficiently attractive in itself to draw the reader in. A curious pair of biblical images suggests itself here, in parallel to the divergent aesthetic dispositions we have been describing. To St. Thomas's bare truth, divested of all ornament, we might compare the Suffering Servant, who "had no form or comeliness that we should look at him" (Is. 53:2). Again, Aelred's beautifully adorned presentation may remind us of the ravishing bride of the Song of Songs, or for that matter, of her equally magnificent bridegroom. How ought we to adjudicate between two such compelling metaphors for theological exposition? Moreover, how well do the accounts so envisaged correspond formally to the theological notions they are intended to convey? We shall take these questions up for the last time when we draw together the conclusions of our whole comparative analysis below.

Erotic versus Scientifically Neutral

In addition to being beautiful, Aelred's theological works may readily be described as erotic. In more traditional Christian terms, the eros so palpable

---

occasion is a description of liturgical innovations of which Aelred clearly disapproves.

53. See, however, chapter 3, n. 147, above (p. 131).

54. Leclercq, *The Love of Learning*, 142.

55. Even, as we have seen, in his preaching. Only the occasional—and exquisite—hymn contravenes Thomas's absolute yielding of literary device to clarity of exposition.

Aelred and Thomas Compared

on every page of Aelred's texts is the desire for God driven by *compunctio*, that quality of the humble, contrite Christian soul so cherished by Gregory the Great.[56] In Leclercq's estimation such desire, rooted as it is in St. Augustine's Christian Platonism, profoundly shapes monastic theology in general.[57] Furthermore, monasticism's keen interest in the eschatological horizon of this desire also finds one of its great spokesmen in Aelred, as we saw in chapter 2 above, and again in the section in this chapter entitled "The Communal, Trinitarian and Eschatological Dimensons of Friendship." Indeed, Aelred's doctrine of spiritual friendship and the erotic character of his whole theological outlook converge in a distinctive eschatological vision: the glorified communion of saints enjoying universalized particular friendship—with one another, with the angels, and with God, the end of all human desire, who "shall be all in all."[58]

It is certainly right to observe that St. Thomas's entire theological project, like that of Aelred, is fundamentally driven by the desire for God. Nevertheless, Thomas, along with the rest of his thirteenth century scholastic colleagues, strove for a scientific neutrality that inevitably exposed the will as suspect, liable to compromise the purity of the intellect's hard-won conclusions.[59] Put more positively, Thomas's relentless pursuit of the indisputable proposition aims at bringing the intellect to rest, and with it, ultimately, the intellectual appetite, or will. In order to maintain clear sight of this goal, desire, even desire for God, must be severely bracketed from the investigation, however much it stands always in the background. On the other hand, Thomas succeeds in reinserting this desire into his account of charity as friendship, at least in propositional form. In his delineation of friendship's eschatological horizon as the *communicatio* of heavenly beatitude, Thomas, for the first time in our findings, significantly evades Leclercq's generalizations concerning scholasticism.[60] At the same time, he succeeds in elucidating, in the singularly un-erotic terms of scholastic science, man's desire for God as the final cause of his divinely infused love—thus *amicitia*—for God. Thus, Thomas accomplishes the curious feat

---

56. See chapter 1, n. 72, above (p. 30).

57. Ibid.

58. See *SA* III.134. See also "Conclusion: Aelred's Monastic Theology of Friendship" in chapter 2, above.

59. Cf. "Thomas's Science of Friendship" in this chapter.

60. See Leclercq, *The Love of Learning*, 220. Cf. also the section "Differences between Monastic and Scholastic Theology: Genre" in chapter 1, above.

of de-eroticizing the original Christian erotic. We may fairly ask what are the limits, if any, to the disparity between form and content of a theological text, beyond which the cognitive and spiritual dissonance likely to be engendered in the reader ought to be considered as proscriptive of the form in question. Given the genuine value of clarity in theological exposition, on the other hand, the dilemma is not an easy one to resolve.

Personal versus Impersonal

We have noted Aelred's ebullient personalism, not only in the dramatic execution of his major works on friendship and charity, but also in his distinctive procedure as a biblical exegete, especially in *Iesu puero* and *O. past*.[61] In each case, Aelred's literary activity may be described as personal in both psychological and grammatical senses. That is to say, Aelred's deep personal investment in his subject, as well as his earnest concern for the spiritual wellbeing of his readers, already evident in so many stylistic nuances, are made transparent by his frequent use of the first and second grammatical persons. In this respect as in so many others, Aelred exemplifies a mode of theological discourse common to the 12th century monastic milieu.

Thomas, on the other hand, in keeping with his commitment to scientific neutrality, adopts a perspective of complete personal detachment from his subject matter. As in Aelred's case, Thomas's stance can be described in both psychological and grammatical terms. Whatever a reader may believe to be Thomas's personal feelings or attitudes towards the many topics he takes up, evidence of such psychological states is not to be found in the text itself, at least of Thomas's systematic works. What may appear at first to be an embarrassing exception to this claim proves the rule eloquently, namely, the invariable use of the first person at the heart of the *quaestio*, in the formulation of Thomas's magisterial opinion. As we have already observed, the "I" in *ST*, while utterly consistent with what we know about the life of Thomas Aquinas, speaks not in the person of the man, but formally, objectively, as the mouthpiece of a thoroughly purified human Reason.[62] Once again, while granting all the benefits of lucidity, precision and objectivity in the theological enterprise, we pose the question here, as in the preced-

---

61. See the sections "Aelred's Theology of Friendship is Dramatic" and "Aelred's Friendly Exegesis" in chapter 2, above.

62. Albeit one presumably illuminated by divine grace. See "Thomas's Science of Friendship" in chapter 3, above.

ing section,[63] whether there is not a certain discord evident between the form of Thomas's scholastic discourse and his subject matter. However we are ultimately to appraise it, this incongruity contrasts remarkably with the harmony we have observed between the same two aspects of Aelred's presentation.

Persuasive versus Demonstrative

We concluded our summary characterization of monastic theology in chapter 1 by describing that theology as typically "sweet."[64] This designation effectively synthesizes the titular descriptions from the last three sections (beautiful, erotic, personal), both in general, and in the exemplary instance of Aelred. Spiritual sweetness pervades the texts of Aelred, not only as reflected in his frequent literal employment of forms of the words *suavis* and *dulcis*,[65] but also in virtue of his very tone. In the latter case, Aelred's habitually gentle turn of phrase and frequent flights of mellifluous prose, not to mention his impetuous eulogy at the death of a friend,[66] render *SC*, a would-be tedious treatise on one of the theological virtues, hardly less heavy with the sweetness of its burden than the honeyed dialogues of *SA*. But to what purpose? In elegant accord with the monastic theological tendency described in chapter 1, Aelred seeks tirelessly to enlist the power of *suavitas* in the service of an act of theological and spiritual per*suasion*. With his spiritual father St. Augustine, Aelred shares the intuition that the sweetness of God's Word, especially his Incarnate Word, Jesus, has the ultimate power to persuade, and so to win man's wayward heart to himself. Aelred's theological style expresses the conviction that the words produced by a member of Christ's Body, who is thereby an extension of Christ Himself, ought always, sweetly, to urge the sinner to conversion. Thus, Christology once more shows itself to be central to Aelred's account of friendship, determinative not only of much of its specific theological content, but even of its underlying form.

---

63. The question should be read as implied at the close of the section on beauty and clarity as well.

64. See chapter 1 the conclusion to the section on "Contemporary Scholarship," above.

65. For a range of Aelred's uses of both words, see, e.g., *SA* III.2–3, 127, 132, and 133 and *SC* I.20.57, III.4.12, 6.19, and 20.48, all previously cited, *et passim*.

66. See *SC* I.34.98–114.

Theologizing Friendship

In Thomas's case, the current chapter's three preceding descriptions of his theological account of friendship (clear, scientifically neutral, impersonal) may similarly be brought together under a single rubric, that of demonstrability. This characteristic scholastic approach inevitably precludes the *suavitas* so typical of Aelred's account. Simply put, Thomas's account of friendship and charity, like *ST* in general, constitutes an effort to move men's minds to intellectual conviction through logical demonstration. Though Thomas's debt to St. Augustine is no smaller than that of Aelred, he opts definitively against the Augustinian theological mode of persuasion through a combination of logical argument and rhetorical skill. Over against this approach, routinely employed by such great monastic authors as St. Bernard and St. Aelred, Thomas attempts through strictly rational argumentation, albeit from first principles provided by revelation, to validate his taut definition of charity as man's friendship for God. The outcome of Thomas's effort, for all its brilliance, presents us once more with the question of whether, and to what degree, the seeming dissonance between the form and content of his account mars the fruit? In the case of Aelred, who has deliberately forged just such a correspondence, it is fair to ask the correlative question: does a noteworthy degree of subjectivism, however carefully choreographed and circumscribed, interfere in the end with theological clarity?

Self-Descriptions of the Two Milieux

To complete this part of our chapter, let us recall one more way in which we previously dichotomized medieval theology along monastic and scholastic lines, namely, according to the various metaphors each milieu associated with its own theological activity. In the case of the monks, we noted numerous different images that pertained to food and eating: bees gathering and storing nectar, "lowly gleaners" collecting the leftovers of the harvest, "mumblers and munchers," ruminating on the divine words of Scripture.[67] On the side of the schools, we appealed to Bernard of Chartres's memorable "dwarfs perched on the shoulders of giants" and to the notion of the Beatific Vision so central to scholastic thought.[68] In short, whereas monasticism gravitates in its self-description towards images expressive

67. See "Differences between Monastic and Scholastic Theology" in chapter 1, above.
68. Ibid.

of the highly concrete sense of taste (and by extension, touch and smell), scholasticism privileges the most spiritual of the senses, that of sight. This difference, in turn, corresponds to a contrast between the fundamentally more experiential, tactile, aesthetic mode of being and thinking embraced by the monks, and the more strictly conceptual, abstract mode of thought cultivated in the scholastic milieu. By now, it will be abundantly obvious how well our two authors instance these general tendencies in their respective works, and specifically, in their theological accounts of friendship. The further question, in keeping with those raised above, is whether one or the other of these tendencies more aptly facilitates a true and accurate theological description of friendship and its relation to charity. With this question in mind, along with those raised in the preceding sections, we come to the last major part of this chapter and of the dissertation. Our procedure for this part will be first of all to lay out our final general conclusions. When this has been done, we will complete our work with a brief delineation of some challenges presented by each author's account to that of the other, as well as some speculative proposals for further investigation, based on our findings.

Conclusions, Challenges, Possible Avenues for Further Exploration

The final synthesis of our findings in this dissertation must be prefaced with a cautionary note, concerning precisely the type and scope of conclusions that admit of being validly drawn in the context of the project at hand. Our grounds for caution, adumbrated in Leclercq's work and confirmed by our own, are as follows: notwithstanding scholarly inclinations to draw the monastic and scholastic milieux of the twelfth and thirteenth centuries closer together[69]—inclinations that include Leclercq's own, albeit in dialectical tension with his major thesis—we must continue to insist on the increasing heterogeneity between the bodies of texts produced by those milieux during that period. An inevitable consequence of this heterogeneity is the implausibility of reaching conclusions that are cut and dried, or sweeping, and at the same time valid: reductionism risks watering down at least one or the other of the two perspectives, in order to provide a too-

---

69. Such inclinations are reflected to varying degrees in the influential works of David Knowles, James McEvoy, and R. W. Southern, as well as in the more narrowly focused project of Richard Egenter, to name a few.

Theologizing Friendship

facile composition from a single palette, finally falsifying both. Instead, we ought to attempt more modestly to descry some generalizations about the theological approaches and notions of each milieu, based on our findings in the works of Aelred and Thomas, and then to gesture cautiously towards possible aspects of the realities underlying these generalizations. To a great extent this is what Leclercq tried to do, though he did not pursue these tactics in connection with the in-depth consideration of any one particular theological *topos*, as we have done in the current study. Having dutifully issued this friendly word of warning to any reader anxious for radical or totalizing claims regarding such a complex and manifold subject as ours, let us proceed.

The Analogy of Friendship

Based on the whole range of our findings from the comparative analysis executed above, we propose that a loose three-way analogy obtains among friendship, reading and theology, on both sides of the monastic/scholastic divide. That is to say: in the works of Aelred, and by extension, in the monastic milieu, we find a monastic notion of friendship that has its correlatives in a certain way of reading and in a certain way of doing theology. On the other hand, we discover in Thomas, and so also in the schools more generally, a scholastic idea of friendship that has its readerly[70] and theological correlates.

Aelred and Monastic Friendship

From our investigation of his thought in chapter 2, we recall the pith of Aelred's notion of friendship: the perfect union of will and ideas.[71] Aelred also states that the ideal friendships are motivated by both reason and affection.[72] Though the two different descriptions might at first glance appear redundant, it is worth keeping both, inasmuch as the motivation to the union

---

70. It is possible that we will be charged with neologism here; however, the word has clear analogical precedent in the form "painterly," now common currency in art criticism.

71. See SA I.59. See also "The Johannine Character of Aelred's Theology of Friendship" and "Conclusion: Aelred's Monastic Theology of Friendship" in chapter 2, especially n. 171, above (p. 88).

72. See SA III.2-3 and SC III.20.48. See also "Friendship and Charity" in chapter 2, above.

and the union itself are by no means identical.[73] Hence, *spiritual* friendship will be that perfect union (rationally and affectively motivated) of will and ideas which is grounded *in Christ*, and therefore *ipso facto* informed by the gift of supernatural charity. All of the other recently enumerated elements of Aelred's theological account of friendship, both material and formal, relate more or less directly to this fundamental idea. Thus, true friendship for Aelred is characterized by charity, precisely because it is Christ-centered; moreover, it has a strongly Johannine coloring, particularly due to the exalted place given by Aelred to the sharing of secrets as a sign of the degree of union between close friends. Furthermore, Aelred expounds the union between spiritual friends as the ideal expression of the rest associated with the sabbath year, the second in his typology of the three sabbaths. Friendship also has for Aelred a profoundly existential, involved or dramatic quality. Significantly evocative of its *voluntaristic* character, this quality is never to the detriment of its simultaneously rational foundation. Finally, friendship tends in Aelred's account to overflow dyadic constraints, both horizontally and vertically, into the broader community (i.e. comm*unity*) of persons, created and uncreated. This is to say that spiritual friendship obtains not only in the present, but also diachronically, linking up living members of Christ's Mystical Body with the glorified communion of saints, including the angels. As such, Aelredian friendship has trinitarian overtones as well. In a similar fashion, the various formal qualities of Aelred's written account discussed above—biblical, aesthetic, erotic, personal and sweet—can readily be seen as either expressive of or strongly resonant with friendship itself as he reckons it.

Correlatively, recalling especially the sections entitled "Friendly versus useful Exegesis" in chapter 2 and "Biblical versus Non-Biblical" in this chapter, we suggest that Aelred's way of reading Scripture is analogous to his theological notion of friendship. Summarizing our analysis in "Friendly versus useful Exegesis" in the pithiest terms, we found that Aelred's way of reading the Bible was profoundly relational, marked by intimately personal addresses to biblical personae, to the authors, to Aelred's own readers, and to God. This unaffected biblical personalism would appear to be rooted in Aelred's identification of the Word as revealed in Scripture with the

73. Thus, one can easily imagine a relationship motivated by both reason and affection that does not in the end achieve the "perfect union" of true friendship. Similarly, on the other hand, one can imagine such a perfect union of will and ideas as the fortuitous development of a relationship that did not in fact begin at the behest of both reason and affection.

Incarnate Word of God. The interpersonal and christological parallels with Aelred's notion of spiritual friendship are clear. We need only add one further dimension to the analogy: just as Aelred's *way* of reading Scripture is grounded in the unceasing monastic *activity* of reading, namely, *lectio divina*, so mature spiritual friendship requires constant practice and nurture.

Finally, we maintain that the analogy of monastic friendship extends even beyond the monastic way of reading to a particular way of doing theology. Insofar as we have shown the applicability of our formal generalizations concerning monastic theology to Aelred's particular account of friendship,[74] our argument is already more than half-made. We need now only recall the evidence, especially in the same preceding sections, of the degree to which each of these formal characterizations—of Aelred's account; of monastic theology—accords with Aelred's fundamental *idea* of friendship. Thus, monastic theology, like monastic friendship according to the exemplary account of Aelred of Rievaulx, is ideally a balanced activity of reason and will, profoundly Christ-centered, existentially grounded in both sensible and spiritual experience, and quintessentially expressed in the perfect union of will and ideas between the persons involved, one of whom is evidently always God, in the instance of theology.

Thomas and Scholastic Friendship

Similar reasoning may be applied to the account of St. Thomas, beginning with his fundamental definition of love of friendship, *amor amicitiae*, as love of another for his own sake.[75] When this bare-bones anthropological definition is taken up into Thomas's theology, friendship becomes the primary way of explicating charity, where the one loved for his own sake is God. The result is another lapidary definition: charity is man's friendship for God.[76] As in Aelred's case, all of the material and formal elements of Thomas's account analyzed earlier in this chapter in the sections "Content of the Two Accounts Compared" and "Form of the Two Accounts Compared" can be correlated more or less immediately with one or another part of this summary description. Clearly, Thomas's definition of charity as friendship

---

74. See the whole of the section "Form of the Two Accounts Compared" in this chapter.

75. See *ST* 1–2.26.4, *corp*. See also "Love and Friendship" in chapter 3, above.

76. See *ST* 2–2.23.1, *corp*. See also "Love, Friendship, and Charity" in chapter 3, above.

for God itself already accounts strictly for the relationship between friendship and charity. Moreover, this spare definition perfectly expresses the transcendent (as opposed to christological, or otherwise divinely Personal) character of Thomas's notion, as expounded in detail in chapter 3. Again, Thomas's root definition of friendship is borrowed directly from Aristotle, who also provides the impetus for delineating charity's order. Indeed, the central definitions in Thomas's theological account of friendship and charity bespeak a scientific rigor again attributable to Aristotle, along with the metaphysical and logical apparatus informing much of Thomas's basic argumentation. Finally, the lack of a well-developed communal or properly trinitarian dimension to Thomas's explicit doctrine of friendship follows, if not as a matter of course, then at least as one of convenience, along the dyadic trajectory to which each of his two basic definitions inclines. On the other hand, the eschatological horizon, as crucial to Thomas's account as to Aelred's, can almost be glimpsed from the Thomistic definition itself of charity, inasmuch as "the friendship of charity is founded upon the fellowship of eternal beatitude."[77]

In addition, as noted summarily in regard to Aelred's work (*mutatis mutandis*), the aforementioned formal qualities of Thomas's account—nonbiblical, clear, scientifically neutral, impersonal and demonstrative—can be loosely aligned with friendship itself in Thomas's conception. If the parallel is slightly less transparent than in Aelred's case, a few brief, general points should serve for clarification. Though the point may appear controversial *prima facie*, we assert that Thomas's notion of friendship is *not* biblical to precisely the extent that it *is* Aristotelian: notwithstanding its theological content, Thomas's model for virtuous friendship is more that of Aristotle than of one of the evangelists, or of St. Paul, or of Moses, David or Solomon, for that matter. By the same token, the Aristotelian "for his own sake" so crucial for Thomas's fundamental psychological definition of friendship may be seen as cognate with his commitments to personal detachment and neutrality, and even, by extension, with his high estimation of clarity and demonstrability.[78]

In parallel with our argumentation concerning Aelred, we discern an analogy between Thomas's mode of reading Scripture and his theological notion of friendship. Our position, already virtually presented in the

---

77. Cf. n. 163, above (p. 148).

78. It is noteworthy that the phrase receives no special emphasis in Aelred's account. Cf. Douglass Roby, in his introduction to *Spiritual Friendship*, 30–31, on Aelred's lack of knowledge of Aristotle's *NE*, in view of Cicero's lack of direct knowledge of that work.

sections "Friendly versus Useful Exegsis" in chapter 2 and "Biblical versus Non-Biblical" in chapter 3 above, is that Thomas tends towards a scientific objectification of the biblical text that inevitably depersonalizes it in the process. We observed that this approach to *sacra pagina* does not remove the Bible altogether from the realm of *amicitia*. It does, however, establish it unambiguously as the subsidiary object of that concupiscent love directed to the good (of truth, wisdom, salvation, what-you-like, associated with fruitful reading of Scripture) desired for the scholastic reader's own sake or for the sake of others. This *amor amicitiae* for Thomas's self and his neighbor, for whose sakes he reads, in turn amounts to an overflow of his primary *amor amicitiae* for God. Thus, in the final analysis, it is Thomas's friendship for God that drives his study of Sacred Scripture.

Last of all, we suggest that scholastic theology itself, like the scholastic reading on which it depends, manifests an analogy to scholastic friendship. As with Aelred and monastic theology, the gist of our argument should be readily apparent from the way Thomas's account of friendship conforms to the formal characterizations of scholastic theology drawn from chapter 1. To render explicit how scholastic theology evinces the Thomistic idea of friendship itself, it is enough to revisit our initial summary of Thomas's notion, as the ideal relation between nature and supernature, in which the latter perfects the former.[79] We can hardly epitomize more succinctly the work scholastic theology set itself to do: In short, Thomas and his colleagues sought to elucidate as clearly as possible both termini of this relation as well as the relation itself, in the bright light of natural reason, yet simultaneously elevated by the brighter light of supernatural grace.

Challenges: Evaluation of the Two Analogies and Beyond

All that remains to be done is to highlight in a rather cursory fashion some mutual challenges offered by our two authors' accounts, beginning with our relative appraisal of the pair of triadic analogies just proposed. We may begin with an important clarification, regarding Thomas's account specifically, that will help us in turn to frame the chief dilemma of the current section. The problem is this: our assertion of an analogy between Thomas's notion of friendship and his approach to theology in general seems to be at odds with our numerous questions above concerning a perceived

---

79. See the section "Relation between the Major Texts within Each Account" in this chapter.

dissonance between the form and content of his theological treatment of friendship. Considered carefully, however, this proves not to be the case. In the preceding section, in elucidating our conclusions, we were careful to state that the analogy we observed was between our two authors' theological approaches on the one hand and their respective *ideas* of friendship, on the other—not between their theologies and the *reality* of friendship itself. In contrast, it is this latter relationship, between theological approach and the reality under investigation, with which the observed discord between form and subject matter is concerned, and to an assessment of which we now turn. The dilemma, then, is precisely the one formulated in the section "Self-Descriptions of the Two Milleux" earlier in this chapter: whether one or the other of the two theological approaches we have examined more aptly facilitates a true and accurate theological description of friendship and its relation to charity.

In terms of our general conclusions in the preceding section, the question is this: granted the consistency within its own milieu of each of our two analogies of friendship (notion of friendship, way of reading Scripture, way of doing theology), which of the two analogical clusters is truer to the Christian *reality* of friendship? The clarifying distinction in the preceding paragraph verges on explicating one line of argument, namely, that the incongruity noticed several times between Thomas's mode of discourse and the subject matter, *amicitia*, can fairly be identified as a weakness of his approach. In other words, we believe, conversely, that a certain recognizable correspondence between the mode in which a subject is presented and the nature of that subject itself has great merit, especially in terms of its capacity for being fruitfully received by a hearer or reader.[80] In our opinion, just such a correspondence is one of the great strengths of Aelred's account. On the other hand, recalling our competing biblical images from the Song of Songs and Isaiah 53:2, we may also ask whether Thomas's stark clarity enables us at times to perceive more lucidly the theological truths at stake in his account. Conversely, the charm of Aelred's account, for all its power to seduce us, may risk intermittently obscuring our Lordly Friend from our vision, in his less comely guise as the Suffering Servant.

A second challenge, this time unilateral, is posed to Thomas by Aelred, concerning their different treatments of the enemy within their respective

---

80. This intuition seems to be cognate with the scholastic dictum, appealed to by Thomas himself, that a thing is received in the mode of the receiver: "Manifestum est enim quod omne quod recipitur in aliquo recipitur in eo per modum recipientis." *ST* 1.75.5, *corp*.

accounts of friendship. In our view, Aelred's account of the enemy, within the grand sweep of his doctrine of the three sabbaths, outshines that of Thomas, for all the latter's fine theological detail. We recall that the terminological rigor of Thomas's account seems to rule out consideration of the possibility that love of an enemy could in some instance become transformative of the relation between the lover and the hateful object of his—according to Thomas, heroic—love. For Aelred, on the other hand, just such a transformation is envisaged as the possible outcome, never to be taken for granted, of the courageous love and forgiveness of one's enemy. Moreover, in a subtler contrast with Thomas's account, the *enemy's* moral agency comes into play, at the same time exposing the original protagonist as less than thoroughly heroic in the relationship. Thus, Aelred states that a person remains "a slave to sin" (John 8:34) until, "himself forgiving and loving, he is forgiven and loved."[81] What is at stake here, in the discrepancy between the two accounts, may prove to be nothing less than the moral imagination. The question is whether the scholastic mode of theological formulation may at times inhibit one's ability to envisage such a redemptive transformation as Aelred's more dramatic, dynamic cast of thought so readily engages. And will the enemy ever in fact become my friend if I have locked him preemptively into an ironclad category?

Finally, one more pair of challenges may be proposed, virtually comprising, as in the first case above, two sides of the same coin. In a real sense, the following questions may be reckoned among the most fundamental challenges to each account, issued this time not by Aelred to Thomas or vice versa, but by us, on behalf of the Church and the Christian Tradition.

Of Thomas, then, we ask whether charity in the end actually comes to eclipse or absorb friendship in his account? One may protest at first that as the genus under which *caritas* is revealed to constitute merely the supernatural species, surely *amicitia*'s place is assured, not only in the local account of charity, but far beyond, given charity's importance to the whole of Thomas's moral theology and ultimately to his vast and comprehensive theological vision. However, a curious phenomenon may be observed to take place as Thomas unfolds his definition of charity in terms of friendship. As we showed in chapter 3, only God is properly loved for his own sake *simpliciter*, as the only being who belongs to no one else and who is therefore capable of being loved without further reference to any other being. But this necessarily entails that the "for his own sake" of a Christian's love of

---

81. See *SC* III.4.11. See also "Spiritual Friendship is Christological" in chapter 2, above. For the Latin citation, see chapter 2, n. 106 (p. 70).

friendship for his human friend must be construed ultimately as included in and subordinated to his primary, and truest, love of friendship, his *amor amicitiae* for God alone.[82] Moreover, we also noted the absence in *ST*, or anywhere else in Thomas's work, for that matter, of a sustained treatment of something like "spiritual friendship," which is to say, the graced friendship between Christian men and women. But if Thomas's account of friendship within the theological framework is always *qua* charity, that is, friendship *for God*, it is hard to see how a mere equation does not result, at the same time effectively evacuating *amicitia* of any distinctive content not already encompassed in the proper understanding of *caritas*. True, friendship still provides a bridge to and from the natural realm, and this is Thomas's main concern as well as his whole point of departure. Nevertheless, we are left to wonder whether intimate friendships between Christians are not inevitably absorbed into expressions of charity itself, in such a way that the particularities of the persons involved begin to look like superfluities, in light of the "truer" and more universal dictates of the greatest theological virtue.

Conversely, we are bound to ask Aelred whether the intimacy of human friendship in his perspective—the perfect union of will and ideas between human individuals—ever risks crowding out Christ? Indeed, pressing further a question raised above,[83] does Aelred's literary subjectivism cost his account the theological rigor necessary to safeguard the commitment by spiritual friends to Christ's presence between and among them? The problem may be turned somewhat on its ear by returning to another question, left unanswered before. The gist of that question was whether friendship *is* something like Aelred's dynamic, dramatic notion, or is it more like Thomas's scientific idea? If friendship is at all like Aelred's notion, it may well be that we have no choice but to do without the sort of safety net that "scientists" of all kinds want so badly to provide. Instead, we may have to rely on our commitments alone, or better, on our trust in Christ's presence at the heart of our friendships. To the question of whether a human friendship between virtuous Christians can itself come to crowd Christ out of its center, we must concede that in this life, the risk is evidently always there. Such an admission, however, merely confirms the aptness of Aelred's spiritual insight and the mode of its expression. It is precisely on account of his deep awareness of such a risk that Aelred bothered composing a work

---

82. See the section "Love, Friendship and Charity," as well as chapter 3, n. 131, above (p. 126).

83. See the section "Persuasive versus Demonstrative" in this chapter.

on spiritual friendship in all of its aspects, among which the frailty of the human condition figures prominently.

Speculative Suggestions for Further Inquiry

Last of all, we wish to propose to the reader some avenues for continuing investigation, gleaned from our own theological research and reflection on the topic of the monastic and scholastic theologies of friendship. We will therefore finish the dissertation by offering brief descriptions of four areas for possible study: "Sources," "Hermeneutical Implications," "Theological 'Style,'" and "Theology versus Philosophy."

First, we might have written several more dissertations devoted solely to the topic of our authors' distinctive uses of sources, especially biblical, though patristic and pagan as well. Though we have tried to say something about Aelred's peculiarly monastic way of reading the Bible and the mutual influence that occurs between that way of reading and Aelred's understanding of friendship, a far more thorough treatment of his biblical usage could certainly fill out the picture; so, too, in the case of Thomas's classically scholastic mode of Bible reading, especially in light of his theological account of friendship. The two authors' distinctive appropriations of St. Augustine could certainly be taken up, with particular attention to the theme of friendship, in far more detail than has been done here. Finally, the very different ways in which Aelred and Thomas enlist the aid of Cicero and Aristotle, respectively, warrant more explicit discussion.

Next, our research into the subject of friendship, especially in the context of monastic and scholastic theological approaches of the twelfth and thirteenth centuries, leads us to believe that a philosophically rigorous notion of friendship may provide a hermeneutical key to understanding authentic personal communication, both written and spoken. Expanded into the theological register, friendship could become instrumental in providing a more adequate account of biblical *inspiration* than has heretofore been articulated. Correlatively, new prescriptions for valid biblical *interpretation* could begin to be envisaged. Finally, the possibility that the thirteenth century constitutes a watershed, in connection to this proposal of a "friendly hermeneutics" being replaced by an ever more distant and inevitably more suspicious relation to the text, demands further study. The figures of Hugh of St. Victor and St. Bonaventure would bear close reading in connection to this thesis.

Aelred and Thomas Compared

Third, the matter of theological "style," engaged at several points in this dissertation, is deserving of a great deal more attention. Poetry, art, beauty, and personal, dramatic, dynamic engagement of texts and other persons, over against scientific neutrality and personal detachment: how such formal characteristics of theological activity impact the content of discovery and transmission is a hugely interesting and important matter for reflection and academic inquiry. In our own investigation, we made the proposal that things ought to be treated according to their own modes of being: thus, to the extent that friendship itself is personal, existential, involved, dialogical, "poetic," etc., its description needs to have these characteristics as well. On the other hand, there may remain room for a complementary "detached" treatment. We recall here Jean Leclercq's suggestion of a complementarity obtaining between the monastic and scholastic theological modes.[84] In the twentieth century, such authors as Thomas Prufer and the novelist Evelyn Waugh have given the question of literary theological style serious consideration[85]; others should follow.

Finally, the transition from the hegemony of a more monastic way of doing theology to the overwhelming triumph of the scholastic approach, which took place over the course of the twelfth and thirteenth centuries, has a great deal of pertinence to the question in Christian academic circles of the relations between Theology and Philosophy, or even more basically, between faith and reason. This enormous area of intellectual work is already being pursued from many different perspectives. We only propose here that the complex relations between the monastic and scholastic milieux and their respective ways of doing theology bear significantly on these questions. Moreover, Aelred's and Thomas's respective theological accounts of friendship can be parsed out along the two sides of the same divide: between a more holistic, integrated understanding of intellectual activity in the monasteries on the one hand, and, on the other, an ever more sharply defined two-pronged approach by the Schools to the primary object of Christian inquiry, namely, God.

---

84. "To speak of two theologies merely means calling attention to the fact that a certain group of Christian thinkers laid more stress on a given aspect of the unique mystery of salvation or on some one of the components of Christian reflection. Accordingly, the two methods which have been described here by means of contrast are merely two complementary aspects of theological method" (Leclercq, *The Love of Learning*, 222).

85. See Waugh, *Brideshead Revisited*; Waugh, "Fan-Fare," 300–304; Waugh, "Literary Style in England and America," 477–81; Prufer, "The Death of Charm and the Advent of Grace," 91–102.

Selected Bibliography

Primary Sources

Latin:

Aelred of Rievaulx. *Aelred Rievallensis opera omnia 1: Opera ascetica.* Edited by A. Hoste and C. H. Talbot. Corpus Christianorum Continuatio Mediaevalis 1. Turnholt: Brepols Editores Pontificii, 1971.

———. *Aelredi Rievallensis opera omnia, Homeliae de oneribus propheticis Isaiae.* Edited by Gaetano Raciti. Corpus Christianorum Continuatio Mediaevalis 2D. Turnholt: Brepols Editores Pontificii, 2005.

———. *Aelredi Rievallensis opera omnia, Sermones I–XLVI.* Edited by Gaetano Raciti. Corpus Christianorum Continuatio Mediaevalis 2A. Turnholt: Brepols Editores Pontificii, 1989.

———. *Aelredi Rievallensis opera omnia, Sermones XLVII–LXXXIV.* Edited by Gaetano Raciti. Corpus Christianorum Continuatio Mediaevalis 2B. Turnholt: Brepols Editores Pontificii, 2001.

———. *Patrologia Latina.* Edited by J. P. Migne. Vol. 195. Paris: J. P. Migne, 1841.

———. *Sermones inediti B. Aelredi Abbatis Rievallensis.* Edited by C. H. Talbot. Series scriptorium S. Ordinis Cisterciensis, vol. 1. Rome: Curiam Generalem Sacri Ordinis Cisterciensis, 1952.

Aquinas, Thomas. *In Librum Beati Dionysii De divinis nominibus.* Edited by Ceslai Pera. Rome: Marietti, 1950.

———. *Sententia Libri Ethicorum.* Vol. 47:1–2, *Sancti Thomae Aquinatis doctor angelici Opera omnia iussu Leonis XIII. P. M. edita.* Rome: Ad Sanctae Sabinae, 1969.

———. *Summa contra Gentiles.* Leonine manual ed. Rome: Apud sedem Commissionis Leoninae, 1934.

———. *Summa Theologiae.* Vols. 4–12, *Sancti Thomae Aquinatis doctor angelici Opera omnia iussu Leonis XIII. P. M. edita.* Rome: Ex Typographia Polyglatta, 1888–1906.

Cicero. *De Amicitia.* Introduction, notes and vocabulary by H. E. Gould and J. L. Whiteley. Wauconda, IL: Bolchazy-Carducci, 1941.

Selected Bibliography

English:

Aelred of Rievaulx. *Dialogue on the Soul.* Translated and with an introduction by C. H. Talbot. Cistercian Fathers 22. Kalamazoo: Cistercian, 1981.

———. *The Historical Works.* Translated by Jane Patricia Freeland, with an introduction by Marsha L. Dutton. Cistercian Fathers 56. Kalamazoo: Cistercian, 2005.

———. *The Life of S. Ninian.* In *The Historians of Scotland*, vol. 5: *Lives of S. Ninian and S. Kentigern.* Edited and translated by Alexander Penrose Forbes. Edinburgh: Edmonston and Douglas, 1874.

———. *The Liturgical Sermons: The First Clairvaux Collection, Sermons One–Twenty-eight, Advent—All Saints.* Translated by Theodore Berkeley and M. Basil Pennington, with an introduction by M. Basil Pennington. Cistercian Fathers 58. Kalamazoo: Cistercian, 2001.

———. *The Mirror of Charity.* Translated by Elizabeth Connor, with an introduction by Charles Dumont. Cistercian Fathers 17. Kalamazoo: Cistercian, 1990.

———. *Spiritual Friendship.* Translated by Mary Eugenia Laker, with an introduction by Douglass Roby. Cistercian Fathers 5. Kalamazoo: Cistercian, 1977.

———. *Treatises; Pastoral Prayer.* Edited by David Knowles. Cistercian Fathers 2. Kalamazoo: Cistercian, 1971.

Aquinas, Thomas. *Catena Aurea: Commentary on the Four Gospels Collected out of the Works of the Fathers by St. Thomas Aquinas.* Edited by John Henry Cardinal Newman. London: Saint Austin, 1997.

———. *Commentary on the Nicomachean Ethics.* Translated by C. I. Litzinger. Library of Living Catholic Thought 2. Chicago: Henry Regnery, 1964.

———. *The Sermon-Conferences of St. Thomas Aquinas on the Apostles' Creed.* Edited and translated by Nicholas Ayo. Notre Dame: University of Notre Dame Press, 1988.

Aristotle. *Nichomachean Ethics.* Translated and with an introduction and notes by Martin Ostwald. Indianapolis: Bobbs-Merrill, 1962.

Augustine. *Confessions.* Translated with an introduction and notes by Henry Chadwick. Oxford: Oxford University Press, 1991.

Benedict of Nursia. *The Rule of St. Benedict.* Translated, with introduction and notes by Anthony C. Meisel and M. L. del Mastro. New York: Doubleday, 1975.

Cicero. *On Old Age; On Friendship.* Translated, with an introduction, by Frank O. Copley. Ann Arbor: University of Michigan Press, 1967.

Hugh of Saint Victor. *The Didascalicon: On the Study of Reading.* Translated and with an introduction and notes by Jerome Taylor. New York: Columbia University Press, 1961.

Secondary Sources

Ayo, Nicholas. *The Sermon-Conferences of St. Thomas Aquinas on the Apostles' Creed.* Notre Dame: University of Notre Dame Press, 1988.

Bejczy, István. *Erasmus and the Middle Ages: The Historical Consciousness of a Christian Humanist.* Leiden: Brill, 2001.

Boswell, John. *Christianity, Social Tolerance, and Homosexuality: Gay People in Western Europe From the Beginning of the Christian Era to the Fourteenth Century.* Chicago: University of Chicago Press, 1980.

Selected Bibliography

Bouyer, Louis. *The Cistercian Heritage*. Translated by Elizabeth A. Livingstone from *La Spiritualité de Cîteaux*. Westminster, MD: Newman, 1958.

Cavadini, John C. "The Sweetness of the Word: Salvation and Rhetoric in Augustine's *De Doctrina Christiana*." In *De Doctrina Christiana: A Classic of Western Culture*, edited by Duane W. H. Arnold and Pamela Bright, 164–81. Notre Dame: University of Notre Dame Press, 1995.

Cessario, Romanus. "Toward Understanding Aquinas' Theological Method: The Early Twelfth-Century Experience." In *Studies in Thomistic Theology*, edited by Paul Lockey, 17–89. Houston: Center for Thomistic Studies, 1996.

Chenu, M.-D. *Introduction à l'étude de S. Thomas d'Aquin*. Paris: Publications de l'Institut d'études médiévales, 1954.

Connor, Elizabeth. "Monastic Profession According to Aelred of Rievaulx." In *Studiosorum Speculum: Studies in Honor of Louis J. Lekai, O.Cist.*, edited by Francis R. Swietek and John R. Sommerfeldt, 53–73. Cistercian Studies 141. Kalamazoo: Cistercian, 1993.

Copleston, Frederick. *A History of Philosophy*. Vol. 2, *Medieval Philosophy*, Part 1: *Augustine to Bonaventure*. Garden City, NY: Doubleday, 1962.

———. *A History of Philosophy*. Vol. 2, *Medieval Philosophy*, Part 2: *Albert the Great to Duns Scotus*. Garden City, NY: Doubleday, 1962.

Courcelle, Pierre. "Ailred de Rievaulx à l'école des 'Confessions.'" *Revue des Études Augustiniennes* 3 (1957) 163–74.

Daniel, Walter. *The Life of Ailred of Rievaulx (Vita Aelredi)*. Translated by Frederick Maurice Powicke, with an introduction by Marsha Dutton. Cistercian Fathers 57. Kalamazoo: Cistercian, 1994.

Doig, James C. *Aquinas's Philosophical Commentary on the Ethics: A Historical Perspective*. Dordrecht: Kluwer Academic, 2001.

Dumont, Charles. "Aelred de Rievaulx." In *Théologie de la Vie Monastique: Études sur la tradition Patristique*, 527–38. Paris: Aubier, 1961.

———. "Aelred of Rievaulx's *Spiritual Friendship*." In *Cistercian Ideals and Reality*, 187–198. Kalamazoo: Cistercian, 1978.

———. "Personalism in Community according to Aelred of Rievaulx." *Cistercian Studies* 12 (1977) 250–71.

Dutton, Marsha L. "The Invented Sexual History of Aelred of Rievaulx: A Review Article." *The American Benedictine Review* 47 (1996) 414–32.

Dutton-Stuckey, Marsha. "Christ our Mother: Aelred's Iconography for Contemplative Union." In *Goad and Nail: Studies in Medieval Cistercian History, X*, edited by E. Rozanne Elder, 21–45. Cistercian Studies 84. Kalamazoo: Cistercian, 1985.

———. "The Cistercian Source: Aelred, Bonaventure, and Ignatius." In *Goad and Nail: Studies in Medieval Cistercian History, X*, edited by E. Rozanne Elder, 151–78. Cistercian Studies 84. Kalamazoo: Cistercian, 1985.

———. "The Conversion and Vocation of Aelred of Rievaulx: A Historical Hypothesis." In *England in the Twelfth Century: Proceedings of the 1988 Harlaxton Symposium*, edited by Daniel Williams, 31–49. Woodbridge, UK: Boydell, 1990.

———. "Eat, Drink, and Be Merry: The Eucharistic Spirituality of the Cistercian Fathers." In *Erudition at God's Service: Studies in Medieval Cistercian History, XI*, edited by John R. Sommerfeldt, 1–31. Cistercian Studies 98. Kalamazoo: Cistercian, 1987.

———. "Getting Things the Wrong Way Round: Composition and Transposition in Aelred of Rievaulx's *De institutione inclusarum*." In *Heaven on Earth: Studies in*

Selected Bibliography

  Medieval Cistercian History, IX, edited by E. Rozanne Elder, 90–101. Kalamazoo: Cistercian, 1983.

  ———. "Intimacy and Imitation: The Humanity of Christ in Cistercian Spirituality." In *Erudition at God's Service: Studies in Medieval Cistercian History, XI*, edited by John R. Sommerfeldt, 33–69. Cistercian Studies 98. Kalamazoo: Cistercian, 1987.

  ———. "A Prodigal Writes Home: Aelred of Rievaulx's *De institutione inclusarum.*" In *Heaven on Earth: Studies in Medieval Cistercian History, IX*, edited by E. Rozanne Elder, 35–42. Kalamazoo: Cistercian, 1983.

Egenter, Richard. *Gottesfreundschaft: Die Lehre von der Gottesfreundschaft in der Scholastik und Mystik des 12. und 13. Jahrhunderts.* Augsburg: Dr. Benno Filser, 1928.

Fiske, Adele "Aelred's of Rievaulx [sic] Idea of Friendship and Love." Part 1. *Citeaux* 12 (1961) 5–17.

———. "Aelred's of Rievaulx [sic] Idea of Friendship and Love." Part 2. *Citeaux* 13 (1962) 97–132.

Gadamer, Hans-Georg. *Truth and Method.* 2nd rev. ed. Translated by Joel Weinsheimer and Donald G. Marshall. New York: Continuum, 2002.

Gallagher, David M. "Desire for Beatitude and Love of Friendship in Thomas Aquinas." *Medieval Studies* 58 (1996) 1–45.

———. "Thomas Aquinas on Self-Love as the Basis for Love of Others." *Acta Philosophica* 8 (1999) 23–44.

Ghellinck, J. de. *Le Mouvement Théologique du XIIe Siècle.* Paris: Desclée-de Brouwer, 1948.

Gilson, Etienne. *History of Christian Philosophy in the Middle Ages.* London: Sheed and Ward, 1955.

Hallier, Amédée. *The Monastic Theology of Aelred of Rievaulx: An Experiential Theology. (Un Éducateur Monastique, Aelred de Rievaulx).* Translated by Columban Heaney. Cistercian Studies 2. Spencer, MA: Cistercian, 1969.

Hubert, M. "Aspects du latin philosophique aux xiie et xiiie siècles." *Revue des études latines* 27 (1949) 227–31.

Hunt, R. W. "English Learning in the Late Twelfth Century." In *Essays in Medieval History*, edited by R. W. Southern, 106–28. London: Macmillan, 1968.

Illich, Ivan. *In the Vineyard of the Text: A Commentary to Hugh's Didascalicon.* Chicago: University of Chicago Press, 1993.

Jordan, Mark. "Aquinas' Middle Thoughts on Theology as Science." In *Studies in Thomistic Theology*, edited by Paul Lockey, 91–111. Houston: Center for Thomistic Studies, 1996.

Kerr, Fergus. "Thomas Aquinas." In *The Medieval Theologians*, edited by G. R. Evans, 200–220. Oxford: Blackwell, 2001.

Knowles, David. *The Evolution of Medieval Thought.* New York: Random House, 1962.

———. *The Monastic Order in England.* Cambridge: Cambridge University Press, 1950.

Kraus, James E. *The Catechetical Sermons of St. Thomas Aquinas: A Comparison of the Popular Doctrine of His Lenten Sermons of 1273 with the Scientific Doctrine of His Other Works.* Rome: Apud Pontificium Institutum Angelicum de Urbe, 1953.

Lackner, Bede K. "The Monastic Life according to Saint Bernard." In *Studies in Medieval Cistercian History II*, edited by John R. Sommerfeldt, 49–62. Cistercian Studies 24. Kalamazoo: Cistercian, 1976.

Leclercq, Jean. *Aux Sources de la Spiritualité Occidentale: Étapes et constantes.* Paris: Les Éditions du Cerf, 1964.

———. *Bernard of Clairvaux and the Cistercian Spirit*. Translated by Claire Lavoie. Cistercian Studies 16. Kalamazoo: Cistercian, 1976.

———. "Conversion to the Monastic Life in the Twelfth Century: Who, Why, and How?" In *Studiosorum Speculum: Studies in Honor of Louis J. Lekai, O.Cist.*, edited by Francis R. Swietek and John R. Sommerfeldt, 201–32. Cistercian Studies 141. Kalamazoo: Cistercian, 1993.

———. "The Intentions of the Founders of the Cistercian Order." In *The Cistercian Spirit: A Symposium*, edited by M. Basil Pennington, 88–133. Cistercian Studies 3. Spencer, MA: Cistercian, 1970.

———. *The Love of Learning and the Desire for God: A Study of Monastic Culture*. Translated by Catharine Misrahi. New York: Fordham University Press, 1961.

———. *Monks and Love in Twelfth-Century France*. Oxford: Clarendon, 1979.

———. *Saint Pierre Damien Ermite et Homme D'Église*. Rome: Edizioni di Storia e Letteratura, 1960.

———. "A Sociological Approach to the History of a Religious Order." In *The Cistercian Spirit: A Symposium*, edited by M. Basil Pennington, 134–43. Cistercian Studies 3. Spencer, MA: Cistercian, 1970.

———. *Témoins de la Spiritualité Occidentale*. Paris: Éditions du Cerf, 1965.

Lubac, Henri de. *Exégèse médiévale: Les quatre sens de l'Ecriture*. 4 vols. Paris: Éditions Montaigne, 1959.

———. *The Mystery of the Supernatural*. Translated by Rosemary Sheed. New York: Crossroad, 1998.

Mâle, Emile. *The Gothic Image: Religious Art in France of the Thirteenth Century*. Translated by Dora Nussey. New York: Harper and Row, 1958.

Malloy, Christopher J. "Love of God for His Own Sake and Love of Beatitude: Heavenly Charity According to Thomas Aquinas." PhD diss., The Catholic University of America, 2001.

Mansini, Guy. "*Duplex Amor* and the Structure of Love in Aquinas." In *Thomistica*, edited by E. Manning, 137–96. Recherches de Théologie Ancienne et Médiévale, Supplementa 1. Louvain: Peeters, 1995.

———. "*Similitudo, Communicatio*, and the Friendship of Charity in Aquinas." In *Thomistica*, edited by E. Manning, 1–26. Recherches de Théologie Ancienne et Médiévale, Supplementa 1. Louvain: Peeters, 1995.

McEvoy, James. "Amitié, attirance et amour chez S. Thomas d'Aquin." *Revue philo-sophique de Louvain* 91 (1993) 383–408.

———. "Notes On the Prologue of St. Aelred of Rievaulx's 'De Spirituali Amicitia,' with a Translation." *Traditio* 37 (1981) 396–411.

———. "The Theory of Friendship in the Latin Middle Ages: Hermeneutics, Contextualization and the Transmission and Reception of Ancient Texts and Ideas, from c. AD 350 to c. 1500." In *Friendship in Medieval Europe*, edited by Julian Haseldine, 3–44. Phoenix Mill, UK: Sutton, 1999.

McGuire, Brian Patrick. *Brother and Lover: Aelred of Rievaulx*. New York: Crossroads, 1994.

———. "The Cistercians and the Transformation of Monastic Friendship." *Analecta Cisterciensia* 37 (1981) 1–63. Reprinted in Brian Patrick McGuire, *Friendship and Faith: Cistercian Men, Women, and their Stories, 1100–1250*. Aldershot: Ashgate, 2002.

Selected Bibliography

———. *Friendship and Community: The Monastic Experience, 350–1250.* Kalamazoo: Cistercian, 1988.

Meilaender, Gilbert. *Friendship: A Study in Theological Ethics.* Notre Dame: University of Notre Dame Press, 1981.

O'Brien, Robert Caldey. "St. Aelred et la 'lectio divina.'" *Collectanea Cisterciensia* 41 (1979) 281–92.

Ohly, Friedrich. "Ausserbiblisch Typologisches zwischen Cicero, Ambrosius und Aelred von Rievaulx." In *Schriften zur mittelalterlichen Bedeutungsforschung,* 338–60. Darmstadt: Wissenschaftliche Buchgesellschaft, 1977.

Prufer, Thomas. "The Death of Charm and the Advent of Grace." In *Recapitulations: Essays in Philosophy,* 91–102. Washington, DC: Catholic University of America Press, 1993.

Raciti, Gaetano. "L'apport original d'Aelred de Rievaulx à la réflexion occidental sur l'amitié." *Collectanea Cisterciensia* 29 (1967) 77–99.

Reeve, Pamela. "Exploring a Metaphor Theologically: Thomas Aquinas on the Beatific Vision." In *Studies in Thomistic Theology,* edited by Paul Lockey, 283–300. Houston: Center for Thomistic Studies, 1996.

Roby, Douglass. "Chimaera of the North: The Active Life of Aelred of Rievaulx." In *Cistercian Ideals and Reality,* edited by John R. Sommerfeldt, 152–69. Kalamazoo: Cistercian, 1978.

Rouse, Richard R. "Cistercian Aids to Study in the Thirteenth Century." In *Studies in Medieval Cistercian History II,* edited by John R. Sommerfeldt, 123–34. Cistercian Studies 24. Kalamazoo: Cistercian, 1976.

Rousselot, Pierre. *The Problem of Love in the Middle Ages.* (*Pour l'histoire du problème de l'amour au moyen âge.*) Translated and with an introduction by Alan Vincelette. Milwaukee: Marquette University Press, 2001.

Smalley, Beryl. "Some Thirteenth-Century Commentaries on the Sapiential Books." *Dominican Studies* 3 (1950) 236–74.

———. *The Study of the Bible in the Middle Ages.* Oxford: Clarendon, 1941.

Sokolowski, Robert. "Phenomenology of Friendship." *The Review of Metaphysics* 55 (March 2002) 451–70.

Sommerfeldt, John R. *Aelred of Rievaulx on Love and Order in the World and the Church.* Mahwah, NJ: Newman, 2006.

———. *Aelred of Rievaulx: Pursuing Perfect Happiness.* Mahwah, NJ: Newman, 2005.

———. *The Spiritual Teachings of Bernard of Clairvaux: An Intellectual History of the Early Cistercian Order.* Cistercian Fathers 125. Kalamazoo: Cistercian, 1991.

———. "The Vocabulary of Contemplation in Aelred of Rievaulx' *On Jesus at the Age of 12; A Rule of Life for a Recluse; On Spiritual Friendship.*" In *Heaven on Earth,* edited by E. Rozanne Elder, 72–89. Kalamazoo: Cistercian, 1983.

Southern, R. W. *The Making of the Middle Ages.* New Haven: Yale University Press, 1953.

———. *Medieval Humanism.* Oxford: Blackwell, 1970.

———. *Saint Anselm and His Biographer: A Study of Monastic Life and Thought, 1059–c. 1130.* Cambridge: Cambridge University Press, 1963.

———. *Scholastic Humanism and the Unification of Europe.* Vol. 1, *Foundations.* Oxford: Blackwell, 1995.

———. *Scholastic Humanism and the Unification of Europe.* Vol. 2, *The Heroic Age.* Oxford: Blackwell, 1995.

Selected Bibliography

Spaemann, Robert. "Die Lehre des heiligen Thomas von Aquin über den amor perfectus." In *Reflexion und Spontaneität: Studien über Fénelon*, 88–106. Stuttgart: Ernst Klett, 1990.

Squire, Aelred. *Aelred of Rievaulx: A Study*. London: SPCK, 1969.

Steel, Carlos. "Thomas Aquinas on Preferential Love." In *Amor amicitiae: On the Love that is Friendship*, edited by Thomas A. F. Kelly and Philipp W. Rosemann, 437–58. Recherches de Theologie et Philosophie medievales, Bibliotheca 6. Louvain: Peeters, 2004.

Studzinski, Raymond. *Reading to Live: The Evolving Practice of Lectio Divina*. Collegeville, MN: Liturgical, 2009.

TePas, Katherine M. "Aelred of Rievaulx: The Correlation between Human Friendship and Union with God." PhD diss., The Catholic University of America, 1992.

———. "*Amor, Amicitia* and *Misericordia*: A Critique of Aelred's Analysis of Spiritual Friendship." *Downside Review* 112 (1994) 249–63.

Torrell, Jean-Pierre. *Saint Thomas Aquinas*. 2 vols. Translated by Robert Royal. Washington, DC: The Catholic University of America Press, 1996, 2003.

Vansteenberghe, G. "Amitié." In *Dictionnaire de Spiritualité*, 1 cols. 500–29. Paris: Éditions Beauchesne, 1937.

Waddell, Chrysogonus. "Simplicity and Ordinariness: The Climate of Early Cistercian Hagiography." In *Simplicity and Ordinariness*, edited by John R. Sommerfeldt, 1–47. Cistercian Study 61. Kalamazoo: Cistercian, 1980.

Wadell, Paul J. *Becoming Friends: Worship, Justice, and the Practice of Christian Friendship*. Grand Rapids: Brazos, 2002.

———. *Friends of God: Virtues and Gifts in Aquinas*. New York: Peter Lang, 1991.

———. *Friendship and the Moral Life*. Notre Dame: University of Notre Dame Press, 1989.

———. "Growing Together in the Divine Love: The Role of Charity in the Moral Theology of Thomas Aquinas." In *Aquinas and Empowerment: Classical Ethics for Ordinary Lives*, edited by G. Simon Harak, 134–69. Washington, DC: Georgetown University Press, 1996.

———. "Peter Abelard's *Letter 10* and Cistercian Liturgical Reform." In *Studies in Medieval Cistercian History II*, edited by John R. Sommerfeldt, 75–86. Cistercian Studies 24. Kalamazoo: Cistercian, 1976.

———. *The Primacy of Love: An Introduction to the Ethics of Thomas Aquinas*. New York: Paulist, 1991.

Waugh, Evelyn. *Brideshead Revisited: The Sacred and Profane Memories of Captain Charles Ryder*. Rev. ed. London: Chapman and Hall, 1945.

———. "Fan-Fare." In *The Essays, Articles and Reviews of Evelyn Waugh*, edited by Donat Gallagher, 300–304. Boston: Little, Brown, 1983.

———. "Literary Style in England and America." In *The Essays, Articles and Reviews of Evelyn Waugh*, edited by Donat Gallagher, 477–81. Boston: Little, Brown, 1983.

Weisheipl, James A. *Friar Thomas D'Aquino: His Life, Thought, and Works*. Washington, DC: The Catholic University of America Press, 1974.

Wohlman, Avital. "L'élaboration des elements aristotéliciens dans la doctrine thomiste de l'amour." *Revue thomiste* 82 (1982) 247–69.

Yohe, Katherine M. "Did Aelred of Rievaulx Think Friends are Necessary?" *Cistercian Studies Quarterly* 35 (2000) 29–46.

Selected Bibliography

Young, William W. *The Politics of Praise: Naming God and Friendship in Aquinas and Derrida*. Hampshire, UK: Ashgate, 2007.
Zeller, Hubert van. *The Benedictine Idea*. Springfield, IL: Templegate, 1959.

www.ingramcontent.com/pod-product-compliance
Lightning Source LLC
Chambersburg PA
CBHW051744230426
43670CB00012B/2157